Private Equity Unchained

Also by Thomas Meyer

BEYOND THE J-CURVE (*with Pierre-Yves Mathonet*)

J-CURVE EXPOSURE: Managing a Portfolio of Venture Capital and Private Equity Funds (*with Pierre-Yves Mathonet*)

MASTERING ILLIQUIDITY: Risk Management for Portfolios of Limited Partnership Funds (*with Peter Cornelius, Christian Diller and Didier Guennoc*)

Private Equity Unchained

Strategy Insights for the Institutional Investor

Thomas Meyer
LDS Partners, Luxembourg

palgrave
macmillan

First published 2014 by
PALGRAVE MACMILLAN

Palgrave Macmillan in the UK is an imprint of Macmillan Publishers Limited, registered in England, company number 785998, of Houndmills, Basingstoke, Hampshire RG21 6XS.

Palgrave Macmillan in the US is a division of St Martin's Press LLC, 175 Fifth Avenue, New York, NY 10010.

Palgrave Macmillan is the global academic imprint of the above companies and has companies and representatives throughout the world.

Palgrave® and Macmillan® are registered trademarks in the United States, the United Kingdom, Europe and other countries.

ISBN 978–1–137–28681–9

This book is printed on paper suitable for recycling and made from fully managed and sustained forest sources. Logging, pulping and manufacturing processes are expected to conform to the environmental regulations of the country of origin.

A catalogue record for this book is available from the British Library.

Library of Congress Cataloging-in-Publication Data
Meyer, Thomas, 1959–
Private equity unchained : strategy insights for the institutional investor / Thomas Meyer.
pages cm
Summary: "Until recently, strategy played little meaningful role in the management of illiquid investments, and what many investors call 'strategy' has been more akin to 'tactics' or 'learned reflexes'. Even large institutions still appear to manage their private equity allocations on such a case-by-case basis. But the environment has changed and returns are no longer 'assured' as they once were. Private equity and other illiquid asset classes have matured, as more players seek to deploy ever larger amounts in a market where opportunities necessarily become difficult to identify and access. The few principles that institutional investors have relied on up to now have been anchored in a less competitive past. Private Equity Unchained deconstructs existing practices and provides insights into how to think strategically about illiquid asset allocations. In order to thrive in markets characterised by extreme uncertainty, investors must first accept the limitations of what is knowable. This begins by leaving behind many of those financial theories that institutions normally cling to as a safe harbour for managing risk. Once divested of such false comforts, investors will be in a position to identify their real options and take an active and strategic approach to alternative investing" — Provided by publisher.
ISBN 978–1–137–28681–9 (hardback)
1. Private equity. 2. Corporate governance. 3. Portfolio management. I. Title.
HG4751.M4 2014
332.63—dc23 2014023172

Contents

Figures and Tables

Figures

Tables

Acknowledgements

Finishing a book is like returning home after having climbed a mountain. Looking at the completed script is an anti-climax and one wonders how one embarked on this journey in the first place. To a large degree this book builds on previous publications over the last ten years, so the thoughts expressed here are the result of the cooperation and discussions with the co-authors of these works: Peter Cornelius (AlpInvest Partners), Christian Diller (Montana Capital Partners), Didier Guennoc (LDS Partners) and Pierre-Yves Mathonet (ADIA). In this context I must also thank Yasuharu Hagi (MCP Group) and Kazushige Kobayashi (Capital Dynamics).

Many ideas stem from the advice and conversations with other industry practitioners. I could list many people with whom I discussed the concepts explained in this book, but I at least should mention Guy Fraser-Sampson, Elias Korosis (Hermes GPE), Hal Morimoto (Astoria Consulting) and John Renkema (APG).

I am extremely grateful for the support of my colleagues Philippe Defreyn (LDS Partners) and Jobst Neuss (European Investment Fund) and for the help of Tim Jenkinson (Professor of Finance, Director of the Oxford Private Equity Institute and head of the finance faculty at Saïd Business School, University of Oxford). I particularly thank Ross Butler (JRA Butler) for his critical review and his help in improving earlier versions of the manuscript.

I also thank my endorsers, Colin Mayer (Peter Moores Professor of Management Studies at Saïd Business School, University of Oxford), Georges Sudarskis (Sudarskis & Partners) and Robert van Zwieten (Emerging Markets Private Equity Association).

Acknowledgements would not be complete without expressing my gratitude to Peter Baker, Gemma d'Arcy Hughes and Jamie Forrest at Palgrave Macmillan, without whom this book would never have seen the light of the day. Julie Rowbotham has done an outstanding job as copy editor and Francesca White as leader of the production process.

I reserve the last acknowledgement to my most important supporter: once more, my heartfelt gratitude goes to Mika Kaneyuki, my wife and best friend, who is my strength and purpose in life.

Luxembourg, May 2014

Chapter 1
Introduction

The focus of this book is institutional investment into the private equity market. That is to say, it is concerned with the deployment of capital into the asset class, rather than its investment into specific companies. For our purposes, private equity refers to an institutionalised way of owning a share of a company that is not registered and not publicly traded on an exchange. The process for investing in such financial instruments is not standardised but rather takes place through a negotiated process.[1] It therefore requires a significant degree of sophistication on the part of the investor, let alone the fund manager who will deploy capital.

In practice, this deployment is a search for opportunities in uncertain, under-researched or overlooked niches, where information is proprietary and where there is little or no competition.[2] It is not for the faint-hearted. The challenge then is how to reconcile these extreme uncertainties inherent in private equity with the needs of institutional investors to define and encompass risks prior to setting out on such a venture. The industry's structure and particularly the intermediation through funds is, at least in part, a response to these extreme uncertainties.[3]

It may seem clichéd to say that the lifecycle of such a fund resembles a trade journey into the unknown, but this is much more than a metaphor – the private equity industry's investment vehicle of choice, the limited partnership, has ancient roots and much in common with traditional ways of financing trade voyages. For instance, medieval Italian merchant families financed trade voyages through 'commendas'. In this asymmetric relationship the 'sleeping partners' (that is, today's 'limited partners') were not liable for debt and stayed at home while the 'travelling partners' controlled the venture and set sail to search for profitable business. 'Travelling partners' (for which, read 'general partner' today) offered skills, experience and the willingness to take high personal risks. At the time of the commenda the high profits were based on venturing across a vast geographical space and there was a concomitant need for trust underpinned by strong alignments of interest.

Centuries later this limited partnership continues to be the structure of choice for skilled and risk-taking professionals to pool funding from wealthy and relatively risk-averse parties for investments in an environment of extreme uncertainty.

Purpose of this Book

This book is primarily written for investment professionals who are already familiar with the key concepts of private equity. However, this is not about the next level of technical detail, but rather how institutional investors can achieve organisational effectiveness in this dynamic and competitive environment. While there have been a number of books published on institutional investment in private equity in recent years, and there is certainly no shortage of books on corporate strategy, there is next to nothing written on strategies for investing in private equity. Meanwhile academia seems far more interested in the deployment of private equity funds and their approaches to value creation and realisation, rather than the initial commitment of capital. Anyone seeking detail on how to develop sophisticated strategies in this area will have been frustrated.

This is also a deliberately un-academic book, because private equity investment is a largely un-academic exercise. The development of an investment strategy involves anticipating and shaping the future, a perspective that is in contrast to that usually taken by academia. Academics seek to understand how and why things work, which is mainly by looking at existing and therefore backward-looking data. Their financial models may give good explanations of the past but their priority is not necessarily a practical application in the future, particularly when dealing with a highly uncertain subject. Academic results reflect a certain setting, come with a number of caveats, and are thus often contradictory, which make them of limited use for practitioners. In the discussion between academics and practitioners, neither side really understands or even tries to understand the purpose or motivation of the other.[4]

Quick Glossary

When referring to '**investors**' in this book we normally mean institutional investors and their organisational entity set up for managing private equity investments. These institutional investors either employ professionals as '**investment managers**' to directly invest in private equity or invest through funds where professional management is provided by intermediaries.

'Funds' in a private equity context are usually set up in the form of a limited partnership and are unregistered investment vehicles for pooling capital. Here institutional investors are the fund's **'Limited Partners' (LPs)** who commit a certain amount to the fund and do not take an active role in its management. The term **'General Partner' (GP)** refers to the firm as an entity that is legally responsible for managing the fund's investments and who has unlimited personal liability for the debts and obligations.

The LPs' **'Commitments'** are drawn down as needed. There is little, if any, opportunity to redeem the investment before the end of the fund's lifetime. A significant part of the capital remains as **'Undrawn Commitments'** in the hands of the LPs.

'Fund managers' are the individuals involved in the fund's day-to-day management. They form the fund's management team that includes the carried interest holders, i.e., those employees or directors of the GP who are entitled to share in the 'super profit' made by the fund.

There's No Such Thing as a 'Good' Private Equity Strategy

The above statement may seem odd for a book on private equity strategy, but it is important to grasp at the outset. Among private equity fund managers – our 'travelling partners' – the concept of 'strategy' is often considered abstract and bearing little relation to their business. Indeed most fund managers appear to go without a 'real' strategy or confuse strategy with tactics, but are successful nevertheless. It is a corner of the investment world that seems to resist 'business school' strategy formulation. One could put this seemingly cavalier approach down to market immaturity. In fact it signals something fundamental about the nature of private equity investment.

Private equity is at odds with most of the rest of financial markets, which depend upon rich datasets, high precision and frequently updated information. In private equity, investments are often made in conditions of extreme uncertainty and, due to the asset class's illiquidity, decisions are often effectively irreversible.

As an asset class, private equity is competing for funds with other asset classes that appear easier to access, understand, research, monitor and manage. Initially there were few players in an under-explored market that offered rich pickings, now many players have become active with money chasing deals. A few years ago 'access' and due diligence were seen as 'everything', but now the landscape has become more competitive and these traditional tools often do not lead to the desired outcomes any longer. The institutional learning about private equity investments and improvements of skills in assessing such opportunities have to a large degree been neutralised by increased inflows of capital into the asset class.

Private equity is still under-researched: relative allocations are still immaterial, and regulation is frozen in financial technologies that go back to the middle of last century. While academics claim to have a broad understanding about performance determinants on the level of a fund, significantly less is known about factors affecting how an institutional investor in funds performs. The existing research about investor performance determinants has been described as scattered and contradictory; and studies on how institutional investors in private equity funds can strategically affect performance through defined investment strategies are virtually non-existent.[5]

The thesis of this book is that investors in private equity tend to experiment too little and put too much weight on track record and that they overestimate their skills in evaluating opportunities. Perhaps because of the rich-pickings of the past, LPs still tend to underestimate the value of flexibility and rarely actively look for it.

In addition, where flexibility exists, LPs often fail to exploit it because of operational deficiencies. To be successful in a more competitive but uncertain environment, investors in private equity need to build an investment process that seeks new opportunities and efficiently exploits them by moving as quickly as possible. Here institutions often fail to be sufficiently committed to a private equity programme, and fail to put the necessary organisation, processes and procedures in place to become sustainably successful.

Private Equity Is More Biology Than Physics

Clearly, a step-by-step guidebook with clearly identifiable tasks that can be executed and as a consequence lead to a highly profitable investment strategy is not possible. Rather than with hard facts, we are dealing with a social system and cannot assume that this system obeys physical laws or that there is mathematical logic linking its various parts. More than other areas in finance, private equity escapes the rules of science that could provide the authority with which engineering can proceed. In this respect, private equity investing is closer to a social activity than to science or art, and thus offers parallels to Clausewitz's characterisation of war.[6] However, military strategy is an analogy that only applies to some degree. It is rather biological systems that enable growth and survival in a changing and occasionally hostile environment, with a balance between predators and prey that holds useful lessons.

There may be good reasons why 'strategy', associated with 'strategic planning' and 'planning' is not embraced by private equity investment managers. As the key to coping with an uncertain environment is flexibility, any plan carries the danger to take away this hard-fought-for flexibility. Strategy defines the rules, constraints, methods and resources. It cannot be a plan, as this would be too rigid and would quickly become maladapted to an uncertain changing environment. Management theorists like Henry Mintzberg have long argued that emerging strategies are more realistic. On the other hand, investors cannot be too opportunistic, as this often results in herding, essentially having no strategy at all and leading to chaos. Putting day-by-day calculation ahead of mission means that all is tactics but that there is no strategy.

However, it is possible to design and plan portfolios in terms of primary commitments where we are occupying positions in a private equity landscape. Planning aims to minimise search costs, i.e., where to search and how to evaluate opportunities. But one must act opportunistically when managing such a portfolio of positions, i.e., relationships, as it generates options to co-invest or to make secondary deals, or for restructurings, dealing with tail-end situations and fee renegotiations.

Baffling the Boffins

Employees in today's financial markets would struggle with Aristotle's assertion that it is the mark of a trained mind not to expect more precision than a subject matter will allow. In institutions that are subject to oversight, and where regulation desires predictability and boards demand an 'unshakable case' for investing, it is easier to rely on 'science' than to admit to have resorted to judgment as this puts the decision-maker's career at risk. Conventional business strategies place emphasis upon planning and control. For most managers it seems inconceivable that one can work in any other way. However, putting formalised strategies onto paper will sooner or later give away the fact that you do not know much and have little control about the future. Investment managers may have strong views regarding the future, but why take the risk of exposing yourself by disclosing your thinking? In many situations they are essentially relying on hunches and are unable to describe all the relevant factors. Institutions may trust their investment professionals, but depending on individuals who may or may not be excellent investment managers is an uncomfortable perspective.

As Guy Fraser-Sampson caustically concludes in *Intelligent Investing* (2013), it is perhaps for this reason that many investors choose not to have an investment strategy: 'If nobody knows what your objectives are, then nobody can say that you failed to reach them.'[7] This is not necessarily caused by a lack of decisiveness but it is rather reflecting realism about the future. Despite the assertiveness most investment professionals demonstrate, they may well be aware of the fact that the ability to predict is weaker than most of us would like to admit.[8] In environments such as the private equity market, which are characterised by extreme uncertainty, actions chosen to achieve objectives cannot be guaranteed to lead to the intended results.

How You Will Benefit

A well framed investment strategy should enable us to identify and achieve an objective with more certainty, quicker or for less cost. These dimensions – predictability, time and costs – are interrelated and not all can be met simultaneously, which is one explanation why there cannot be an 'optimal' strategy.

This book is intended to help you define some rules of the game to be followed to 'deserve' success in the sense that this substantially improves your chances, but by no means guarantees success.[9] It is like in chess, where an understanding of the rules, the notation and even memorising the big games of the past does not make you a grandmaster. Nevertheless, it is a start.

Chapter 2

A Neo-Classical Asset Class

Depending on your perspective, private equity investing is either very new or very old. There are repeated examples throughout human history of organisational structures that look remarkably like today's private equity limited partnership structure and some of which we will analyse in detail later on. Few, if any, have a direct evolutionary link to today's industry, but they are nevertheless revealing about the nature of private equity investment.

The story of 'modern' private equity is very much a post World War II phenomenon and commonly seen as post-1970s. However, even this story is more complex than it seems, and resists the neat evolutionary narrative that is sometimes attached to it – for instance, from junk bond raiders to mega buyout funds say. What follows, therefore, is not an industry chronology but a reassessment of the classic 'story' with the goal of enabling a clearer analysis of the fundamental nature of private equity and its long-term cycles.

The Modernist Narrative

David Rubenstein, the co-founder of the Carlyle Group, describes the development of the private equity industry between the mid-1970s and mid-2007 in four different stages.[1] The period from 1974 to 1984 is viewed as the infant industry's 'Stone Age', with small 'bootstrapped' deals raised on a transaction-by-transaction basis, with a handful of lenders and largely irrelevant to the financial world.

The 'Bronze Age' from 1985 to 1990 saw opportunities arising from the restructuring of bloated US industry, a wider investor base, the junk bond revolution and outsized returns, culminating in KKR's record breaking leveraged buyout of RJR Nabisco. For the first time the use of leverage drew major adverse publicity.

By the early 1990s, however, the economy slowed and the junk bond market collapsed. Several high-profile buyouts resulted in bankruptcy, and with the development of takeover defences and protections, the leveraged buyouts of public companies virtually disappeared. After reaching a peak in 1989 commitments to buyout funds fell back to the early 1980s level, before slowly increasing again thereafter.[2]

The 'Silver Age' dawned in the mid-1990s after the 'LBO kings' had used their relative hibernation for a professional makeover. The industry adopted 'private equity' as a new name in an effort at this, and a lower interest rate environment was followed by a dramatic increase in the number and size of deals. Instead of giving preference to incumbent managers in MBOs, corporate vendors preferred to sell large divisions through auctions, leading to an increasing number of investor-led buyouts in the late 1990s.[3] Multibillion dollar funds emerged with global investors and lenders and a public pension funds dominated investor base supported many new funds, albeit in an increasingly competitive market.

Buyout activity accelerated after 2002 in both Europe and the US and until 2007 private equity really took off, a period which can indeed be described as its 'Golden Age'. The private equity industry gained a dominant position in the world with its firms becoming, in the words of *The Economist*, the 'New Kings of Capitalism'.[4] Private equity researcher Steven Kaplan estimates that within a quarter century commitments to this asset class increased by a factor of thousands, i.e., from $0.2 billion in 1980 to over $200 billion in 2007.[5] Firms became large, sometimes even listed, but with the glamour again came public criticism and political backlash.

Cornelius (2011) added as a fifth period the 'Great Deleveraging' since 2008, with less leverage and more equity in deals, smaller funds and smaller deals. Raising money from investors became more difficult and commitments to buyout funds reverted to the levels of ten years before. The 'Golden Age' of private equity appears to have given way, to stay with the analogy, to the 'Age of Iron and Rust' with increased demands of firms to focus on strategic and operational improvements, the need to operate globally, in emerged markets, and to deal with corporate social responsibility (CSR) as risk management. This period saw losers but also winners, such as private equity firms emerging as the new merchant banks.

The Elephant and the Shrew

Rubenstein's observations are no doubt shaped by his experiences as a large US buyout investor, and they are commonly held. While this modernist narrative certainly has its fair share of upheaval and reinvention, it is far from the full story. In fact, there was private equity before what he saw as the 'Stone Age', and its history since has been more varied.

It was a handful of venture investments in the late 1950s that triggered the development towards what we know of today as private equity. The dawn of modern venture capital was a predominantly American phenomenon, taking place against a backdrop of great social and technological upheaval, the emergence of television, mass communication, massive military expenditures, the space age and computers. Venture capital could be seen as the brainchild of General George Doriot, the pre World War II Harvard Business School professor, who organised the first non-family VC firm, American Research and Development (ARD), as a publicly traded, closed-end investment company, subject to the Investment Company Act of 1940.

ARD was a pioneering organisation but with a structure that was plagued by a number of problems and with an ultimately failing business model. It was mainly the intermediation through limited partnerships that fostered a widespread adoption of private equity in institutional portfolios. In the early twentieth century increasingly limited partnerships were used in the US to raise capital for prospecting new oil fields. In 1959, Draper, Gaither and Anderson (later renamed Draper Fisher Jurvetson) adopted this structure and raised what, in all likelihood, was the first limited partnership in the VC industry.

Initially buyouts and venture capital were barely differentiated and many firms now recognised as private equity specialists had their roots in venture capital. Building on his experience of co-running the corporate finance division of Bear Stearns, Jerome Kohlberg, together with Henry Kravis and George Roberts, set up KKR in 1976 and in 1978 raised the world's first dedicated leveraged buyout fund as a limited partnership based on the venture capital model with a size of just $30 million.[6] The limited partnership proved to have a better fit with the business environment and could be argued to be the 'ideal' vehicle for private equity investing.[7]

Today, the gap between venture capital and buyout investing is filled with every conceivable permeation of private equity – growth capital, mezzanine, and increasingly infrastructure (such as bridges and roads) and real estate funds are argued to be counted as private equity too. In many ways, the differences between these types of investment are great. The target of buyouts are established businesses – generally privately held or spin-outs from public companies – that need financial capital for restructuring and changing ownership. Whereas buyout investors tend to use high levels of debt for buying whole companies, for growth equity they provide financing in exchange for just a share in the company. Venture capital on the other hand provides high-risk, high-reward finance designed for young companies that have different asset structures, cash flows and growth rates than mature companies. The term 'mezzanine' generally refers to a layer of financing between a company's senior debt and equity. Structurally, it is subordinate in priority of payment to senior debt, but senior in rank to common stock or equity. In acquisitions and buyouts, mezzanine can be used to prioritise new owners ahead of existing owners in the event that a bankruptcy occurs. However, it is typically used to finance the expansion of existing companies.

In practice the delineation between the various forms of private equity is not clear cut and there are even overlaps with hedge funds and the debt financing provided by more traditional financial institutions such as banks. Even the line between private equity and public markets can sometimes be difficult to draw. It is easy to see why simple narratives tend to prevail. A large buyout investor today has little in common with a venture capital investor, and trying to explain the link would confuse people. But, like the elephant and the shrew, fundamental characteristics are not necessarily the most obvious.

Another complexity is that while there is a literal evolutionary link between the buyout elephants and the venture capital shrews of today, there is not necessarily such a link from historical uses of the private equity or limited partnership structure. In fact, the limited partnership structure could be rightly called 'time proven' as very similar structures had emerged in Babylonian times. These structures are not necessarily the ancestors of the modern private equity industry, but they have been 'rediscovered' as what arguably is the 'machine of innovation'. It is all the more puzzling, then, that limited partnerships have attracted so little attention in the fields of financial modelling and investment strategy.

Beast with a Thousand Faces

Rather than attempting to map a coherent narrative of private equity history, those that will draw effective lessons from the past would do better to identify the common themes that precipitate market change and reinvention. We tend to see the past either as more 'primitive' or 'more pure' and by contrast view our current state as either 'evolved' or 'debauched'. More commonly, evolution (or devolution) is a response to external factors, and private equity has shown an amazing ability to adapt itself to changing environments. One clear theme that follows each adaptation is a move from rich pickings to saturation.

The modern private equity industry's roots lie in the enormous US economic expansion following World War II where growth was often favoured over efficiency and assets were mainly acquired for the sake of growth. The resulting conglomerates proved most of the time financially disappointing and thus provided rich opportunities for the newly emerging market for corporate control.[8]

The approach pioneered by Jerome Kohlberg during his time with Bear Stearns was targeting manufacturing companies with stable and steady revenues in dependable but generally unglamorous niche markets. These companies were bought in partnership with their management teams but were essentially paying their own acquisition by themselves borrowing the major part of their purchase price. This technique exploited the US tax code that allowed the companies to treat their debt like capital expenditures, i.e., as an operating expense that is deducted from profits through the depreciation tax schedules. The resulting significant reduction in taxes allowed the companies to retire these massive loans at a fast rate. Finally, the buyout firms sold these investments as soon as possible, usually within four to six years.[9]

The early successes led to the remarkable level of takeover activity during the 1980s. The LBOs by firms that were viewed as 'raiders', as there were no obvious synergies between them and their targets, quickly resulted in adverse publicity and political scrutiny. What annoyed the public and politicians alike was the fact that the investee companies were supposed to sell off their own core assets for repaying the debt incurred in the acquisition. These allegations of asset stripping have never since left the worldwide political debate on private equity.

Law of diminishing returns

In the 1980s, while the industry was still small, it was comparatively easy to identify opportunities, and private equity firms could generate their returns through good deal judgment, essentially 'buying low and selling high'.[10] With an increasing number of new firms entering the market and much higher amounts invested in private equity, this became more challenging, requiring financial engineering combined with powerful incentives, which became the dominant strategy during the 1990s. Like in all entrepreneurial undertakings, profits attract competition and imitators and markets mature. Baker and Smith (1998) estimated that in 1997 there were about 800 'LBO equity' partnerships. The proliferation of funds led to stronger competition for assets, to a degree that traditional sources of private equity value creation process are bid away in auctions. This forced investors to spend more time and effort on the search for opportunities that matched their profile. Private equity funds started to operate internationally, not only in Europe, but increasingly also in emerged and still emerging markets, holding regionally or even globally diversified portfolios of companies. Firms also targeted an internationally diversified investor base. According to Cornelius (2011), large US pension funds had committed around one third of their private equity allocations to non-US funds.

As GPs had to just invest about 2 per cent of a fund's equity and not only received a 20 per cent carried interest but also were receiving various fees, they had a strong incentive to buy bigger businesses, raise larger funds and manage several funds in parallel. This, in combination with growing investor demand for high returns, led to an increasingly competitive environment. In 2006 and 2007, institutional investors, such as pension funds and university endowments, committed a record amount to private equity, both in nominal terms and as a fraction of the overall stock market.[11] The private equity business model so far has been highly lucrative for fund managers, even if their investors were not earning as much. It therefore seems that the industry attracts entrants up to a point where LPs are not sufficiently rewarded and the average performance of private equity is low.

Change as a way of life

While many forms of investment classes, including certain equity investment classes, thrive on stability, private equity's oxygen is change. Facilitating and exploiting the need for change is the sector's raison d'être. Once that change is established, private equity becomes redundant, and so private equity moves from niche to niche, identifying gaps and market failures. Once these opportunities have been spotted, private equity swarms, taking early gains and effectively rebalancing the system.

While such a process tends to keep the system as a whole healthy, some groups may lose out in the process and their anger can often be directed at the surgeon rather than the illness. The past ten years have been a pertinent example of this, where LBO-financed companies were characterised as being stripped of their assets and workers being laid-off, led to public outrage and calls for politics to protect the American people against Wall Street 'parasites'. In Japan, foreign firms such as Ripplewood or Lonestar, who entered the market in the late 1990s and initially dominated the restructuring scene were often referred to as 'hagetaka' (vultures). In 2005, a German mainstream politician, without differentiating between private equity, hedge funds and other financial firms, condemned them all as 'swarm of locusts that fall on companies, stripping them bare before moving on'.[12] Parasites, vultures, locusts, raiders, pirates: these names capture what the public thinks about private equity, and when the financial crisis started in 2008, politicians in Europe and the US saw tightening regulation as a 'locust control' opportunity. Regulatory clampdown as a result of hostile public opinion, often stoked by vested interests, can therefore be seen as an ever present threat to private equity.

Institutional investors in private equity

While modern private equity is a young industry, significant institutional investing into this asset class is even younger. The early investor base – mainly family offices and high net worth individuals – could be described as 'entrepreneurial' and few institutions, for instance insurance companies, had committed to private equity before. For pension funds, such investments were initially considered to be imprudent and inappropriate. However, in 1979 the US Department of Labor clarified its 'prudent man rule' under the Employee Retirement Income Security Act (ERISA) in a way that explicitly allowed pension funds to invest in assets that were perceived to be highly risky. According to Cornelius (2011), in many ways the emergence of the institutionalised private equity industry can be traced to ERISA. In the early 1980s LBOs had also achieved sufficient respectability to attract investments from pension funds and the fiduciaries of educational institutions, such as Harvard University's endowment fund.[13]

The institutionalisation of the industry also lead to demands for more data and industry statistics for benchmarking. At certain times, however, investors were certainly willing to invest under significant uncertainty. Although hardly any research has been undertaken on infrastructure and mezzanine funds, it has not stopped investors from pursuing such opportunities which between 2004 and 2007 attracted a lot of funding.[14]

What's Next?

Modern private equity has moved from an 'exotic' financing technique at the peripheries of corporate finance to the mainstream.[15] Its techniques have been imitated by banks (buying companies using leverage) and major corporations, following private equity's underlying principles, such as alignment of interest between managers and shareholders, rigorous board oversight and focus on execution. This has eroded the opportunities for outside investors.

Will private equity morph into something else? The practices established by a young private equity industry were more compatible with entrepreneurial than institutional investors. Blackstone, Carlyle and KKR are examples of players that have gradually institutionalised and created organisational structures that would outlast their founders. These firms built broader alternative asset platforms and are doing private equity, hedge funds, hedge funds-of-funds, as well as real estate. Many observers predict that institutionalisation will slowly convert private equity partnerships into investment banks, thus 'making the industry poorer as a whole'.[16] The Darwinian struggle we see in this industry regularly raises the spectre of a wider shake-out.[17]

Private equity's demise is frequently and so far erroneously predicted, but we should be alive to the ways in which such a demise could occur. There is a clear danger of being a victim of its own success, attracting too much money, attention and regulation. This would result in a bifurcation of the industry with losers that cannot cope anymore with the new constraints imposed by investors and regulators, and winners who are protected by entry barriers and drift into the merchant banking area. For modern private equity, certain industry trends appear to be irreversible. Regulation will not allow private equity – in its current form at least – to slip under the radar screen again. The industry's poor reputation seems durable.

What lessons, then, can be drawn from this varied and complex portrait of private equity? Resist the temptation to simplify into a narrative. Such a story bias will inevitably lead to false conclusions. Secondly that private equity doesn't have a hereditary line like English monarchs, but springs up as a consequence of external need, and can just as quickly die away. And thirdly that private equity tends to repeat itself. Whenever there is a need through history, the private equity concept tends to be reinvented. It is a time proven phenomenon. So those that describe the model as broken or dead are more likely to be describing a misapplication, poor application or an absence of need.

Speed Read

- One clear theme in private equity's history is a cycle, moving from rich pickings in overlooked niches to saturation and an increasingly competitive environment. Modern private equity has become a victim of its own success, attracting too much money, attention and regulation.
- The private equity concept tends to be reinvented and is a time proven phenomenon. Throughout history, humans have found similar organisational structures to tackle similar challenges.
- The common denominator, the limited partnership structure, is tried and tested with very similar structures present through several millennia. These structures are not necessarily the ancestors of the modern private equity industry, but they have been 'rediscovered' as what arguably is the 'machine of innovation'.
- Those that describe private equity and notably the LP model as 'broken' or 'dead' are more likely to be describing a misapplication, poor application or an absence of need. Indeed, so far little consideration has been given to financial modelling or investment strategy in an LP context.

Chapter 3

The 'Repair Shop of Capitalism'

Those seeking a clear-cut definition of private equity will be disappointed. Even in this most basic of requirements, the asset class resists neatness and order – a trait it shares with other so-called 'alternatives'. This may seem nothing to lose sleep over, but how investors conceptualise and categorise private equity fundamentally affects their assessment of its risks and rewards. Private equity is not even necessarily 'private', nor is it always just 'equity'. For instance, publicly listed private equity is regulated, mezzanine is closer to debt than to equity, securitisations of private equity funds offer access to the bond markets, and secondary transactions are viewed by some as a solution to overcome the asset class's illiquidity. Moreover, other institutional investors have recognised that the core skills of private equity firms – governance and operational engineering, incentives and financial structuring – create value, and so they increasingly imitate private equity's modus operandi.

Definable Traits

Private equity does have some definable traits. It is a structurally illiquid asset class which is commonly understood by institutional investors to carry a compensatory risk premium. To benefit, they must have a liability profile that allows them to lock capital in for a period of usually ten years or even more.[1] But this premium is constantly under attack from forces that would bring private equity into the mainstream. Institutional investors typically focus on the organised private equity market with investing conducted either directly or through funds as unquoted vehicles. Private equity funds are pooled, privately organised investment vehicles administered by professional managers. They are organised on behalf of qualified investors, i.e., they are not open to the public. Because of their structure they can take advantage of exemptions in regulation and legitimately exploit opportunities associated with intransparency. However, a tightening in regulatory requirements across private

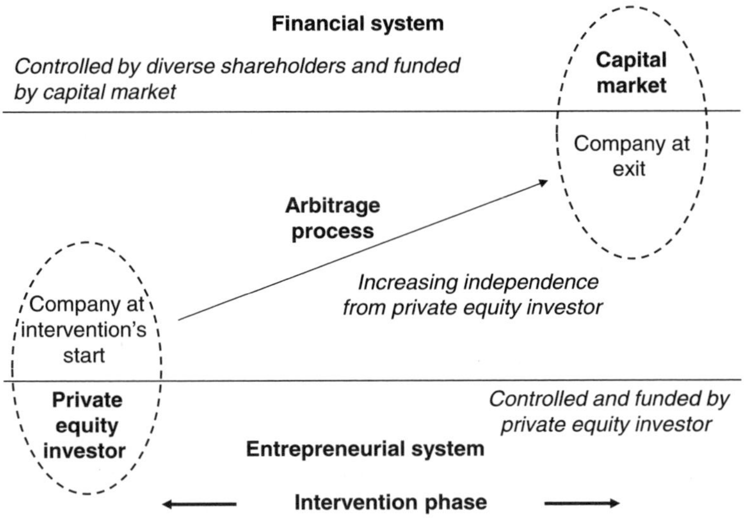

Figure 3.1 Private equity as arbitrage

equity's traditional funding sources – banks, insurers and pension funds – as well as for alternative investment managers, plus a convergence of regulations, led to fewer exemptions that the private equity industry could possibly exploit. Consequently, the space for private equity to operate in profitably appears to be shrinking.

If the best definition of something is in what it *does* rather than what it *is*, then the core of a private equity investment is its strategy to search for arbitrage opportunities in under-researched or overlooked niches, where information is proprietary and there is no or little competition. In addition, crucial for a satisfactory definition of private equity is that here investments are only held temporarily – with a pre-planned or contractually fixed maximum term, which we term here as the 'intervention phase' (see **Figure 3.1**) – with the intention of profitable divestment.

Arbitrage, but Not As You Know It

Within the *financial* system, where financial securities are bought and sold, the term 'arbitrage' has connotations of speculation and mechanistic exploitation of disparities in the pricing of commodities. In this realm, regulation aims to protect the unsophisticated investor and assure fair treatment among all participants, particularly the most vulnerable investors, i.e., those with limited means and short time horizon. Consequently, liquidity has high importance, requiring a high degree of transparency and standardisation to allow high volume and frequent transactions. A large financial sector engages in measuring, dealing and transferring risk.

However, in the *entrepreneurial* system, where entrepreneurs create new goods, services, methods of production, and new forms of industrial organisation, access to information is privileged and information gaps can be legally exploited. Contact between investors and entrepreneurs is direct; indeed, the line between investor and entrepreneur is often blurred. All transactions are negotiated, and such deals are rare and take time. Investors need to have sufficiently deep pockets, must not be subject to short-term liquidity needs and must possess a range of skills. They are providing capital at their own peril and are not, and should not, be protected by financial regulation. High selectivity is key, there is limited scalability, and investments are undertaken in a highly uncertain context. Those seeking opportunities in the entrepreneurial system will not find them on Bloomberg.

It is a fair assumption that wealth creation is driven primarily by the entrepreneurial system with the financial system acting more as enabler and better suitable for wealth protection. As Schumpeter argued, innovation is 'doing things differently' in the realm of economic life and the entrepreneur is the driving force of capitalist development, freed more or less completely from the responsibilities of the financier. While this delineation is not always clear-cut, the super-profits available to private equity investors can be seen as a function of extreme arbitrage between the two systems. In the absence of a better term, this could be described as 'entrepreneurship-arbitrage'. Private equity managers access the financial system for capital, and deploy it within the entrepreneurial system before seeking increasing interaction with, and an eventual exit within, the financial system.

Arbitrage based on information asymmetries

Private equity practitioners commonly emphasise their ability to facilitate operational improvements within investee companies as the main driver of returns. However, a less flattering interpretation is that they merely financially engineer, taking advantage of tax breaks, superior information, or rely on timing and mispricing between debt and equity markets.[2] Whether the equity is listed or not, it is argued to have the same intrinsic risk characteristics. Private equity is often viewed as an asset class that is essentially identical to public equity in terms of its role in a company's capital structure, except for its substantially higher degree of illiquidity.[3] Un-listed companies may need to be given more time to be acquired or sold off but otherwise should follow the same value development and be subject to the same market influences as listed ones.

This certainly holds true for large privately held companies that are operating close to public market competitors. Finding suitable opportunities – highly scalable businesses in attractive sectors and acquiring stakes without heavy leverage – is highly research driven and aims to exploit the general lack of information on certain niches. An example is the successful approach followed by TA Associates L.P.:[4] this firm is systematically identifying and contacting predominantly privately owned, high-growth businesses in its preferred sectors. Owner-managers are called to talk about whether they might be interested in selling the company or growing it and exiting it subsequently. According to Bishop (2012), TA Associates is contacting 10,000 firms a year and visits between 1500 and 1700 of those, which typically results in 15 new investments. However, Steve Kaplan has researched this subject and found that the explanation that private equity firms exploit information asymmetries was unconvincing.[5] This is, for instance, evidenced by the fact that during market booms investors regularly overpay in their leveraged buyouts and experience losses.

Arbitrage based on structural deviations

'Private equity' is markedly different from 'privately held'. Companies deviating from their peer group creates an arbitrage opportunity. An important area of improvement is in the governance of an investee company to make it more palatable to public markets or potential acquirers. Buchanan et al. (2012) describe corporate governance as 'the product of a complex institutional environment shaped by historical forces that are distinct to every national market.' Particularly in emerging markets, many companies either diverge from this model or have not adopted such practices yet and are therefore off the multinationals' radar. This opens opportunities to what could be called 'governance arbitrage' that private equity investors could exploit.[6] This approach makes sense in situations where private-equity-held companies are supposed to be acquired and integrated into publicly quoted companies, or eventually will be exited via an IPO.

Another way private equity firms can 'close the value gap' is by introducing missing management experience, systems, processes, structure, infrastructure, clients, products, services and so on;[7] and by selling off or closing down excess infrastructure, resources, products, services etc. Private equity firms invest with a thesis based on a 'value creation plan' developed with the company's management and comprising, for instance, management changes, hiring of staff, people management, cost reductions, marketing, productivity improvements, strategic changes or repositioning, acquisition envisaged. During the intervention phase, this value creation plan is implemented towards a specific and challenging three- to five-year goal.[8] Firms often establish specialist operations teams that focus day to day on the implementation of 100-day plans to quickly introduce the appropriate management systems and to address problems that need to be fixed urgently. This approach is best summarised by Harvard Business School Professor Malcolm Salter's description of a private equity firm as the 'the repair shop of capitalism'.[9]

Exposure to Market Risk

If we accept that the essence of private equity is 'entrepreneurship-arbitrage' – a process requiring tangible changes to be implemented over an intervention phase spanning several years – then we are clearly talking about something quite different compared to public equity. In which case, our view of market risks will also be affected.

Sell discipline

The key to private equity investing is its sell discipline. Not only is there a strong incentive to perform, and pressure to reach the milestones targeted under the value creation plan, but also the constant buying and selling result in learning curve advantages that private equity firms hold compared to other types of investors.[10]

Prior to such a sale, private equity ownership effectively shields investee companies from distracting communications requests, from noise, from rigid reporting requirements and regulations (compared with listed companies, for instance), and from the vagaries of market sentiment, through consistent financial and managerial support.[11] Such a shield becomes particularly crucial in turnaround situations, or for fledgling businesses seeking to compete with much larger rivals. As we will discuss in more detail later on, private equity funds organised as limited partnerships are designed to shield vulnerable portfolio companies in their early stages and those in need of being restructured from disruptive market influences and to assure these companies' continued financing.

From this perspective it is, as Cornelius et al. (2013) argue, conceptually problematic to look at the market value of a private-equity-held company, especially at an early investment stage and implies that market values, and thus risk, need to be looked at in the context of the investing firm, which at least during the early stage of the intervention process is inseparable from the portfolio company. During the intervention phase, the market value of such an investee company is essentially undefined; secondary sells to other private equity firms are often not the correct reference point to judge market risk, as the price's underlying assumption is that the acquiring private equity firm will continue with the implementation of the, occasionally updated, value creation plan.

Leverage

A key ingredient of private equity investing is leverage – the borrowing that is done in connection with the transaction. Leverage not only amplifies the financial returns but can also increase the company's value, as in many countries interest payments are tax deductible. Equity investments could be seen as offering some protection from capital markets as there is flexibility regarding payments: here management is in control and dividends can be reduced or eliminated as market conditions change. Leverage, however, weakens the protection from the capital market as the creditors decide on the loan's terms and conditions. While operational improvements can create value no matter the direction of the stock market, leverage is very inflexible, increases the probability of the company becoming financially distressed, and amplifies market movements.

In the context of private equity, the risk associated with leverage needs to be looked at from another perspective. This is not only a risk, but also a powerful incentive: leverage creates pressure on the management to focus on the implementation and not to waste time and money in order to make interest and principal payments. Higher leverage than, for instance, observed for publicly listed peers, therefore only constitutes higher risk if the milestones in the value creation plan were missed. As such, leverage can only ever be a temporary value driver because the advantage only lasts while owned by the private equity financer, which is why the debt must be paid down during the intervention period.

Buy-to-hold

Not every privately held company is subject to a private equity investor's intervention following the entrepreneurship-arbitrage model. Fraser-Sampson (2013) differentiates between private equity investors who buy-to-sell and strategic buyers who 'buy-to-hold' (or 'buy-to-keep'). Some institutional investors, such as sovereign wealth funds, pension funds and also corporations, follow the private equity modus operandi and implement a value creation plan, but here, after the intervention phase, instead of a sell-off follows an indefinite 'holding phase' where investors become rather passive and the portfolio companies are exposed again to the market.

As Achleitner and Albrecht (2011) pointed out, equity can be held over very long time periods, allowing the build up reserves that are linked to inflation and the overall growth of the economy. Such reserves are of considerable importance for life insurance companies, which can smooth returns and through realisations help achieve the predictable and stable investment results expected by both shareholders and customers. This is an important advantage compared to what we have described as private equity, where the intervention phase is limited, but on the other hand, there is no remaining potential for entrepreneurship-arbitrage.

The Limits of Financial Models

Financial models that assume a more or less liquid market, despite the rich set of analytical tools available, are of limited use for this discussion: even if they are valid for what we termed here the financial system, most of their critical underlying assumptions do not hold for the entrepreneurial system. Private equity investments are regularly mispriced because they still are developing or being restructured. The approach relevant for our further discussion is the arbitrage based on structural deviations, implying a restructuring over a defined intervention phase.

Despite a hypothetically large size of the market for non-quoted companies, relatively few fit the private equity investors' profile of an ideal target for entrepreneurship-arbitrage. Identifying highly scalable businesses in attractive sectors and acquiring stakes without heavy leverage is challenging in mature economies but may work better in emerging markets. The willingness of conglomerates to sell orphan units that can be restructured and exited profitably moves very cyclically.

Speed Read

- Private equity investors seek opportunities for wealth creation in the entrepreneurial system. The super-profits available to private equity investors can be seen as a function of extreme arbitrage between the entrepreneurial and the financial systems.
- We suggest a clearer differentiation between 'private equity' investing and 'privately held' companies. Private equity investing follows a 'buy-to-sell' modus operandi with what we termed here 'entrepreneurship-arbitrage' and where during an intervention period portfolio companies are shielded from market risk. Privately held companies, on the other hand, are 'bought-to-keep' and do not undergo the intervention of a private equity led restructuring. They therefore have the same intrinsic risk characteristics as their public market peers.
- In the entrepreneurship-arbitrage process, private equity firms access the financial system for capital, and deploy it within the entrepreneurial system and invest with a thesis based on a 'value creation plan' developed with the company's management. After successful completion of the private equity intervention, portfolio companies are eventually exited within the financial system.
- During this intervention phase the concept of market value and market risk is not fully applicable, which requires a refinement of how we think of risk from the private equity investor's perspective.

Chapter 4
Strategy Challenges

The lack of published thought on private equity strategy is surprising, even when you account for the confidentiality that is so highly prized in this industry, and consequent attempts to preserve competitive advantages. This chapter gives an overview of strategy challenges that an institutional investor in private equity will face.

It's important to detail upfront what is outside the scope of this chapter. It does *not* consider the specifics of deal-structuring; the value creation process by GPs during the intervention phase (for instance through margin improvements and strategic sales); how private equity investors build value in portfolio firms, as this goes beyond the question of investment strategy. It also ignores the competition against other asset classes such as hedge funds or real estate funds and avoids detail of a private equity company's business strategy, such as how to differentiate from other asset managers. Such questions have effectively been dealt with in a wide body of management literature, including such classics as the works of Michael Porter and Gary Hamel. Instead we focus on the pure investment activity, i.e., investment 'proper', and provide an introduction into aspects that will be explored in greater detail later on.

Strategy – Martial and Biological

'Strategy' is a term commonly used in management, but its root is the Greek word 'stratēgos' for 'general' or 'commander', which in return derives from two words: 'stratos' and 'ago', the ancient Greek words for 'army' and 'leading', respectively. Whether military battle is a good analogy may be debatable, but many practitioners and academics see no better metaphor for business than warfare: writers on business strategy regularly refer to Sun Tzu's, *The Art of War*, written around 500 B.C. and von Clausewitz's, *On War*, from 1832. For example, in the context of investments Guy Fraser-Sampson defines strategy as 'an action plan designed to achieve specific objectives', believing that this would be consistent with von Clausewitz's view.[1]

Another soldier, Colonel (retired) Dr. Harry Yarger, gives a definition of strategy which applies to military as well as business: 'In simplistic terms, strategy at all levels is the calculation of objectives, concepts, and resources within acceptable bands of risk to create more favourable outcomes than might otherwise exist by chance or at the hands of others'.[2] This definition recognises the fuzziness of risk and the shifting objectives investors are faced with in reality. Importantly, it acknowledges a lack of resources as a major reason for thinking about strategy. In other words, if one is unrestricted in this respect, inefficiencies and mistakes will not really matter. Essentially therefore, strategy is about dealing with constraints, such as having too few resources – in terms of capital or time – to achieve desired outcomes, or to have too few opportunities for given resources.

Strategy in the context of war, and often in business, acknowledges the presence of opponents and competitors. For private equity markets, however, it often does not make sense to see competitors as adversaries. They are certainly rivals but they are also partners with whom to combine resources and coordinate activities. In this environment competition is to a large degree not a zero-sum game. One investor's advantage is not necessarily another investor's disadvantage. Markets have no final outcome, there is no 'last man standing' and even weaker market participants survive in their specialisation. In other words, we are looking more at 'strategies' such as those in biological systems, where private equity investors occupy niches in the market, building on advantages such as better vision, size, speed, specialisation, flexibility and reflexes in situations where there is no time for leisurely analysis. The private equity landscape is clearly a highly Darwinian environment, where pressure to perform is relentless and adaptation is key.

Reflexes specifically attune with an uncertain and changing environment are built into what could be described as the private equity industry's 'operational code': keeping costs as low as possible, focus on efficiency and simplicity, and reliance on diversification. Other parts of this operational code include reliance on 'stealth', so not to invite hostile public reaction or attract competition, 'diplomacy', i.e., to avoid confrontation and litigation and rather work in alliances and relationships with trusted parties where interests are aligned and tasks are delegated, and a high degree of 'patience' to be able to ride out adverse market cycles.

There is No Such Thing as a Passive Private Equity Investment Strategy

Haight et al. (2007) defines investment strategy as 'the plan(s) and methods that will be employed to realise the investment return goals'. One common way of approaching this is by classification, for example, as 'venture capital' or 'leveraged buyout'. Here strategy is essentially reduced to a description of a target, which can also be refined, such as 'experienced high quality GPs'. Another approach is to describe strategies as 'active' or as 'passive' or as a combination of both. Passive strategies aim to match the returns of predetermined indices and to minimise transaction costs. Active strategies seek returns that exceed such indices, but require an expensive research process and high transaction costs. Private equity does not really fit this distinction because there is no passive investment strategy in the real sense, although funds-of-funds could be seen as the closest thing to passive investing for alternative asset classes. Such definitions of strategies are anchored in the world of efficient markets and are implicitly based on the assumption that investors operate in an environment that nearly follows the laws of physics. Here investment strategy would be closer to applying relatively fixed rules with clear relationships between causes and effects, which is not the case for private equity.

In a wider context, investment strategy needs to address how a private equity firm invests and how financial principles are used to generate value for its investors. But do we really need to go beyond what we have described before as 'reflexes'? In theory, having an investment strategy should provide better outcomes than having none. But how far do we need to go and how rigid must an investment strategy be? In private equity, 'investment strategy' appears to be very often just grandstanding that greatly inflates what most of the time could be described simply as 'technique'. Clearly, strategy cannot be a rigid box-ticking exercise but what is superior: the structured and methodical approach which is consistent, teachable and transparent, or the unsystematic approach followed by many practitioners who rely on 'gut feel' but have experience and, like experts in art appraisal, can see the 'big picture'?

Historically industry practice has tended towards the latter, but particularly the Great Recession demonstrated that private equity as an illiquid asset class comes with complications that suggest more reflection is necessary. Here wrong investment decisions cannot be corrected through selling positions off, at least not without a high likelihood of incurring losses. Industry observers point to securitisations and secondary transactions, but these avenues to liquidity only work to a limited degree and tend to dry up precisely when they are needed. Instead, an investment strategy should be based on the assumption that many decisions are irreversible in practice and specifically address the asset class's illiquidity, which limits the applicability of the rich tool set available for managing traded assets.

The obvious reason why an investment strategy is needed is to attract capital for investing, i.e., to make the case when seeking funding that agreed objectives are likely to be met or even exceeded. While the investment strategy should be plausible and explain what will be done for success being 'deserved', practitioners fear that giving too much detail will be overly constraining and jeopardise the flexibility needed to cope with a changing environment.

Access to Capital

The question how to attract capital is probably the most difficult one, as all other thoughts become academic without resources for investment, and, in fact, many newly founded private equity firms never overcome this hurdle. Capital can be provided 'deal-by-deal' and 'just-in-time', i.e., when a suitable opportunity is identified, which, however, will usually result in significant delays needed to convince investors, during which the opportunity often vanishes. Consequently, the private equity industry has preferred funds as a way to buffer capital and in order to only have to raise capital from time to time. Some established and 'proven' performers have developed strong relationships with investors and aim to defend these privileged positions. The need to get access to capital triggers continuous innovation by first movers, regarding the markets and clients targeted, the financial instruments applied and the channels used. An entire industry of gatekeepers has developed around fundraising and there is unfortunately no magic formula. Clearly there are also interdependencies: having proved to be able to generate high financial return certainly helps to attract further capital.

If we exclude behemoths such as the Blackstone Group, the Carlyle Group or KKR – who could justifiably be described as 'fundraising machines' that based on their strong brands are able to ride out cycles – private equity is what Michael Porter described as 'fragmented industry', populated by a large number of predominantly privately-held small and medium-sized firms.[3] Its important characteristics are diseconomies of scale related to the number of investments as well as assets under management and low overall entry barriers, at least during boom periods in the market. Private equity strongly depends on experienced investment professionals, requires a high degree of customisation in the investment approach with a strong creative content, and relies on personal networks. In fragmented industries, increased value added and a low cost basis is critical.

There are a number of ways of entering such a market and of coping with fragmentation: the typical way to operate is as a specialist for an industry, geography or product type (such as mezzanine or preferred equity), at least during the market entry stage. Another approach is a specialisation by customer type. One example (albeit already quite dated) for innovation that helped to broaden the investor base is securitisation of private equity funds. Such so-called Collateral Fund Obligations (CFOs) proved over the years to be an attractive fundraising tool. From a distribution's point of view, CFOs have broadened the potential investor base by opening the asset class to fixed-income investors. Also, listed private equity is a way to widen the investor base as it promises liquidity and a quick entry into the asset class. Arguably, listed private equity caters for the needs of less sophisticated investors, who may not know much about this asset class and do not fulfil the requirements an LP needs to meet. Listed private equity may also be an option for institutional investors subject to regulatory restrictions and who cannot invest in illiquid and risky alternative asset classes, as it meets the requirements of regulation, tax efficiency and transparency. Another aspect of getting access to capital, in this case internally available resources, for investing in private equity is the question of asset allocation, a question we will revisit in the next chapter.

Costs

Justifiably, private equity can be labelled as a very expensive asset class. Therefore costs and how to keep them under control is a major concern of most investors. Financial intermediation in the context of private equity is often looked at from a cost vs. benefit perspective, questioning whether intermediaries such as gatekeepers – funds-of-funds, consultants, account managers and

GPs – offer sufficient value. Often there is a clear case for such intermediation, notably for the pooling of resources for investing. The value added by the various intermediations offered by external parties is increasingly questioned, but this is rather a question of outsourcing vs. in-house approaches.

Another function of financial intermediation is the transformation of risk characteristics of assets, which is differently interpreted in the context of the private equity industry's extreme uncertainty. Here delegation to trusted fund managers at least in part becomes a necessity, in order to be flexible and assure quick reaction in a changing market environment.

Moreover, there is a clear link between market size and its efficiency. Smaller niches that are under-researched and do not attract material amounts of capital offer the best opportunities for the private equity model. Some investors believe that they can save costs, mainly related to fund management fees, and achieve higher returns by investing directly. However, there are clear limits for investing directly and with increasing capital to be allocated to private equity, institutional investors have no choice but to become highly diversified and thus involve fund managers.

The attraction of focusing on costs is that as a 'strategy' it shows immediate results: costs can be reduced, for instance, by negotiating management fees downward, or through seeking just minimum compliance with the organisation's needs or regulatory obligations. However, LPs should move beyond the myopic focus on the specific fund's compensation structure and rather look at the entire compensation over the lifetime of their relationship with a GP. LPs need to think about incentives not costs; paying high management fees for spectacular performance ultimately is better than paying no management fees for underperformance. Instead they need to manage relationships with GPs, which form the backbone of an institutional portfolio and support co-investments, i.e., the syndication of a financing round between a private equity fund and one or more of its LPs, and direct investments.

So now we have our money, what strategic approach and skills are required to achieve our objectives; how should the portfolio be constructed in order to achieve a targeted balance between risks and returns and how can these be quantified in an uncertain environment? Finally, what techniques and processes are required to execute on all this? As we shall argue, investors in private equity tend to experiment too little and put too much weight on track record, overestimating their skills in evaluating opportunities and underestimating the value of flexibility and the effort needed to make use of this flexibility.

Accessing Talent

LPs are relentless in their quest for the best GPs, and trust in their own skills to identify them. Many publications and presentations on private equity give the impression that this is just about picking the 'first quartile' and that the key to investment success is found in the access to such 'top performers'. The example of other industries with arguably comparable dynamics, such as arts, movies and fashion, suggest caution regarding overly relying on one's selection skills. Compared to determining whether a fund will be 'top', predicting whether a movie becomes a 'hit' appears to be a comparatively simple exercise, notably given the wide experience with hundreds of film productions each year. Hollywood producers are convinced that they are able to do this, but the economist Arthur De Vany looked at the empirical evidence and concluded that this conventional wisdom has to be rejected, demonstrating that outcomes cannot be predicted.[4] Even big budgets with stars have resulted in 'turkeys' (for instance, *Waterworld*, the most expensive movie at the time with the then-megastar Kevin Costner), while on the other hand, huge hits have been produced without stars and with low budgets (such as *My Big Fat Greek Wedding* or *Slum Dog Millionaire*). In fact, De Vany points to the 'curse of the superstar': with star movies having only a marginally higher chance of making a profit than those without famous actors, the higher fees claimed by the stars almost make sure that their movies make losses – a situation to some degree resembling that of oversubscribed funds. The novelist and screenwriter, William Goldman, legendarily defined the law of Hollywood to be that 'no one knows anything.' Consequently, under this extreme uncertainty, money can only be made through diversified portfolios of movies and by managing costs so that big 'hits' pay for the unavoidable 'turkeys'.

Maybe LPs have problems in identifying them, but is the spread between top and bottom performers in private equity really mainly caused by skills? The private equity industry points to the GPs' performance persistence, i.e., that more experienced and competent fund managers will perform significantly better than others. When looking at another area of the alternative asset space, the arts market, there is another signal that cautions us not to rely too much on this as well. Common advice given to their clients by art dealers is to buy the best (i.e., most expensive) artworks they can afford. This presumes that masterpieces of well known artists will outperform the market. Economic research, however, found strong evidence that expensive paintings tend to underperform the art market index and suggested that investors should not be obsessive with masterpieces and they need to avoid overbidding.[5] In fact, art lovers as well as investors would be better advised to consider emerging artists. Examining the return-risk ratio of the various sectors suggests that modern and contemporary art offer the highest risk-adjusted return.[6] Of course, as in the case of first-time funds in private equity, the challenge is to recognize the rising star artists – which clearly requires experience and judgment.

Performance persistence is a seductive argument, but it can prompt over-optimism, for instance, of the chances that strong performance shown in previous funds will persist even though, for instance, the targeted industry sector is in decline. As a consequence, LPs may become complacent and not quickly enough reduce or even stop the relationship with a GP and fail to increase their commitments to other firms instead. Also as a consequence of the high reliance on persistence as decision criterion, the market is biased against smaller and less known players. But, as every proven business model will attract further investment and competition, is relying on a, probably outdated, track record really a good way for investing in private equity? Despite all efforts to be better in selecting investments than the competition, the outcome may be a better protection against failure but systematic outperformance through selection skills alone does not appear to be realistic.

With a maturing asset class the talent of fund managers has been converging, fund managers without skills are unlikely to make it through an ever-tightening due diligence sieve. Innovations become commoditised. Rigid, standardised due diligence makes it difficult to invest in smaller funds without or with shorter track records. This, however, works against Darwinian pressure and protects the industry's 'dinosaurs' leading to evolutionary stasis.

Measuring Risk

Conventional wisdom suggests that private equity is more risky and therefore offers higher return than public equity. However, the high return potential is not confirmed by research. Are institutional investors worldwide getting it wrong and investing irrationally? There is a vicious circle where private equity is perceived to be very risky, resulting in small, if any, allocation to this asset class. Due to the immaterial exposure, no great effort is put into modelling risks, and investors just use simple but misleading methods, which make private equity again look too risky.

Despite their wide acceptance, the traditional ways of valuing funds – and as a consequence of measuring – their risk are too simplistic. They also distort our perception of how this asset class performs. The perception that risk for private equity is 'very high' may be true for individual investments and despite all efforts to conduct high-quality due diligence even industry standard private equity funds have a significant probability of losing capital. On a portfolio of funds level, however, gains tend to more than compensate for these losses.

Regarding portfolio management, views are diverging and most practitioners try to model private equity as simply an inefficient area of the financial market. Overwhelmingly, thinking about portfolio construction is anchored in the Efficient Market Hypothesis (EMH) and Markowitz's Modern Portfolio Theory (MPT) and depends on high-quality market data. Private markets do not provide such data and questions around return, risk and correlation are impossible to answer with the precision needed to meet the MPT's assumptions. Much effort is spent on attempts to eliminate uncertainty and make private equity predictable, to a degree where the asset class's significant irreducible uncertainty is even denied.

Dealing with Uncertainty

The first requirement of dealing with uncertainty is to accept it exists. This does not necessarily mean that traditional investment management techniques must be torn up, but they require a different interpretation in this context. Dealing with uncertainty can be tackled with resources in the form of 'deep pockets' and time (both of which limit the type of investors that can become active in private equity), monitoring, diversification, flexibility and real options.

While effective strategies are oriented towards a specific objective, the time available to meet a particular goal is also a crucial factor. Private equity practitioners advocate buy-and-hold and, based on anecdotal evidence, the market rewards investors who steadily invest through the vintage years and are consistent. Stern and

Deimler (2006) pointed out that rather than being an obstacle, uncertainty is the very engine of transformation in a business, a continuous source of new opportunities, and as a strategic weapon, 'time is the equivalent of money, productivity, quality, even innovation.' Time, usually associated with illiquidity and seen as a negative, in fact is the basis for investment success, as it allows for the riding out of adverse market cycles and the searching for opportunities. Rather than looking at a risk and return relationship as the mechanics of efficient markets imply, investors look at a relationship between patience (i.e., acceptable waiting time) and return potential.

One extension of the EMH is the so-called Adaptive Market Hypothesis (AMH) put forward by Andrew Lo from the MIT Sloan School of Management. It has several implications that differentiate it from the EMH and offers a more convincing model for the private equity market space. The AMH acknowledges the existence of arbitrage opportunities and assumes that the investment landscape is fuzzy and continuously changing. Consequently, data is non-existent or unreliable and specifically relationships between risk and returns are not stable over time. The AMH follows an evolutionary approach. The sole objective for market participants is survival, which is enabled, for instance, through delivering competitive financial returns.

Generally in alternative assets, investors search for arbitrage opportunities where they can operate with no or little competition and based on proprietary insights. Opportunities for arbitrage emerge and vanish after a while. Continuous innovation is needed to search for pockets of inefficiency in the private equity market, and adaption to changing market conditions helps to achieve a consistent level of targeted returns. The interpretation of private equity as arbitrage resonates with the approaches to finding uncontested market spaces described in *Blue Ocean Strategy*, a book on corporate strategy by INSEAD professors W. Chan Kim and Renée Mauborgne. They argue that competition should be made irrelevant by finding uncontested market spaces that offer opportunities for highly profitable growth. They refer to these spaces as 'blue oceans' and contrast them to 'red oceans' of crowded market spaces where there are clear boundaries and cut-throat competition turns the water bloody.[7]

As a generalisation, and being applicable in the EMH as well as in the AMH context, we view the cause of risk and the associated opportunity as doing something different or doing things differently. 'Doing' can refer to action as well as inaction. Increased risk is taken when investors experiment and deviate from the practices followed by the majority of the market participants, which is close to the idea of 'mutations' in biological systems.

Generally transparency, often viewed as synonymous with publicly available high-quality data, is believed to reduce risk. However, moving towards market niches with higher uncertainty does not necessarily imply higher probability of failure. Decision-makers should not confuse the absence of high-quality quantitative data with risk. Paradoxically, for private equity more data of better quality is an indication for high risk to underperform.

Balancing between diversification and focus is problematic, as diversification is not a value-creating strategy for an LP, whereas focus requires the ability to forecast, which is in contrast with a highly uncertain environment. Diversification is viewed as one of the strongest tools to mitigate risk but for private equity there is a point where it becomes too expensive. Diversification could be argued to take a further meaning in the context of AMH. Here diversification is not just protection against uncertainty but also aims to minimise the costs related to the search for new opportunities. Diversification needs to be seen in the context of creating real options; to be able to exercise them requires that the investors have put the right processes in place.

Due to the non-scalability of this market, the main approach for LPs to create a basis for competitive advantage is to search for new relationships, and to exploit and maintain existing relationships. Investors new to the private equity market have little choice, but rather need to take the gamble with emerging managers or need to settle with easy-to-access but also unexciting funds. Privileged access to the 'golden circle' of private equity firms allows the LP to invest the desired ticket size, but relationships are fleeting; they become strained or get depleted. In fact, this type of access becomes a 'fight for territory', not unlike a military strategy. Moreover, such funds tend to be oversubscribed and thus unwilling to reduce fees or offer other concessions to their LPs. Instead the solution is to escape onto the 'blue ocean' of smaller and emerging funds and markets. To search for and build new relationships in emerging market spaces is very expensive and requires 'connoisseurs' with diplomatic skills. Reconnaissance and intelligence to search for strategic positions is a people business and also has only limited scalability.

Inherent in the fact that we are dealing with investments under uncertainty, there is a high reliance on professional judgment, which often results in mistrust on the side of investors, the public and regulators. Clear size limitations, with opportunities often too small with fleeting 'pockets' of profitability, imply delegation, with many investors struggling to find the right balance between too little control and micromanaging. Geographically, as well as metaphorically, LPs are relatively mobile, whereas GPs are far more tied to their position in the market place and need to adapt to changing market conditions in order to assure their survival. Adaptation inevitably leads to questioning such 'style drifts', but instead flexibility needs to be encouraged as long as it does not involve straying away from a firm's core competencies. The only way to assure initiative and resilience against adverse market changes is through decentralisation, subsidiarity and trust.[8]

Another important concept for dealing with high uncertainty is the 'real option', i.e., the right, but not the obligation, to take an action. Real options are an important but often overlooked tool for institutional investors. They allow for dealing with uncertainty and amplify the impact of positive developments. Because traditional valuation approaches such as the Net Present Value (NPV) ignore flexibility, real options have become powerful tools for investment strategists.

By way of illustration, take the example of the Spanish fashion retailer Zara. Zara effectively acknowledges that it has no idea what shoppers will buy the next season. Instead, it adopts what Watts (2011) called a 'measure-and-react strategy', which is basically building a portfolio of real options. Instead of betting on tomorrow's 'hot look', Zara waits to see what customers are actually buying – and then makes it. Agents are sent out to scour gathering places like shopping malls in order to observe what people are already wearing. Based on these observations, Zara produces a large portfolio of styles, fabrics and colours, but initially makes each combination in only a small batch. Samples are sent to stores, where one can then observe directly what fashion will be adopted. In order to exercise its real options, the cornerstone of Zara's strategy is the process, i.e., the ability to design, produce, ship and sell a new garment anywhere in the world in just over two weeks. In this way, it can react quickly to the information that is coming directly from the stores. The styles that are not selling are dropped immediately, thus saving costs even if there is relatively little left-over inventory anyway, and successful products are scaled up rapidly. Zara is never associated with any one style which could fall out of fashion.[9]

In private equity investment decisions are largely irreversible in practice, but to some degree they can be staged. We interpret, for instance, follow-on investments, co-investments, 'top-ups', or access to secondary opportunities as real options for an LP. Portfolio management needs to be based on engineering flexibility in the form of real options and creating a process to exercise them efficiently.

Implementation

Investment strategies typically comprise a limited number of set decision-making rules. Such rules are set against a simplified model of the market and they are very often overwritten by management judgment. This renders the purpose of the entire exercise somehow questionable. We are now faced with conflicting perspectives: on one hand we need to design – in other words, plan – portfolios but on the other hand, flexibility – or to put it differently, opportunism – is the key characteristic of private equity investing. Certain things need to be planned – commitments are technically irreversible – others cannot be. The answer to this conundrum lies in the differentiation between strategy and tactics, where General Dwight D. Eisenhower observed: 'The doctrine of opportunism, so often applicable in tactics, is a dangerous one to pursue in strategy.'[10]

That strategy is not to be confused with planning does not mean that planning in the sense of engineering a portfolio has no role in strategy. In the beginning, investors in private equity were largely wealthy individuals but new capital flowing into the asset class now mostly comes from larger institutional investors. These tend to be more risk-averse, less willing to accept illiquidity and volatility and also, due to their fiduciary duties, are unable to make bold contrarian bets and rely on consultants who tend to give uncontroversial recommendations. In this situation, a formal 'strategic plan' can build in the bold contrarian bets, for instance, in the form of a limit system and can address the flexibility and quick reaction needed in the form of processes and procedures. Developing a formalised strategy could be interpreted as a 'war game' which facilitates communication within an organisation about the possible scenarios which could materialise. While no strategic plan can address the uncertainty, the discussions around this are necessary to improve the understanding and get agreement within an organisation that allows a quicker and more appropriate reaction when investing. If we need to constantly analyse at every turn, we would be paralysed and unable to act. Instead, planning and processes help to support flexibility.

Strategies in private equity address the intermediate time horizon in order to find a balance between steadily investing and holding on to the investments on the one side – basically ignoring the current market environment – and reacting to opportunities that are in the process of emerging on the other. So strategy may be more relevant as a framework for various tactics to be employed in a specific situation. Strategy is the overall concept whereas tactics are the actual means used to implement it or to respond to changing conditions. Strategy answers the questions 'where', 'what' and 'which location', whereas tactics define 'how' to compete within the constraints set by the strategy and by the dimension of time.[11] The time horizon may help to differentiate between tactics and strategy.[12] Strategy is about the more distant future, whereas tactics are often a fairly instant action and take advantage of opportunities. Moreover, tactics are closer to the idea of techniques, which only work temporarily, while strategies as method should work for the long term. In practice, of course, the distinction is less clear cut and what is one person's strategy may be another's tactics.

The steps set out in the action plan that aims to achieve an objective are tactics, not strategy, and are typically short-term oriented. Associated with the various strategies, there are several tactics investors in private equity apply. Such tactics, for instance, aim to reduce or limit costs, for instance related to management fees charged by funds, to an excessive diversification in too many funds, or to one's own value chain. There are also tactics that aim to assure 'survival', like diversifying and waiting, which tend to be expensive and thus are in conflict with the aim of reducing costs. Other tactics are related to 'search', i.e., researching, identifying and analysing promising opportunities. Then there are tactics for managing relationships – relating to GPs as well as to other LPs – in order to secure and protect access to investment opportunities.

An important aspect of any strategy is continuity and particularly in the context of a long-term oriented and illiquid asset class not having built up the necessary skills and processes, short-termism and radical shifts in allocations appear to have contributed most to the disappointments investors have experienced with private equity. There is the old military maxim, allegedly coined by General Omar

Bradley, that 'amateurs talk strategy; experts talk logistics'. In other words, the best strategy will not be of help in achieving stated objectives unless there is the ability to execute it. The strategy could be viewed as the concept, tactics as the actions to turn the strategy into reality and logistics as the provision of the resources necessary for such action. A major part of strategy is allocating resources and assuring the organisational commitment necessary to deliver – what could be referred to as logistics. When talking about logistics we are essentially looking at setting up and continuously improving and adapting the value chain that supports the investment process.

Rather than individual decisions, creating a process and following it methodically appears to be the key. Many institutional investors in private equity could be argued to suffer from 'GP envy', trying to imitate their behaviour and modus operandi. What appears to be overlooked is that, compared to directly investing, LPs are (or should be) following a different investment process. This investment process is neither simpler nor more difficult, it is just distinctively different and requires other methods and skills. LPs have strategic choices that go beyond the picking of funds, for instance related to managing relationships with GPs or their portfolio's composition, that drive investment performance. Most institutions invest directly as well as through funds and are thus facing the challenge of making these two different investment processes work together effectively.

Strength Derived from Method

Luttwak (1976) succinctly defines strategy as 'strength derived from method'. The organisational preconditions for success have to be created in the form of a business model, for instance, by developing and building the value chain for private equity investing. This is in line with some investment managers' perception that strategy is 'beyond three years', which also appears to be a realistic time frame for building up resources, methodologies (such as for research and due diligence), skills, staff and infrastructure. As Michael Porter observed, strategy cannot be continuously reinvented. Also, to assure continuity this realistically can only be driven by somebody 'hierarchically high'. An investment strategy needs to be explainable and one needs to be able to check whether it is implemented or not.

Speed Read

- There is little writing on the topic of private equity investment strategy, which is less belligerent and deliberate, and more akin to biological systems. Players cooperate, minimise risks, and inhabit niches based on skills and character advantages.
- There is no such thing as a passive private equity strategy, or at least you will not survive long. Even for those that view 'natural reflexes' as sufficient, the ability to articulate a strategy is usually a requirement in order to raise capital in the first place.
- The right starting point for dealing with uncertainty is to accept it exists. Investors should be careful when applying concepts such as 'performance persistence' or traditional management techniques to private equity. The Adaptive Market Hypothesis (AMH), put forward by MIT professor Andrew Lo, which acknowledges the existence of arbitrage opportunities and assumes an environment of constant flux, seems relevant to private equity.
- Private equity flourishes in an environment of extreme uncertainty. Rather than being an obstacle, uncertainty is a continuous source of new opportunities and the very engine of innovation. A private equity investment strategy has to embrace uncertainty and emphasize experimentation, adaptability and flexibility.

Chapter 5
Strategic Asset Allocation

Investment strategy is often viewed as synonymous with asset allocation.[1] Asset allocation answers what asset classes to invest in and what would be an optimal mix of these. A large body of economic research suggests that asset allocation is the main driver of investment performance and that the added value provided by the selection of a particular asset within the class is minimal. While this may be debatable in the case of private equity, where selection is still viewed to be paramount, asset allocation is nevertheless a key concept in investing. Its fundamental justification is the notion that different asset classes perform differently in different market and economic conditions, and as a consequence, this type of diversification has been described as the 'only free lunch' available in financial markets.

Relevant questions in our discussion are how much to allocate to private equity relative to other asset classes and how much to commit in absolute terms. How private equity is embedded in a broader asset allocation, with for example publicly quoted assets, is touched on in, for example, Swensen (2000), Fraser-Sampson (2006) and Cornelius (2011).

What is an Asset Class?

A definable asset class should have distinct risk–return properties, be homogenous, mutually exclusive and diversifying.[2] An asset class should have the capacity to absorb a significant fraction of the investor's wealth to allow a meaningful allocation within a portfolio.

Categorisations and definitions of asset classes are less clear than often perceived. There are significant overlaps; for example, should publicly quoted private equity be categorised as public or as private equity? Under Solvency II, listed private equity would sit within the public equity risk allocation with a significantly lower shock buffer. Is private equity 'equity', including public equity, or does it belong to alternatives, including hedge funds, or is it just illiquid funds, including real estate, infrastructure, and can we count debt such as mezzanine as belonging to the asset class as well? The more detail with which one tries to define an asset class and segregate it from others, the more one is confronted with overlaps and fuzziness. With such fuzzy definitions, allocations are to a large degree subject to management's judgment.

Modern Portfolio Theory

Nobel laureate, Harry Markowitz, developed the idea that because assets have unique risk and return characteristics, they can be combined in a way that maximises return for any given level of risk. This Modern Portfolio Theory (MPT) is based on the fundamental principle of diversification and has proven to be a powerful idea that since it was put forward in 1952 has dominated the thinking around investing. Underlying the MPT is the Efficient Market Hypothesis (EMH), assuming markets are perpetually in equilibrium and 'informationally efficient'. In this world, price changes cannot be forecasted as they should fully incorporate the information and expectations of all market participants. MPT suggests that for efficient markets, allocation choices are simple. Investors choose the appropriate combination of the risk-free asset and the market portfolio that is in line with their level of risk aversion.

To apply MPT, investors should be able to evaluate returns, risk – as measured by the standard deviation of returns – and correlations for all considered assets to determine an efficient asset allocation. Models based on MPT may be adequate for the universe of publicly traded instruments. But for private equity correlations, volatilities and returns cannot be determined with any degree of reliability and most of the MPT's critical underlying assumptions are not met.[3]

Allocations based on MPT are usually described as 'static'. Investors react when the portfolio composition deviates from the target allocation or when limits are breached. Data are reliable and precise only over short periods of time and thus require a regular and quick rebalancing. Actually, such models should rather be viewed as 'dynamic', in the sense that regular rebalancing of the portfolio is required and assumed to be possible. This clearly does not work for an illiquid asset class and particularly allocations to private equity funds are in practice 'irreversible'.

The Yale Model

The 'Yale Model' – also known as the 'endowment model' of investing – was developed by the Yale endowment's David Swensen and Dean Takahashi. It is described in Swensen (2000) and is said to have embraced the principles of MPT, albeit in a simplistic but robust way. It is based on diversification across asset classes with dissimilar correlations to maximise risk-adjusted investment return.

The Yale model is essentially a naive diversification approach, broadly of dividing a portfolio into five or six roughly equal parts and investing each in a different asset class. The portfolio should be rebalanced on a regular basis back to the original weightings of the asset classes. Such naive diversification recognises that the risk–return relationship for long-term oriented assets cannot be effectively quantified. By rebalancing, investors in theory would be selling private equity positions on secondary markets when prices are high (or, to say it differently, discounts are low), and buy 'low', i.e., committing to funds when there is a scarcity of funding and portfolio companies can be acquired at attractive prices.

Central to this is an equity orientation to the detriment of asset classes with low expected returns such as fixed income and commodities. The novelty of this model is that liquidity is to be avoided rather than to be sought out, since it comes at a heavy price through lower returns and that it has relatively high exposure to alternative asset classes including private equity, compared to more traditional portfolios. Swensen (2000), however, gives no in-depth guidance on how the private equity portfolio itself is built.

Who Can Invest in Private Equity?

Liquidity – the ease and speed with which an asset can be sold at a fair price – is an important factor in an allocation decision and, as a consequence, constrains the allocation to illiquid assets. On the other hand, it is precisely this illiquidity risk, and more specifically the associated risk premium, that attracts investors to these asset classes. Therefore only long-term investors, whose liability profile allows them to lock capital in for a prolonged period of time (usually ten years or even more), can harvest this risk premium.[4] These constraints restrict private equity to institutional investors, which have been defined as 'an organisation whose primary purpose is to invest its own assets or those it holds in trust for others',[5] and would include pension funds, insurance companies, banks, investment companies, endowments, large family offices, corporate investors and government organisations.

Sophisticated investors

Despite the limited attention academics so far have given to this question, industry observers are traditionally arguing that 'sophistication', i.e., knowledge of the asset class, is important and investor types differ in their investment success. For example, compared to other large investor groups, university endowments are reported to have been particularly successful in their private equity investments – which intuitively makes sense, as endowments have far longer investment horizons than other institutional investors and are less constrained by regulatory requirements that otherwise would force higher allocations to liquid assets. LPs apparently enjoy different strengths and advantages, also depending on the underlying fund types.[6] Also linked to this narrative is the performance persistence argument, i.e., that skilful LPs are said to be able to pick better funds.

Recent research, however, would be consistent with LPs generally having gained experience with private equity investing and suggests little difference in return for investors in different global regions.[7] Nowadays there are not as many inexperienced LPs as during the industry's 'Stone Age' but the growth of experience in the LP community appears to have been cancelled out by the significant growth of inflows into private equity and the resulting scarcity in 'low hanging fruits'.

Investor profile

Institutional investors reveal significant differences in their approach and dedication to private equity investing. Asset managers investing in private equity, for example funds-of-funds, depend on raising external capital. What could be called 'hybrid investors' invest capital from the balance sheet of their parent organisations but also manage funds on behalf of external entities.[8] 'Balance sheet investors' manage only their own capital. Typical institutions falling into this category are public pension funds, endowments and family offices. They do not need capital from external sources and just invest directly from the balance sheet of their own organisation. Another group of balance sheet investors are 'non-financial' institutions, comprising government agencies and corporate investors, which do not invest in private equity mainly for financial reasons, but to try to promote other objectives, such as regional development, employment creation, technological development or access to innovation.

However, some institutions are constrained by regulation biased against illiquidity and non-marketable assets. There can also be restrictions, such as the exclusion of investments in industries such as alcohol, tobacco, pornography, gambling or arms. Also, pension funds and life insurers need to take the average age profile of their policyholders and the resulting liability profile into account. As a consequence of regulations and organisation-specific restrictions and preferences, portfolio compositions typically deviate from what MPT implies as lying on the efficient frontier.

University endowments favour higher allocations to alternative assets under certain circumstances.[9] For a higher ratio of donations to endowment fund size, a less liquid portfolio can be held, as the donations provide a direct source of liquid cash. A similar argument relates to tuition fees. Universities do not maximise tuition revenue but instead balance the need for funds with their desire for quality students. Prestigious universities can be more selective and consequently can take on greater portfolio risk as the excess demand for entrance allows smoothing portfolio fluctuations via revenue flexibility. Another possible factor is that the more selective universities have higher-quality board members with greater financial sophistication and therefore support the higher allocation to alternative assets.

On the other hand, there appears to be greater conservatism in investment strategies with higher allocations to traditional liquid assets – mainly fixed income. Universities with greater income risk or high debt-to-assets ratios tend to avoid alternative assets such as venture capital. Public universities also invest more in fixed income. As such universities are predominantly funded by public means through a national or sub-national government, one could argue that such universities receive their endowment from the outside. Research-intensive universities need to hold significantly safer portfolios than liberal arts colleges, as their funding needs are higher and more volatile. Therefore their endowment funds need to be more liquid.

As private equity is highly illiquid and despite the ability of the endowment to sustain long investment horizons, it is rather payout policies and associated liquidity constraints that may dictate more conservative investment strategies. Like university endowments, sovereign wealth funds and family offices are able to control their liabilities, which gives them more flexibility when investing in illiquid assets. Pension funds and insurers need to be careful about their Asset Liability Management (ALM), looking at both assets and liabilities when trying to optimise the trade-off between risk and reward.

Targeting Allocations

Significant allocation is necessary for private equity to have an impact on the overall portfolio's return, but apparently few institutional investors dare to implement this. Simplistically, assuming that private equity can outperform the public markets by about 500 basis points, at least 5 per cent of the entire portfolio needs to be allocated to this asset class.[10] Swensen suggests allocation of less than about 15 per cent would be difficult to justify. Fraser-Sampson (2013) thinks that 10 per cent may be preferred for large investors, but about 15 per cent to 20 per cent remains a good guideline for smaller institutions. He believes that the failure to recognise and observe this principle is one of the most common mistakes made by investors and consultants around the world, as evidenced in the fact that 'meaningless' allocations as low as 1 per cent to private equity can be observed. Even if occasionally significant allocations to private equity are reported, it often relates to a much wider definition of the asset class, for instance, including infrastructure and real estate.

Mechanistic rules and denominator effect

Maintaining pre-set target investment allocation levels is an important part of an institutional investor's prudential apparatus, and there are strict guidelines particularly when committing capital to illiquid assets. For example, guidelines set targets such as 10 per cent allocation to private equity, 20 per cent to hedge funds and 10 per cent to real estate, and either quarterly or annually these investment percentages are checked against these targets. However, measuring asset allocations is not as well defined as perceived and there are complications when managing towards the associated targets.

The problem with the definition of allocation targets is that it largely ignores illiquidity. The adverse effects started to show during the market downturn from 2008 onwards when, for instance, US university endowments found themselves hugely overweight with alternative assets. In the case of Harvard, about one-third of its operating revenues were supposed to come from the endowment. To realise this liquidity and to get back to its 13 per cent target allocation in this asset class, the endowment was reported to be offloading $1.5 billion in private equity.[11] Likewise, Stanford's exposure to illiquid assets make up one-third of its investment assets and their endowment attempted to dispose of as much as $1 billion of combined funded and unfunded commitments to private equity funds, real estate partnerships, timberland investments and so on. This effort to liquidate hard-to-sell assets was driven by the large and unfunded part of commitments made prior to the credit crisis.[12]

Other investors were reported to sell off such positions as well. They were said to have reacted to the so-called 'denominator effect'. During market downturns several related events typically happen. The prices of liquid assets fall and with this the value of the overall portfolio, or the denominator, shrinks. On the other hand the NAVs reported by funds hardly change as write-downs in their valuations lag behind those of quoted asset classes. As an effect, the percentage actually invested in illiquid assets looks much higher than the targeted allocation. Moreover, fund repayments do not happen at the expected rate anymore, which hinders LPs' ability to recycle capital. An LP who needs to quickly address the denominator effect or realise liquidity has only one option: sell down some holdings, which is typically only possible at a substantial loss. Indeed, for unquoted assets a 'fire sale' mentality is problematic – here the market might fail to work and one cannot sell it at any price.

Adding insult to injury is the fact that the apparent increase in allocations to limited partnership funds is not real. Instead it is caused by temporary depressions in public equity prices and time-lags – and in the case of private equity to some degree also reluctance to mark-to-market their NAVs. The hoped-for 'natural' solution to the denominator effect, of course, are economic upswings. But together with public market rallies, valuations for alternative assets will also rise. In fact, there are significant conceptual differences between prices investors can trade on in markets and values for unlisted assets which are subjective by nature. That illiquid assets have often held their value does not necessarily reflect the intrinsic value of these assets, but rather the fact that they are unlisted.

Reactions to such asset allocation problems are often improvised and driven by 'tactical' considerations. Occasionally investors, in line with their other assets losing value, aggressively write down their private equity assets to be able to maintain overall asset allocation. Also in many cases private equity, despite its fundamentally different dynamics, is lumped together with public equity portfolio as one asset class 'equity' to avoid premature sell-offs. The illiquid nature of traditional private equity funds prevents tactical asset allocators from quickly increasing or decreasing allocations to the asset class. Idzorek (2007) suggested that listed private equity indices, and the introduction of products based on them, enable investors to quickly and easily make tactical shifts. On the other hand, this is rather defining the problem away, as listed private equity's liquidity is likely to evaporate in times of market stress.

More relevant appears to be the increase of allocations to the secondary market. For example the California Public Employees' Retirement System (CalPERS), the largest public pension fund in the US, was reported to essentially hedge the disposal of $2 billion of private-equity partnerships in 2008 through investing in secondary funds. They sold when times were relatively good, and bought back at lower prices at what was called a '50% plus "all sellers, no buyers" discount'.[13] A refinement of this approach is to sell off only part of the investor's stakes in partnerships – interests of about 10 per cent to 20 per cent – along with the commitments that stick with them, as opposed to its entire ownership in specific partnerships.[14]

Ambiguities

Mechanistically administered portfolio allocation rules can be too simplistic and can be at odds with MPT which does not assume a rebalancing through distressed sales with potentially large losses. As demonstrated by the denominator effect, such rules often have unintended and undesirable consequences.

When talking about asset allocation the aim is to describe the status of a portfolio, but for illiquid assets we cannot view this as static. In efficient public markets the resources allocated to asset classes reflect the market prices and thus the market's valuation for these assets which can, through selling them again, be turned into resources available for rebalancing the portfolio. Here prices are, at least under usual market conditions, close to valuations and the consensus on the future development. For private equity funds, however, there are significant differences between resources allocated, prices, values and resources available. Moreover, not all allocation decisions can be assumed to be reversible. The problem from an active portfolio management point of view is that 'what goes in', i.e., resources allocated to create value over a longer time period, is not equal to what can be 'taken out' of the allocation. In fact, there are a number of conceptual problems with the asset allocation's definition:

- Target allocations should be implementable, that is, if the targeted allocation is X and current allocation stands at Y, then (X-Y) should be added or, as the case may be, subtracted. Depending on how allocation is defined (e.g., is the funds' undrawn capital included?) this may not be possible: for example, a target allocation based on the funds' invested capital is not under the LP's control.
- Commitments are typically drawn down over a number of years and distributions usually begin coming back before all the capital is called. The uncertain schedule of capital calls – clustered in the early years – and unpredictable distributions of cash or securities to the investors closer to a fund's maturity together make it difficult to make accurate predictions and integrate private funds in a strategic asset allocation. Doing this effectively requires modelling of the funds' behaviour over time. Also the time-lag to access new funds is an obstacle to active portfolio management. Commitments must be made to new funds as mature funds make distributions and ultimately wind down. Unlike with traditional asset classes, matching an investor's asset allocation target with the actual investments in private funds is not straightforward.

In theory an asset allocation should have the characteristics of a partition in mathematics.[15] At any point in time, the percentage of the total assets allocated to different asset classes has to add up to 100 per cent, but this is not how many investors appear to view their asset allocation. They factor in overcommitments, i.e., the ratio between total commitments and the resources allocated to asset class exceeds 100 per cent. For the Harvard endowment, to give an example, it was reported that their portfolio, for a number of years, was '105% invested'.[16]

Flexibility in allocation models that allow for temporary deviations are perceived to be more robust but may lead to complacency.

A formally satisfying definition has to capture the time dimension of the funds. Particularly for fund assets, target allocations are only enforceable at the time of the management decision, not afterwards. Here assets could even be seen in various states: allocated, committed but not yet invested, and invested.

Flexible allocation policy

To ensure that at each point in time allocations add up to available resources and comply with investment guidelines, the definition of allocations should also include operations, such as increasing and decreasing allocations. Changing from current to a targeted allocation requires defining the various steps and the time needed dependent on the resources available. For example, investment guidelines should foresee that the denominator effect will be addressed just through the resources available. The available resources will increase over time through reflows or through realisations. Whereas valuation determines target allocations, the market price determines the tactical implementation. With a flexible allocation policy the allocation to private equity can fluctuate over time. While there may be a target allocation, a flexible allocation approach allows for a bandwidth within which deviations from the target are tolerated, and thus helps to avoid or at least mitigate the denominator effect.

Asset Liability Management

There are several problems that make asset allocation decisions related to private equity difficult: major assumptions underlying MPT do not hold as the asset class is illiquid and has limited scalability, and it is difficult to get access to high-performing funds. Rather than risks, returns and correlations being the determinants of portfolio compositions, like in MPT, scale considerations, profile of liabilities and 'additionalities' appear to drive allocations to private equity. Here portfolio structure is less a product of design but more of an evolutionary pressure in reaction to quite different institutional profiles. Day-to-day demands and constraints over time 'push' an institution's asset allocation into an area where it presents a feasible trade-off.[17]

Background risk

Research suggests that if an economic agent is endowed with a non-tradable risk – background risk – this should decrease their appetite for other risks even if all sources of risk are statistically independent. Market imperfections should have a large impact on portfolio choice and in situations where there is exposure to background risk, investors should optimally choose unique portfolios which best hedge their personal risks. Dimmock (2008) looked at background risk in the context of university endowments where he defined it as the volatility of a university's non-financial income. His results strongly support the hypothesis that this risk drives the endowment fund portfolio composition. They suggest that endowment managers choose portfolios that lower the overall risk of the entire university entity, comprising both its endowment fund and its non-investment operations.

Because universities are infinitely lived, theoretically their endowment investment strategies should not be overly risk-averse. On the other hand the endowment needs to spend on a regular basis to meet the operating needs of the university. The same argument applies to foundations and family offices. Foundations can scale back their grant-making, but museums or schools, for example, depend on endowments to cover their budgets.[18]

Cash flows and prices

Essentially, MPT views a portfolio as 'flat' in the sense that every asset at any point of time is up for sale in order to achieve a targeted portfolio balance. Some long-term investors, however, tend to look at their portfolios as layered, or 'hierarchical', where a portion of their portfolio can be locked in for longer periods of time with illiquid assets last in line, only to be sold if all other options are exhausted.

Practitioners may challenge this statement and point to the often quite buoyant market for secondary stakes in alternative asset funds. Secondary markets, however, should rather be seen within the context of an opportunistic investment management. For risk management purposes, such as swift rebalancing of a portfolio of funds or quick realisation of liquidity, secondary markets will fail to offer a practical solution. Illiquid funds have unique characteristics, so it will be time-consuming to find a willing counter-party trade for trading in this specific asset, particularly if a seller is acting under compulsion and even more so if under time pressure. While illiquidity is usually modelled as cost related to a transaction, assuming that a trade can always take place at a cost, illiquid funds cannot be traded or liquidated for significant periods of time, even if an investor so desires. In this context, commitments to funds become irreversible in the sense that trying to exit them usually is too costly to make this part of a routine investment strategy. In contrast with MPT, an active portfolio management is thus not possible and we also need to deal with a hierarchy of assets, ranging from highly liquid to illiquid ones.

Regarding allocation to private equity, the two different worlds of market prices and cash flows could be argued to collide. Investors use VaR, reflecting apparent market prices, as a basis for determining their capital adequacy and measuring traded risk. Non-financial firms, however, have found this concept difficult to apply in their risk management, as value mainly takes the form of real investments in fixed assets that cannot be monetised easily. Industrial companies tend to look at the Cash-Flow-at-Risk (CFaR) as a more relevant measure for their risk exposures. The CFaR is the maximum deviation between actual cash flows and a set level (such as a budget figure) due to changes in the underlying risk factors within a given time period for a given confidence level.

Under the MPT, asset allocation is driven by market prices, but illiquid funds could be seen as 'cash flow assets', which we would describe, in the absence of a common definition, as assets that usually cannot be traded profitably, create cash flows and – because the opportunity costs associated with undrawn commitments require explicit or implicit overcommitment strategies – need to be sustained through a timely provision of liquidity. To make tradable assets and cash flow assets comparable we can either map market prices onto a cash flow model or use a cash flow model to determine a fair value, assuming that this would fetch the same price in the market.

Relationship between patience and return potential?

The tradable asset model in many ways is not in line with what we have put forward before, where private equity investing essentially shields portfolio companies from adverse market influences. The time horizon clearly has an impact on how to approach portfolio management. Pension funds or insurers with liabilities of, say, 20 years duration will be inclined to think of portfolios of funds. Family offices, investing on behalf of generations not born yet, sovereign wealth funds, aiming to support future generations, or endowments, on the other hand, can be considered to be essentially 'immortal' with investment horizons beyond 200 years,[19] and should therefore rather look at managing portfolios of relationships with private equity firms that raise series of funds. As 'very long-term' investors they are able to follow different strategies.

According to Swensen (2000), having a long horizon, or more generally the right liquidity characteristics, is a necessary but not a sufficient condition in order to obtain high returns. This should not be misinterpreted as causality in the sense that private equity gives high returns due to a liquidity premium.[20] Nevertheless, having a long time horizon makes it possible to be selective. The less time available, the more investors are subject to luck rather than methodology. Rather than looking at a risk and return relationship as the mechanics of efficient markets imply, investors implicitly look at a relationship between patience (acceptable waiting time) and return potential.

Too Much Imitation?

Instead of trying to apply any modelling, many investors appear to simply imitate the allocation policies of their peers or follow historical experience. Acharaya and Dimson (2007) quote a bursar: 'Consultants have their limitations in relying too much on historically based statistical models. They also believe that you should set a long-term investment policy and rebalance the portfolio automatically in response to market movements, which seems tactically inefficient.' Over the years financial regulation has increasingly embraced MPT, which limits what regulated institutions can allocate to illiquid asset classes such as private equity. The cause and effect relationship can be debated; it is possible that regulation does not consider these asset classes as they often represent immaterial allocations in any case.

The question how much to allocate to private equity is still underresearched. There is a danger of allocating too much but most investors appear to not spend much time thinking about this question, and in so doing allocate too little to private equity. Despite its apparent success, Swensen's Yale model is something of a quick fix – and endowments did not escape discomfort during the Great

Recession – but the fact that this model has attracted so much attention shows the impact of strategic asset allocation. As we have seen, private equity is an arbitrage between the entrepreneurial and the financial systems, and sits in some way outside of both. This is not a critique of the EMH or MPT, it is simply that many of their underlying assumptions are not met in a private equity context and it is therefore necessary to look at other frameworks.

Speed Read

- For private equity correlations, volatilities and returns cannot be determined with any degree of reliability and most of the Modern Portfolio Theory's critical underlying assumptions are not met.
- Only long-term investors, whose liability profile allows them to lock capital in for a prolonged period of time (usually ten years or even more) can harvest private equity's risk premium. Allocations are more dictated by the investor's 'background risk' associated with payout policies and liquidity constraints.
- Simplistic mechanistically-administered portfolio allocation rules can be at odds with MPT, which does not assume a rebalancing through distressed sales with potentially large losses. While there may be a target allocation, a flexible allocation approach allows for a bandwidth within which deviations from the target are tolerated, and thus helps to avoid or at least mitigate the denominator effect.
- Rather than looking at a risk and return relationship as the mechanics of efficient markets imply, investors in private equity implicitly look at a relationship between patience (acceptable waiting time) and return potential.

Chapter 6
The Sky is Not the Limit

Private equity does not 'scale up' easily. Attracting more capital could make it a victim of its own success, with 'too much money chasing too few deals' the new industry mantra. This sector-level constraint has size and strategy implications for GPs and the institutions investing in private equity, as LPs alike. In its broadest definition, the private equity market is about twice as large as the market for public equity,[1] but the size of the institutional private equity market is by necessity, far smaller. The opportunities for entrepreneurship-arbitrage are rare and most potential targets are not suitable for institutional investing: companies are too small, their owners unwilling to sell, offer too little growth prospects, do not have the quality of cash flows to bear leverage, and so on.

In practice, this selectively seems to have inhibited the growth of private equity-owned assets which are estimated to be less than 16 per cent (depending on whether before or after leverage) of what hedge funds gather and less than 2 per cent of all assets managed internationally.[2] Academics have attempted to quantify the maximum or optimum size of the industry. Ludovico Phalippou of Oxford Saïd Business School believes the maximum amount that one investor could put profitably into buyout funds has historically varied between €1.2bn and €4bn per year. For venture capital this range is narrower with around €200m per year.[3] LPs seeking to get a proper allocation to venture capital need to invest internationally, as in any given country there are likely to be too few good funds.[4] Whatever the precise amount of capital that may be effectively absorbed by the industry (assuming there is a precise amount at all), the size of commitments, in both absolute terms and relative to the size of the GP and LP organisations, will have significant implications.

The LP Sizing Problem

In theory, large amounts of assets under management enable institutional investors to pool risks and thus allow them to be closer to an optimum relationship between risks and returns. They may also have better access to investments that are not available to small players. There are significant fixed costs for researching the asset class, recruiting qualified investment teams and providing them with incentives. Building skills and gaining experience are an advantage when investing in one of the more complex asset classes. The ability to transact in large volumes leads to scale economies. There are high costs related to structuring the limited partnership agreements and to monitoring funds, favouring larger stakes in funds and, consequently, the bigger LPs. Size may also lead to a better bargaining position – a point we will revisit below. Smaller investors are disadvantaged in several ways. Their portfolios will be more concentrated, often with direct investments, and they are less able to absorb losses stemming from the unavoidable failing investment.

However, while there may be less competition at the larger end of the market, the number of suitable targets will typically also be lower. Large investors such as sovereign wealth funds, for instance, are unable to put as much money to work in private equity as part of their allocation to equity as they would like to.[5] Some institutional investors are also constrained by minimum ticket sizes (in the area of $100m) and not wanting to own more than, say, 20 per cent of a fund, which implies minimum fund sizes of $500m.

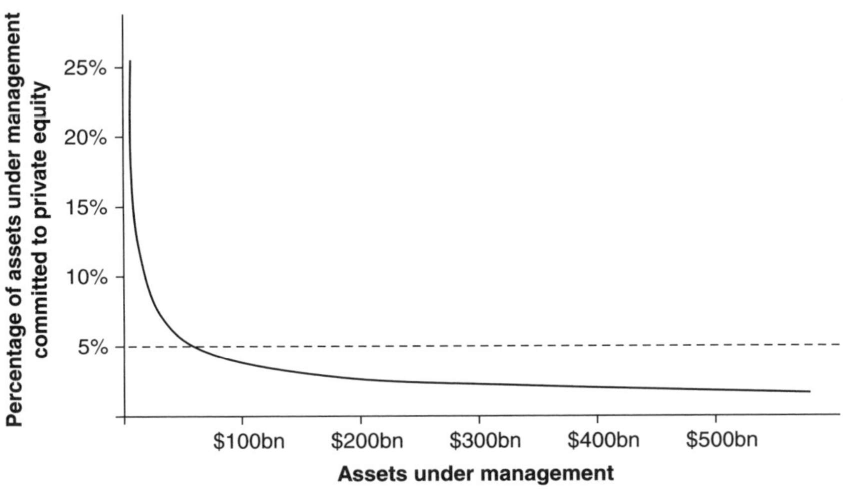

Figure 6.1 Commitments to private equity by large institutional investors[6]

In fact, with increasing assets under management the typical allocation to private equity typically falls below the level of 5 per cent (See **Figure 6.1**). While some larger institutional investors appear to have larger allocations, they may be based on a more 'elastic' definition of private equity, e.g., including, as discussed before, infrastructure investments.

The need to put large amounts of capital to work can also compromise operational standards. Too many fund commitments could increase workloads, weaken due diligence standards, and result in an overall poorer fit with the targeted portfolio. There could be a temptation to crowd into uncontroversial standard funds and overlook emerging opportunities. While, in the rush to meet allocation targets, LPs may not bargain sufficiently and accept less favourable terms and conditions, which leads to a worse portfolio quality on average. There could also be a tendency to invest more opportunistically outside the LP's area of expertise.

The GP Sizing Problem

GPs argue that larger fund sizes, implying – as will be discussed in more detail in **Chapter 9** – higher management fees, help to build up and maintain teams of experienced investment professionals, which is likely to result in higher quality assets. At the larger end of the market, investors may have less competition and that should result in higher potential returns. Moreover, larger investors often have access to more flexible and lower cost financing than their smaller competitors. The size of the funds depends to some degree on the GP's quality, with smaller fund sizes occasionally being a reflection of a less convincing investment case.[7] Marginal differences in initial 'talent', and probably a high degree of luck, result in vastly larger fund sizes and much higher income.

The associated cost of compliance, as well as regulatory burdens such as the EU's AIFM Directive, favours larger players. Also, performance seems to be related to fund size, with larger funds tending to generate better returns than smaller ones, but only as long as the fund is not too large.[8] Even if the funds managed by a GP have grown beyond the optimal point, it is easier for a large firm to shrink as markets fall without losing the ability to operate. In order to survive, GPs need to adapt, but adaptation is expensive as many are too small to survive if their initial attempts to adapt are unsuccessful. This can make another GP the 'last man standing' when the markets recover again, particularly if the GP is drawing management fees for several funds managed in parallel. Overlapping investment periods also increase its survivability in case one of the funds turns out to be a bottom performer.

GP limits to size

Fund size is an enemy of performance and some LPs believe that it is better to focus on funds with concentrated portfolios than on those where capital is spread over many deals. Some research evidence suggests that this result is related to organisational diseconomies of scale.[9] While larger GPs have the resources to survive longer, they may still be threatened because they cannot adapt quickly.

Cornelius (2011) found that small funds invest virtually exclusively in small companies. However, middle-sized and some large buyout funds are less focused on the size of transactions, and deal and fund sizes are less correlated. This allows them to pursue opportunities across a wider range of deal sizes but it may also reflect the difficulties in identifying larger targets with sufficient return potential. Conventional wisdom suggests that in smaller funds, managers work harder. This is particularly relevant for emerging GPs. In theory, smaller funds that specialise and focus on profitable niches also should have advantages. On the other hand, with limited resources there is also less flexibility. Both factors make extreme outcomes – either strong outperformance or complete failure – more likely for smaller funds.

Venture capital is characterised as more labour-intensive and buyouts as more capital-intensive. The crucial difference between the buyout and the venture business derives from the fact that a buyout manager's skill can be applied to extremely large companies, whereas a VC manager's skill can add value to small companies only. This implies increased scalability, allowing buyout firms to sharply increase the size of their funds, which is not the case for VC firms.[10] Particularly in the case of VC funds, capital inflows will likely lead to a decline in performance.[11] In this situation GPs limit their fund sizes and become choosy about their LPs – a behaviour documented for the 'elite' Silicon Valley firms such as Benchmark, Draper Fisher Jurvetson, Kleiner Perkins Caulfield & Byers and Sequoia Capital. This phenomenon is not restricted to venture capital. Also, some buyout firms, such as Clayton, Dubilier & Rice, have resisted the temptation to raise and invest ever-greater sums of money.[12]

In situations where the existing investors are convinced that a fund management team will continue delivering high performance, fundraising will be very quick as the relationship between fund managers and investors simply continues. If they do not manage to convince, LPs will take their money elsewhere and generally with several poorly-performing funds the GP is close to extinction: two strikes and you are out.

Occupying Positions

When building a portfolio of funds LPs can either rely on their skills in choosing better performing funds or build on their access to top GPs. Manninena et al. (2010) found that LPs themselves are persistent in the returns of the portfolio of funds they manage, not because of their skills, but due to the GPs' performance persistence and the tendency of an LP's reinvestments producing the average returns of all the funds available to that LP. This perspective implicitly assumes that performance persistence holds for the GPs and that the decision to invest in the first fund managed by this GP is crucial for the LP because of the longer-term effect by enabling access to subsequent funds – an assumption where we hold some reservations which will be discussed in **Chapter 12**. This access could be seen as an LP's position giving it a sustainable competitive advantage and enabling it to earn greater profits than its peers. An alternative explanation is that LPs are consistent in their approach on how to evaluate and select funds, which as a consequence leads to reinvestment returns that are, on average, close to the portfolio average.[13]

Power matters as well

Because of the private equity market's limited scalability, institutional investors are looking at a 'territory' that has to be 'reconnoitred' and 'conquered' with their competitors as strategic adversaries. Alternatively, investors can move to new areas and occupy positions. Positions need to be defended, for instance, by keeping success a secret. Reputation and track record helps to outpace competitors in fundraising. Team spin-outs are a typical form of entry into this defended market. Industry players can also collude and, through their influence on investors and private equity associations, erect barriers to entry. Evading competition and 'fleeing' to protected niches helps to survive.

Discussing investment strategies without the power to execute them is meaningless. LPs as well as GPs are characterised by various levels of 'game strength' that constrains what they can do. Consider an LP's stake in a fund. A large share would be associated with a high ability to extend the relationship with a GP to future funds and to alter terms and conditions in one's favour. On the other hand, the impact of, for example, co-investments will be marginal compared to the LP's commitment to the fund. Smaller shares, on the other hand, imply a lower bargaining power but a higher ability to scale up the exposure through what we later describe as real options.

The sway LPs hold over GPs relies more on the possible sanction to end the relationship by not committing to future funds rather than trying to change the course of the currently managed fund. GPs differ in regards of size, reputation – often bordering at the verge of 'myth' – and the strength of their LP backing. Depending on the available capital for follow-on investments, VC firms have a different strength regarding their ability to dilute other VC investors in a portfolio company or, should this not be possible, imitate the idea and finance a competing company instead. In private markets, deal-making cannot be enforced like in public markets, where a level playing field is assured. Instead LPs and GPs need to rely to a much larger degree on diplomacy to advance their agenda.

Funds-of-funds as intermediaries between institutional investors and the private equity industry compete mainly on the power they hold over the GPs and the associated ability to get access to their funds. This will depend, among other factors, on the share in the GP's current fund but also on whether the fund-of-funds came in the first closing and also whether it was a backer of the GP's first fund. While for funds-of-funds the track record is difficult to verify, the number of GPs that can be accessed and the power held over them is better observable.

Patience is a virtue

While the LP commitments are contractually fixed, this is not 'carved in stone'. During market downturns, inflow of capital combined with a substantial decrease in investment activity create overhang of unfunded commitments that cannot be efficiently put to work.

Rather than volumes, it is the acceleration and the deceleration of capital deployment that appears to be most detrimental to fund returns. Nevertheless, many LPs simultaneously with other investors, increase massively their allocation to private equity, resulting in disappointing returns. Likewise, for instance in times of downturns in financial markets, allocations are cut and even in reaction to the denominator effect stakes are sold off in secondary markets, leading to further losses. Demaira (2010) finds that, 'paradoxically', it is the pension funds who are looking for high absolute returns who contribute the most to the declines in private equity returns by committing too much too quickly, which the market is unable to absorb.

Suitable Profiles

It is a fair assumption that there is a link between market size and its efficiency. Smaller niches that are under-researched and do not attract material amounts of capital offer the best opportunities for arbitrage. The limited size of a market leads to other imperfections, as institutions tend to allocate too few full-time staff to selecting and monitoring investments. Without being able to focus on private equity these professionals will lack the experience to achieve the best outcome in negotiations. Right-sizing is one of the central questions investors are faced with: large enough to have an impact on the overall portfolio's returns, small enough to allow access and selectiveness. Nevertheless and not surprisingly, as their management fees depend on it, private equity firms have a huge incentive to downplay the limited scaling potential of their targeted markets.

To achieve a competitive relationship between risks and returns, investors need to have a suitable profile, such as being of a reasonably limited size to be able to commit amounts that the market can absorb profitably while being large enough to pursue investments over the long term. Large institutions can recruit the best investment professionals and be technically sophisticated, but due to their size limitations they find it difficult to generate sustainably high returns and also need to leave many market niches aside.

Speed Read

- While in theory very large, the private equity market is not scalable because very few situations are applicable to it.
- Scale limitations apply to GPs and LPs. Both must be large enough to command the necessary resources, but not too large

to overwhelm the available opportunities for entrepreneurship-arbitrage.

- The key to investment success in private equity is avoiding crowded niches. Paradoxically, the small institutional investors who could benefit most from independent research into overlooked niches are overwhelmingly unwilling to pay for this and instead tend to follow the convoy of large players who often are not the right example.

Chapter 7

The Limited Partnership as Part of Humanity's DNA

Today the limited partnership structure is virtually synonymous with the modern private equity industry, yet similar partnership structures, based on the Code of Justinian, the pre-Islamic long-distance caravan trade in the Arabian Peninsula or the medieval commenda were repeatedly used in history to solve the same combination of challenges.

The Limited Partnership

A partnership is a contract, whereby two or more individuals consent to carry on an enterprise, contributing to it by combining property, knowledge or management, and to share its profit. Private equity funds are generally structured as asymmetric limited partnerships where LPs relinquish their ability to manage the business in exchange for limited liability for the partnership's debts.[1] While terms and conditions, and investor rights and obligations have long been defined in specific non-standard partnership agreements, the limited partnership structure – or comparable structures used in the various jurisdictions – has evolved over recent decades into a 'quasi-standard'. The fund usually has a contractually limited life of seven to ten years. The fund manager's objective is to realise all investments before or at the liquidation of the partnership. Often there is a provision for an extension of two or three years.

Partnerships, and the pooling of resources, have existed throughout most of recorded history, and have proven particularly useful for large or especially risky enterprises. The fact that they cut across cultures[2] and legal systems led Borden (2009) to suggest that humans have a natural tendency to form partnerships to conduct business. His study revealed that ancient and modern partnerships, in all of their forms, have numerous common characteristics.

Although the partnership structure is often seen as an innovation for private equity investing, its origins date back to ancient times. The lifecycle of a private equity fund resembles a trade journey into the unknown. The limited partnership structure is said to have medieval roots, where Italian merchant families were financing trade voyages through 'commendas'. In this asymmetric partnership the capital risk of the 'sleeping partners' was reduced since they were not liable for debt and stayed at home while the 'travelling partners' controlled the venture and set sail to search for profitable business. The sharing of risks and rewards was also asymmetric, making a good reputation, a fair alignment of interest and trust critical.

A number of factors contributed to the profit-sharing arrangement:[3] the sleeping partner wanted a reasonable return on his investment and the travelling partner sought a reasonable profit from his services. As they could not achieve this objective in isolation they had to combine their resources. Of course, the sleeping partner could have sought a fixed return, but he, as well as the travelling partner, mainly participated in the venture in the belief that its profits would significantly exceed a fixed return threshold. For a fixed return, the sleeping partner would not have benefited from any unexpected gains of the venture. The sharing of profits also motivated the sleeping partner to study the venture and add their own expertise to the decision-making process. Likewise the profit-sharing encouraged the travelling partner to exert his maximum effort throughout the venture, whereas with a fixed fee he may have been less inclined to work to obtain additional profit for the sleeping partner.

The commenda flourished across Europe after its introduction into Italy, and from the mid-thirteenth century onwards it became highly successful for financing the maritime trade, as it was a convenient way of combining capital with merchant entrepreneurship.[4] The seafaring merchants brought to the venture their trade network, nautical experience and considerable leadership in managing their crew. At the height of Venetian trading power, the sleeping partners made small investments in a large number of commendas to spread the risk, thus resembling today's diversified portfolios of private equity funds held by funds-of-funds and other institutional investors.

Colbert's Ordinance on Commerce of 1673 and the Napoleonic Code of 1807 reinforced the commenda's limited partnership concept in European law. Britain enacted its first limited partnership statute in 1907, while in the US limited partnerships became widely available in the early 1800s. Initially a number of legal restrictions made the structure unpopular for businesses, but during the early twentieth century limited partnerships were increasingly used to raise capital for another situation of extreme uncertainty – that of oil field prospecting. Finally this structure was adopted by the private equity industry where it has become the virtually uncontested vehicle of choice. This model is arguably the most successful worldwide.

Usury Versus Partnership

To suggest Columbus's expedition financed by Queen Isabella as forerunner of the modern private equity industry clearly is a stretch. The point is rather that repeatedly in history humans came up with very similar structures to solve the same combination of problems for investments under high uncertainty.

The limited partnership's core concept is that risk is fully apportioned among several participants and the value of obligations and rewards is not fixed but rather reflects an undertaking's true worth over long periods of time. This approach is in contrast with conventional interest-based systems, which are constrained by the fixed value of obligations and rewards for different enterprise participants.[5] For their rare skills and their significant financial and personal risks, the travelling partners rightfully expected to take a fair share of the profits. Therefore trust and fairness are critical for overcoming the principal agent problem between the sleeping and the travelling partners.

Trust

Both travelling as well as sleeping partners benefited from the other's contributions, but 'tracing' problems prevented the parties from knowing the exact source of profits received from the venture. Borden (2009) also pointed out that private equity funds, for example, face such tracing problems and therefore use profit apportionment to affect behaviour and to align interests. When fund managers significantly participate in profits, both they and the investors increase returns when their services and the investors' capital produce at maximum capacity. Moreover, the performance of the fund managers attracts or repels potential investors.

The travelling partners engaged in these trade journeys were effectively several months away from their financial backers or any other central authority and reports about agent malfeasance would be severely delayed and a long time would pass before this could possibly be penalised. In any case, such information would be mostly by word-of-mouth, so self-interested action or underperformance could not easily be detected. As a consequence, the travelling partners as agents were necessarily operating with huge autonomy. Private equity is often described as a 'reputation market',[6] so we also find here the element of trust to be critical and violation of trust leads to ostracism of the offenders. Trust also goes the other way: for a seafaring merchant running high financial and personal risks, the last thing he would want to worry about is haggling over his fair share in the spoils after he hit gold and managed to come back from the journey.

Fairness

Therefore fairness is another important part of the discussion and has several aspects: some stakeholders have concerns regarding the morality of investing whereas others see more importance in a fair compensation of the various parties involved. In the ancient world, there were two generally approved methods of lending money:[7] voluntarily to relieve poverty and as a duty before whatever god you served to help a neighbour in need and where the lender was to expect nothing more than the return of the principal amount. Secondly, for a business venture where the lender was to receive an agreed percentage of the actual profit made. Lender and borrowers shared the risk, because the lender lost money and the borrower had opportunity costs. This shared risk creates a partnership, in contrast to the banker borrower relationship. In fact, all major religions have prohibitions against usury because it is seen as detrimental to a functioning society: owners of wealth would be able to take advantage of the not so wealthy by lending them money on highly unfavourable terms or by creating a situation in which a debt is unlikely to be ever repaid.

One important driver of the commenda and comparable structures, indeed, is the avoidance of usury. Noonan (1957) defines usury as terms in a loan transaction departing from fairness or justice, but usury is originally any interest on a loan that is predetermined and not based on the actual profit and loss of the investment. The prohibition of charging interest in Islam – as in other religions – is based on the concern for fairness.

On The Origins of Carried Interest

For the modern private equity industry, actual profits made are typically apportioned in a split of 80 per cent for LPs and 20 per cent for the GP, the so-called 'carried interest'.[8] The carried interest was also a feature of the medieval commenda where each party received income from the combination of property and services: if a sleeping partner invested £200, for his own investment of, say, £100, the travelling partner would be entitled to a 25 per cent share in the profits as 'tractator' and to a further third as an investor. He also stood to lose his £100. While the commenda's structure for sharing risks and rewards is universally accepted as fair, the question remains which split of the profits is fair? The 25/75 per cent split is mentioned by a number of authors, such as Swabey (2008) or Borden (2009). Also for modern private equity funds, a 25/75 per cent carried interest split is in use, although this is seen as 'premium carry' for elite funds only. The origins of the 20 per cent as a quasi market standard, however, are obscure. Toll (2001) explains that the standard carried interest figure may have its roots in the oil and gas business, where taking 20 per cent of the profit has long been the rule for companies engaged in exploratory drilling. Several early VC firms chose the 20 per cent rate, which established it as a market practice.

One could assume that 20 per cent carried interest is mainly driven by LP considerations, i.e., this split is just 'economically rational' in the sense that it provides adequate remuneration for fund managers to make them work hard while keeping them 'hungry' enough to raise further funds – which would be certainly in the interest of the LP.[9] This explanation is not satisfying, as 20 per cent carried interest is paid irrespective of fund size and therefore results in wide ranges of remuneration levels. Secondly, successful fund managers would be the first to be satisfied and more tempted to retire early than unsuccessful ones. In fact, it is puzzling that despite all the discussions around fee levels, even during the market downturn following the Great Recession, the 20 per cent carried interest has rarely been seriously challenged.[10]

20 per cent as 'focal point'

Rather than a figure that is endowed with any particular logic, it appears that the private equity market standard of 20 per cent carried interest is what Nobel Prize winning American economist

Thomas Schelling, in his 1960 book, *The Strategy of Conflict*, called a 'focal point', i.e., each person's expectation of what the other expects him to expect to be expected to do. Admittedly this is a confusing definition, so to put it into other words, a focal point (also called a 'Schelling point') is a solution that people will tend to use in the absence of communication, because it seems natural, special or relevant to them.[11]

There are a number of examples that support the assumption that 20 per cent is such a focal point. For instance, the book of Genesis mentions a 20/80 per cent profit split in the context of what could be described as an 'asymmetric partnership'.[12] Bernstein (2008) explains Islam's astonishingly rapid initial spread as due in no small part to the fact that stealing from fellow believers was forbidden, but not from infidels. Soon after he was expelled from Mecca in 622, the Prophet's troops began attacking that city's infidel caravans. One-fifth of the booty snatched from the non-believers was earmarked for Allah and the community while the rest was divided between the victorious troops and their leaders. Another example is the Castilian crown's practice whereby voyages had to be privately financed, and the backers were indemnified by a fifth of the profit of any trade, for a term of ten years, and the governorship of the conquered lands.[13]

In the so-called 'ultimatum game' we find an asymmetric set-up comparable to that of the limited partnership structure: the ultimatum game is an experimental economics game where two players, a proposer and a responder, divide a sum of money that is given to them. The first player proposes how the sum is divided as an ultimatum. There is no arguing allowed over the proposal, and the second player can either accept or reject it. If the responder accepts, the money is split in line with the proposal and both players are richer by the respective amounts. The second player, however, holds significant power as he can also reject the proposal, in which case neither player receives anything. How much should the proposer offer?

Pan economicus

According to economic theory the proposer should offer the smallest non-zero amount possible which the responder will always accept.[14] Research on the ultimatum game conducted in 2007 by the Max Planck Institute of Evolutionary Anthropology in Leipzig, Germany suggests that unlike humans, chimpanzees conform to traditional economic models.[15] Chimpanzees were offered a choice of trays containing raisins in sets of 10 raisins in total that were divided differently, for example a 'fair' offer of five raisins each, a 'hyper-fair' offer of eight raisins for the proposer and two raisins for the responder or a 'hyper-unfair' offer of ten for the first chimpanzee and none for the second.

The first chimpanzee would propose an offer of raisins to the responder by partially pulling out the chosen tray of raisins as far as he could. The second chimpanzee could accept the division of raisins by pulling the tray the rest of the way and the two would be able eat. Alternatively he could reject the offer by not pulling the tray and as a result neither of them would get anything to eat. In this experiment any offer was accepted regardless of the split between proposer and responder, and rejections only occurred when the receiver was offered no raisins at all. The researchers came to the conclusion that chimpanzees were not concerned with the concept of fairness, supporting the hypothesis that an aversion to inequitable outcomes plays a key role in human social organisation and distinguishes us from our closest living relatives.[16]

Humans as arbiters of fairness

The ultimatum game first sparked the interest of economists because it is highly replicable but results clearly departed from the standard behaviour of self-interested income maximisers. Studies have demonstrated that humans do not act 'rationally' in the economic sense, but act like arbiters of fairness: too low proposals are rejected, apparently, as researchers hypothesise, to punish the greed of the proposer. Unfairness tends to be punished because humans recognise that very few things are one-time deals. In the limited partnership structure we can recognise the LP as the proposer and the fund manager as the responder.[17]

Of course, in reality the GP is proposing the deal, but from an abstract viewpoint the LP controls the 'pot of money' that determines the reward to be split. We have to recall that private equity investors do not have average returns in mind, as this amounts to preparing for failure. Likewise, no captain would have embarked on a perilous journey to distant lands unless he believed it would make him 'filthy rich'. The payoff may have been unknown, but it was often enormous, and therefore it was wise to agree on the split between travelling and sleeping partners before setting sail. Both parties assume that the reward is to be big – the GP because of his market insight, the LP because of his due diligence – and therefore the LP would feel penalised if the deal were not accepted by the GP. The ultimatum expires, in this interpretation, when the fundraising goes stale.

For the ultimatum game the experimental results show that, surprisingly, in many cultures the proposer offers a 'fairer' split of between 40 per cent and 50 per cent of the total. Camerer and Thaler (1995) found that responders usually accept the 'fair' offers, and typically reject offers lower than 20 per cent. Research has found cultural preferences. For example, there are contrasting perceptions of what is considered as fair in ultimatum bargaining in Japan and the United States. Oosterbeek et al. (2001) found that Mongolian proposers tend to offer even splits even when very unequal splits would be accepted as well. Similar results were found in small-scale societies. This made some researchers conclude that 'reputation' is seen as more important than any economic reward – a finding that is of particular relevance in the private equity market with its strong role of reputation. Finally, for industrial societies, offers below 20 per cent are rejected with a probability of 0.40 to 0.60. And, as in the ultimatum game, 20 per cent also emerges as the focal point for limited partnerships' carried interest. One could add that this is possibly the 'Western' focal point and that 'premium carry' of 25 per cent to 35 per cent that Japanese and Korean funds have been moving swiftly towards may also be rooted in a different perception of fairness.[18]

The limited partnership as part of the human's 'genetic code'

The desire to trade is also not only the cause of many of the most important human developments, but technological innovation has also been a driver of trade.[19] Trading is one of the oldest human instincts and it often goes together with a desire to explore the unknown. As the *National Geographic* observes, '[y]et as a species we're curious enough, and intrigued enough by the prospect, to help pay for the trip and cheer at the voyagers' return. Yes, we explore to find a better place to live or acquire a larger territory or make a fortune. But we also explore simply to discover what's there.'[20] Indeed, a number of researchers are suspecting an 'explorer gene'. Therefore the limited partnership may not only be central to the success of private equity, but also – as evidenced by its ancient pedigree – part of the human's 'genetic code'. Its asymmetric sharing of risks and rewards together with 'fairness' appears to be a kind of 'killer application' for economic growth in an environment of uncertainty and change. If we accept this hypothesis, there are implications regarding how one should think about matters such as risk management or regulation.

The moral sense of fairness is 'hardwired' into our behaviour and is an emotion shared by most people and primates tested for it. Nevertheless, one should not rule out 'homo economicus' who is rational, self-maximising, and efficient in making choices. One argument put forward in this context is that fairness is of less relevance than it was in our prehistoric past. In modern society there are supposedly more one-time deals that are to be evaluated on their economic merit as one rarely does a deal with the same party again, and therefore we would get away with our greed at the expense of the community. But when Gordon Gekko talked about 'greed is good', he was not discussing morals, he was referring to efficiency: greed is right because it works to efficiently allocate resources in a market with a large number of atomistic participants. Market efficiency assures that on average participants are not treated unfairly; acting in a rational and self-maximising manner under such circumstances is not contradicting humanity's preoccupation with fairness.

Limitations of the Limited Partnership

The commenda is well-suited to address illiquid investments in innovation as it appears to be designed for trade voyages in an environment of uncertainty and change. Essentially the lifetime of this venture is limited by the time of the journey, and there was limited scalability, as shipping space was restricted. To some degree this formed a corporate governance mechanism, as only the successful travelling partner was able to fund the next journey. He needed to show success (i.e., track record), and again needed to convince investors that there was still more out there that justified another journey – the response to uncertainty is basically 'trial and error'.

Response to uncertainty, not to risk

Investors in a limited partnership trade off the efficiency, scalability and transparency associated with modern large corporations against the flexibility of, and the communication within, small teams that allow a much quicker adaptation to changing market conditions and newly arising opportunities. This structure should rather be seen as the answer to uncertainty, not to risk. According to Hans Lovrek, who to the knowledge of this author was the first to point to the similarities between the commenda and the modern private equity industry, in general the commenda competed with the 'sea loan' and – as today – the limited partnership is used in environments with high information asymmetry, where the sea loan is the 'cheaper' form in more stable environments.[21] The requirement to liquidate capital at the end of each voyage puts limited partnerships at a disadvantage compared to other company forms. For instance, with increasingly established trade routes the English East India Company followed the example of its Dutch counterpart and in 1654 adopted a perpetual existence, becoming a joint-stock company in 1658.[22]

Investors should ask themselves whether the environment a fund is supposed to operate in is predominantly characterised by uncertainty and whether the fund managers really add value and take personal risks to generate the returns. If not, the case for investing through a limited partnership vehicle is weak and other structures may be more appropriate.

Co-existence with public markets

Like cells multiplying and mutating, new private equity fund management teams tend to branch out of established firms once new opportunities are perceived. However, GPs are likely to 'die out' when change and innovation starts to slow down or opportunities become too scarce to support this costly investment modus operandi, with its cumbersome fundraising cycles, its relatively high management fees and its restricted scalability.

The limited partnership is a financial instrument that has proven effective for private equity investing. In fact, many interpret the limited partnership as a critical part of the private equity model. If one accepts this hypothesis – certainly a 'big if' – what are the implications? In the 'Golden Age' of private equity some observers started to wonder whether limited partnerships were even beginning to challenge the public corporation as a form of corporate governance.[23] Based on the arguments put forward above, however, funds structured as limited partnerships cannot be a panacea. It is not the structure per se that makes private equity investing successful, but it appears to be the best adapted instrument for a very specific situation that reflects private equity in its purest form: venture capital. That means a situation where investors are faced with extreme uncertainty, a temporary opportunity and high asymmetries regarding skills and experience. For investment opportunities that are accessible over longer time periods, in industries that are generally well understood, where data is available, risks quantifiable and the various parties' contributions are traceable, the limited partnership structure ceases to be efficient.

Instead, historically the limited partnership structure has been used to explore, driven by pure necessity – such as to avoid the effects of hunger or droughts – or the human instinct to venture out into the unknown. In the context of private equity investments, the use of the structure is predicated on the assumption that there are actually opportunities 'out there', or that industries face uncertainty and change and require a supportive ownership structure to help them through the transition. The strength of the public market, on the other hand, lies in its ability to efficiently exploit stable environments. By comparison, limited partnerships are expensive for their investors, as rationality and efficiency are in effect sacrificed in favour of an appetite for experimentation and adaptability.

A Broken Model?

Despite its apparent virtues, the limited partnership structure has often been criticised. It is sometimes argued – especially during market downturns – that the limited partnership model is broken and destined to disappear.[24]

Illiquidity as the source of the expected upside

Limited partnership funds belong to the most illiquid assets, but their illiquidity is known in advance, as opposed to asset classes whose liquidity may dry up unexpectedly during periods of financial turmoil, for instance. Investors in private equity deliberately accept illiquidity to harvest a premium, with the limited partnership providing an adequate framework. Here illiquidity does not represent a market failure but is an essential characteristic to generate excess returns.

Thanks to the institutional capital provided outside listed markets, unquoted portfolio companies are able to sustain difficulties or successes without having to release information that could be detrimental to the success of the investment due to the adverse behaviour of competitors, suppliers or clients. In fact, in private equity a key purpose of the fund structure is to shield fledgling portfolio companies in their early stages and those that are being restructured in turnaround situations from disruptive market influences. Similar considerations apply to explorations and green field projects that are particularly susceptible to sudden changes in investor sentiment and are at a high risk of being cut off from sources of funding. To allow the value of such investments to increase, financial resources need to be provided on a sustained and predictable basis within a reasonably long time frame. From this perspective it is conceptually problematic to look at the market value of a fund's underlying investments – especially at an early stage of the intervention phase.

There are additional interpretations of the illiquidity of limited partnership shares. Private equity valuations are determined by a small number of experts rather than a large number of market participants. This implies a significant margin of errors and that market values can only be approximated through appraisal techniques. Outside investors in theory are faced with the 'lemon problem', because they have less information on the quality of the fund; this effect makes them less willing to pay what may actually be a fair price for a fund share; under certain market conditions, they might not be willing to buy a share at all. Also the GPs may face a 'lemon problem' when having to replace LPs for subsequent funds, because outsiders are less able to determine whether the manager is of poor quality or previous investors were hit by a liquidity shock. By choosing the degree of illiquidity of the security, GPs can influence the type of LPs the fund will attract.[25] This allows them to screen for 'deep-pocket' investors who have a low likelihood of facing a liquidity shock and are able to back future funds.[26]

Why not evergreen funds?

One important criticism is related to the self-liquidating nature of funds structured as limited partnerships. It has been argued that in the typical fund structure, managers need to show quick hits to prove they deserve a new fund. However, this is working against the raison d'être of investments in areas where patient capital is particularly needed. One frequently cited example is venture capital, where deals are sometimes found to be exited prematurely relatively to what would have been the optimal holding period of the investment. In principle, the solution may be sought in 'evergreen funds', that is, funds that do not mature but instead have an – at least theoretically – infinite lifetime. But why does the alternative asset industry still use what Love (2009) calls 'archaic LP structures that are spectacularly ill-suited' to long-term investing? One answer lies in the particular way the limited partnership addresses uncertainty and grants control rights to investors.

'Evergreen' vehicles are often promoted as a solution to the alleged inefficiency associated with the regular need to fund raise, but they are also criticised as there is no mechanism for them to return capital to investors and they provide little incentive to managers to force exits from their investments.[27] The question 'why are funds not evergreen?' could be compared to the question 'why do publicly quoted companies pay dividends?' One argument put forward by economists – the dividend irrelevance theory – essentially indicates that dividend payments should have little to no impact on stock price. Investors are not concerned with a company's dividend policy since they can sell a portion of their portfolio of equities if they want cash.[28] On the other hand, a high dividend payout is important for investors, because dividends provide certainty about the company's financial well-being.

As, among others, the Madoff investment scandal demonstrated, Ponzi-like schemes where investors are paid from their own money or those of subsequent investors can go undetected for quite a while in the case of evergreen structures, particularly where the underlying portfolio companies are difficult to value. Limited partnerships address this problem as fund managers only get rewarded once cash has been returned and true performance has been revealed. Similarly, there is a strong argument to be made for self-liquidating funds in private equity. Take venture capital, for example, where valuations are notoriously difficult and are often seen by investors with considerable doubt. To be sure, it is not that the fund managers are not seen as trustworthy; rather, it is the recognition that in any appraised asset class, valuations are highly judgmental. The only way to give investors confidence is by exiting portfolio companies, thus liquidating investments and showing investors that valuations are 'real'.

Another explanation for the significance of the dividend policy lies in control, i.e., retained earnings are under the corporation's control while the ability to issue new equity control is transferred to shareholders.[29] The more the corporation pays out as dividends the more often its shareholders can exercise their control. The shareholders' power rests in their ability to make the provision of new finance conditional on changes deemed necessary to rectify the company's underperformance.

It's also about control

While fund managers may prefer evergreen funds as such structures give them the opportunity to access capital on a permanent basis, investors often shy away from being locked up under such conditions. In contrast to evergreen funds, limited partnerships follow a fundraising cycle in the sense that GPs return to the market at – more or less – regular intervals to raise capital for a new fund. Funds set up as limited partnerships should rather be seen as shares with limited lifetimes that effectively have built-in the end of the relationship between the GP and its LPs. Like all organisations, GPs eventually go into 'decay', are faced with conflicts within their teams, lose motivation, or become overconfident and arrogant. Organisational changes are difficult and often only outside pressures can force them. The requirement to raise another fund is a check and balance, with the GP's future depending on it. In the extreme case, where no new funds are raised at all, full liquidation eventually becomes inevitable as management fees on old funds under management dry up. Heikkilä (2004) views this periodic liquidation of private equity funds as essential for the LPs in the funds, because the exit and reinvestment cycle allows them to withdraw capital from less competent fund managers or managers whose industry expertise has become obsolete. It also allows setting back the clock for new investors, who do not need to value and pay for an existing portfolio. The fund management team's track record and reputation is critical for the successful closing of follow-on funds. Typically, limited partnership agreements do not allow follow-on funds with the same strategy by the same manager before the end of the investment period or before a high percentage of the active fund is invested.

It also allows the GP to start with a clean sheet and to improve the team dynamics by bringing in new members and changing incentives. LPs are forced to think whether to reinvest rather than whether to disinvest. Without this predetermined breaking point, GPs are likely to engage in rent seeking, pursuing lower risk strategies but charging a compensation in line with high-risk and high value added. Instead, the fund's limited lifetime forces its managers to regularly return to the capital markets and ask existing or new investors to back the next fund. Rather than having a 'magic formula' that guarantees success, fund managers periodically need to convince investors that they provide superior investment opportunities. This requires fund managers to closely listen to their investors and to adapt rapidly. LPs can exercise 'evolutionary pressure' through selection and monitoring and are therefore an essential component of the 'alternative asset ecosystem'. Of course, this is not a factor in situations where investors in funds also have management control. Indeed, evergreen funds tend to include only a few LPs as investors and, in most situations, are funds operating on behalf of a single family office.

Competing structures

Investing through limited partnerships is not uncontroversial and, in addition to the evergreen funds discussed above, a range of competing approaches have been marketed to investors over the years, including listed vehicles, deal-by-deal investments, direct and co-investments.[30] However, these approaches have generally produced mixed results.

Rather than the public listing itself, the lack of self-liquidation appears to be the core problem with quoted vehicles, as there is no guarantee that accounting and real value will converge. In fact, self-liquidation is not confined to non-quoted vehicles. For instance, Jon Moulton's Better Capital is quoted but is distributing realisations to its shareholders, which may be one of the reasons why it is one of the very few listed private equity vehicles to have traded at a premium its NAV.[31] However, retail investors are detrimental to investment success in private equity as they usually lack the 'deep pockets' to sustain investments with high failure rates and, due to their typically small relative share in the listed vehicle, have limited power to change the behaviour of its management and are less able to exercise any 'evolutionary pressure'.

A 'deal-by-deal' approach shares certain characteristics with investing directly. At first glance, this seems to look highly attractive from a LP's standpoint. It not only appears to reduce management fees, it also gives LPs the possibility to opt out, for example, in situations where they are liquidity-constrained, and to build up a portfolio that is more in line with their targeted asset composition. Increasingly, institutions have turned towards investing directly, a subject that requires reflection and to which we will turn in the following chapter.

The Limited Partnership as Endangered Species

The limited partnership is criticised and under attack from various sides. To be sure, the limited partnership may have important shortcomings, which lie not least in their self-liquidation and their limited life span. However, it has stood the test of time and provides a framework for long-term investing, which is typically associated with a high degree of uncertainty where no superior structure has evolved yet.

No superior structure

To paraphrase Sir Winston Churchill, the limited partnership may be the worst form of investing in private equity, except all those other forms that have been tried from time to time. Some innovations such as co-investments aim to address some of its weaknesses while other proposals such as evergreen structures or direct investment are either replacing one ill with the other or are even aggravating the problems.

While the limited partnership's illiquidity, opacity and long investment horizon are viewed as disadvantages, these characteristics are key to its success. And given their long heritage, one might expect there to be a greater understanding of the risk properties of LP funds, from the standpoint of a diversified investment portfolio. Instead, investments in limited partnerships are often treated in the same way as investments in traditional asset classes. As we discuss in the remainder of this book, such treatment may have unintended consequences. Instead, a risk management approach is needed that reflects the specific characteristics of the limited partnership.

Unintended attacks

Some of the attacks are unintended. For example, regulation obliges LPs such as banks to 'look-through' and risk weight the underlying exposures of a fund as if the exposures were directly held. Economically, the limited partnership is rather one entity that appears to have components, but they are in reality indivisibly connected.

This misunderstanding gives an incorrect picture of the risks that tend to be exaggerated and of the rewards, which are overlooked or downplayed. Repeated attempts from policy makers to impose heavy-handed regulation on the private equity industry can be counterproductive, as such efforts aim to structure and steer, on behalf of many unsophisticated participants, something that would be better kept as flexible as possible. Attempts to press a private equity fund into the 'one size fits it all' public market corset will be counterproductive as it conflicts with the raison d'être of this vehicle. Regulators put a premium on liquidity at, in the case of private equity, the expense of commitment to long-term investing.

A warning from the past

Colin Mayer in his book, *Firm Commitment*, describes the corporation as a rent extraction vehicle for the shortest-term shareholders that allows them to hold all other stakeholders, including longer-term shareholders, to ransom by threatening interventions such as takeovers and hedge fund activism.[32] As a solution he suggested different classes of shares, where those willing to hold shares for the long term should receive voting rights, whereas those not willing to make that commitment should not – an approach which could be argued to be embodied in the way private equity firms raise a sequence of funds. In their book, *Why Nations Fail*, Acemoglu and Robinson argue that a series of contractual innovations – among which the commenda is mentioned as the most famous – made economic institutions much more inclusive and thus formed the key bases for the economic expansion of Venice. Having studied official documents, the authors concluded that the commenda was a powerful force in fostering upward social mobility: these documents are full of new names, people who had previously not been among the Venetian elite. They explain the republic's end of prosperity with its switch towards more extractive economic institutions and an increasingly narrow elite monopolising the main lines of business and eventually banning the commenda. More than a structure for intermediation, the limited partnership is an engine for innovation.

Speed Read

- The origins of the limited partnership structure date back to ancient times. Its profit-sharing arrangement is echoed in the medieval commendas, where both parties had an expectation that the venture's profits would significantly exceed a fixed return threshold; the sharing of profits also motivated the sleeping partner to study the venture and add their own expertise to the decision-making process. Likewise the profit-sharing encouraged the travelling partner to exert his maximum effort throughout the venture.

- The limited partnership may not only be central to the success of private equity, but also – as evidenced by its ancient pedigree – part of the human's 'genetic code'. Its asymmetric sharing of risks and rewards together with 'fairness' appears to be a kind of 'killer application' for economic growth in an environment of uncertainty and change.
- Investors in a limited partnership trade off the efficiency, scalability and transparency associated with modern large corporations against the flexibility of, and the communication within, small teams that allow a much quicker adaptation to changing market conditions and newly arising opportunities.
- The limited partnership may have important shortcomings, which lie not least in their self-liquidation and their limited life span. However, it appears to be the best adapted instrument for specific situations, i.e., where investors are faced with extreme uncertainty, a temporary opportunity and high asymmetries regarding skills and experience.
- More than a structure for intermediation, the limited partnership is an engine for innovation. The more surprising is it that so far neither the financial industry nor academia has spent much effort on modelling its specific characteristics.

Chapter 8
Do-It-Yourself?

From the institutional investor's perspective there are many different routes to investing in private equity, such as through funds, directly into portfolio companies, co-investing alongside funds into portfolio companies, or even employing an additional layer of intermediation, such as a fund-of-funds (see **Figure 8.1**).

In a theoretical market of perfect information and friction-free exchange of goods there is no need for intermediation. As we have seen, private equity is about as far from a perfect market as institutions are likely to get. There are substantial costs associated with searching, evaluation, structuring and transacting investments and related risks that can be shared between parties that pool their capital. Intermediaries may also have superior information on markets that require special knowledge. As a result it has been noted that private equity appears to be 'a textbook case where the benefits from financial intermediation – in this case, specialized funds – would be substantial'.[1] So why are some large institutions choosing the 'do-it-yourself' approach?

Private equity investment through limited partnership funds is an expensive affair. Some estimates put the cumulative cost of an LP's compensation structure, including fees and carry, at 5 to 7 percentage points per year.[2] In theory at least, the cost saving of cutting out the fund 'as middle-man' are significant. No wonder, therefore, that a prominent LP like OMERS PE, the private equity investing arm of the Ontario Municipal Employees Retirement System, a C$55bn pension system, has spent the past decade shifting commitments from funds and into direct investments, with a target of 85 per cent direct exposure out of their total commitment to the asset class.[3]

It's a Fee Reduction Thing

Other institutional investors have taken note, with consultants generally supportive of the strategy. The main arguments put forward

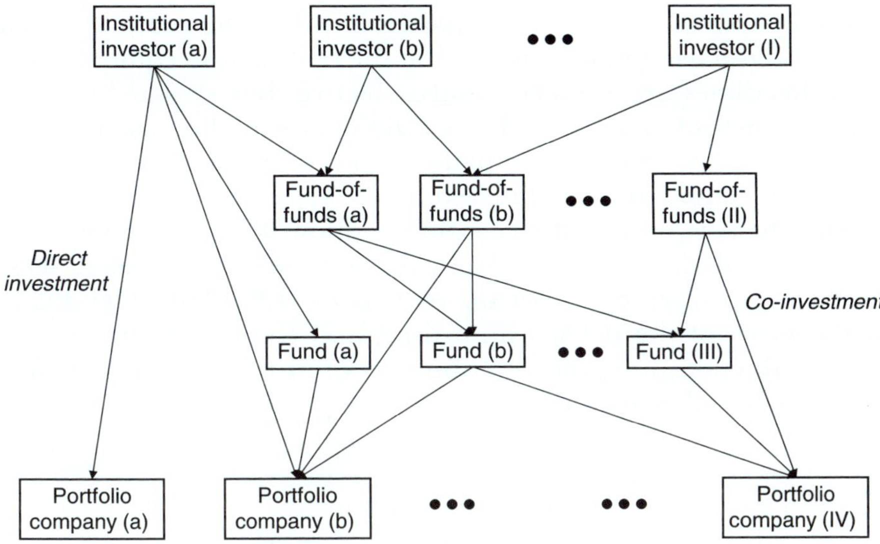

Figure 8.1 Institutional investing in private equity

relate to cost reductions, increased control over investee companies, better tailoring of the portfolio to the investor's specifics, and better quality of the investments selected. While the 'directs movement' has been pioneered by the large Canadian pension funds, one of the Toronto-based Canada Pension Plan Investment Board (CPPIB), with C$183bn of assets under management, has adopted a more cautious approach for private equity. Despite having built a direct investment team since 2006 it is continuing to mainly rely on third party managers. In 2013, CPPIB was reported to have still invested two-thirds through funds, albeit with the intention to increase direct investments significantly. However, this would be implemented through a 'symbiotic' relationship with its closest fund managers. That is to say, through co-investments.[4]

The concept of the fee-taking financial intermediary who adds little or no value to the process has become well-established in the consciousness of investors and policymakers as the bogey man of efficient and fair markets, and even of inequality of wealth. 'High' fees have become a political anathema and politically accountable institutions, such as public pension funds, are consequently sensitive to those investments that seem to carry disproportionately high charges. Various commentators, such as Will Hutton in *The Guardian*, referred to a study by Citigroup, suggesting that if pension funds and insurance firms had borrowed money themselves and invested in a basket of companies in which the funds invested they would have outperformed even the best private equity firms.[5] Such headlines are powerful and seductive, but should be taken with a pinch of salt, since the question remains how an investor could get access to these companies without knowing the universe the private equity firms are investing in.

And there is no doubt that compensation structures offered by GPs, particularly in combination with the fund's management fees, do have a profound impact on returns for LPs. This dilemma is at the heart of the debate, and direct and co-investing is seen as a 'fee reduction thing mostly'[6]. But does this really work or is this perspective rather myopic?

There is no free lunch

Mark Wiseman, President and CEO of CPPIB has commented: 'We don't pay what Blackstone and KKR pay, but it's fairly close. We do attract extraordinary people'. The comment suggests that direct investing might not be quite the free lunch its proponents imply, and that this debate may actually be, as with funds-of-funds, rather about outsourcing versus running the process in-house. Indeed, it is not clear whether running an in-house direct investment programme that can reasonably expect to achieve the same gross returns will actually be cheaper than investing through funds as intermediaries.[7]

Then there is 'career risk'. Interim losses, occasionally steep losses, are a price investors need to pay if they want to reap the rewards of alternative investments. Directly investing without involving intermediaries clearly makes an institution's managers more accountable but makes them justifiably fearful of jeopardising their prospects in an organisation. Moreover and as a general observation, in larger organisations, and with an increasing size of the cooperating group, it becomes increasingly difficult to monitor the individual contribution of members and various forms of opportunistic behaviour become prevalent. Here, taking less risk is more attractive, since without compensation comparable to that of fund managers there is nothing beyond a 'thank you' for phenomenal performance. If things go wrong it is likely to have a negative impact on one's career. Instead of 'pulling the plug' there will be a tendency to delay action in the hope that the problem can be avoided, overlooked in a larger portfolio of direct investments or at least will only blow up after one has moved on in the organisation.

This issue is relevant not only for direct investments but also for investing into funds. Also here contrarian bets will not be rewarded and the way to play safe is to invest where others do, i.e., to go for brands, and focus on the large buyouts. Here, it is easier to explain under-performance than for lesser-known firms in more interesting niches. To conclude, for salaried managers working for institutional investors and even more so for their consultants, the disincentive of being 'wrong' usually by far outweighs the reward of being 'right'.

Toward greener pastures?

The reward for spectacular performance is typically promotion into other areas or increased managerial responsibility. Also it is a fair assumption that highly qualified people join large organisations because they are looking for a career spanning several functions and hierarchic levels. This is at odds with the long-term nature of private equity investing and can also have a negative effect on the important networking in this industry. Only ownership and investment by qualified individuals provide an alignment of interests in an environment where high risk and uncertainty need to be taken and borne over longer time periods.

According to Chassany (2013), Canadian pensions make the point that while they are paying less, dealmakers do not have to worry about fundraising. Taking the economics of private equity into consideration, joining such institutional investors may be a way for private equity professionals to maintain their track record while essentially 'hibernating' in what has repeatedly been described as the most difficult fundraising environment on record.[8] Under more favourable circumstances and situations where professionals start to develop a knack for this type of investing, they are likely to move to traditional partnerships.

An ongoing debate

In fact, the debate is not new and institutional investors have tried direct investing before, for instance in Europe through captive structures during the 1990s. The experiences highlighted some significant challenges, such as how to create a governance structure that gives investment authority and decision-making power to the investment professionals, and how to manage the difficult interaction of the private equity focused entities with the rest of the organisation. As a result of these issues, the share of institutional investors investing directly had decreased significantly before this debate started to again gain momentum in the years after 2008.

Finally, cost savings may not be the only reason for pursuing direct investments. Another factor is the difference between investors who buy-to-sell and those who buy-to-hold. For the latter, building up reserves over time frames longer than the typical fund's ten-year lifetime, a more flexible and targeted portfolio management and market timing are often of higher importance, which is difficult to achieve through exclusively investing in funds.

Empirical evidence

Fang et al. (2012) found that direct investments have actually significantly outperformed standard fund investment benchmarks and notably co-investments. These results provide an economic rationale for the disintermediation trend and may also be explained by institutional learning and a growing familiarity with the private equity investment modus operandi. On the other hand, the advantages of the 'solo deals' over co-investments were found to be greater for local and later-stage companies that perform less R&D. For local deals, institutions' investment professionals may have an informational advantage, while for later-stage investments less specialist know-how is required, so here involving private equity firms would bring no or fewer advantages.

Regarding co-investments, Fang et al. (2012) describe an essentially passive approach, where institutional investors only co-invested in deals offered to them, apparently based on the deal size, probably as 'lemons', and that were substantially (nearly five times) larger than the funds' average deals. That co-investments are viewed as being offered by the funds to their LPs reflects a specific approach that is not necessarily representative.[9] Practitioners point out that it is important that an LP generates his co-investment deal-flow like any other direct investor through communicating to the fund managers his specific interest and regularly following-up through calls and meetings.[10]

When comparing across co-investments, Fang et al. (2012) found that larger deals substantially underperform smaller deals. As one of the authors of this study, Josh Lerner, explained: 'The problem was, it seems, that the co-investments were doubly cursed [...] They were done at exactly the worst possible time in the cycle and, second, these deals tended to be substantially larger than what the fund managers used to do, in the order of three times larger – and those deals seemed to perform poorly.'[11] This outcome, however, should not come as a surprise: co-investment strategies are mainly touted as an approach to get around management fees, so it is logical that investors who solely focus on costs had poured too much into this activity.

Organisational Considerations for D.I.Y.

Direct investing will never be for everyone. For a start, there are regulatory restrictions that make a direct private equity investment difficult for some institutional investors. For instance, Dutch pension funds are not allowed to take a majority stake in a company as this is seen as entrepreneurship and not an investment role by the regulators. The regulatory flip side to this is increasing costs related to compliance with newly emerging regulation, such as AIFMD, which some institutional investors hope to avoid by going directly, as they are subject to a different regulatory regime. Other investors may invest in publicly listed equity and thus in theory may receive material, non-public information on listed companies from their private equity side. In this case they would need to stop trading in the listed shares, unless extensive Chinese walls are in place. Therefore, incorporating a private equity organisation in an asset management firm is often costly and only worthwhile for larger organisations.[12]

Skills and commitment

According to Barber and Goold (2007), private equity investing requires skills both in investing and in streamlining operations. Investors who try to replicate this technique should ask themselves whether they have the network and can spot and correctly value opportunities. GP skills related to the knowledge of which industries are worth investing in can well be imitated. This mainly analytical side is rarely a problem for larger institutions. However, it is unlikely that LPs can 'steal' GP skills related to a comparative advantage in screening or monitoring investments.[13]

Few institutional investors will be able to build and maintain a team with skills and experience to turn a poorly performing business around. This requires the capability to identify a business's critical strategic levers that drive improved performance, putting financial controls in place and keeping a focus on meeting milestone objectives. Moreover, it would involve putting in place a strong, highly motivated and highly incentivised management and the ability to poach talent, which indirectly may cause friction as in-house investment teams will be faced with quite different compensation packages and incentive structures.

From the LPs' perspective one major perceived disadvantage of fund investments is their illiquidity, but the solo deals' advantage of better market timing may be illusive. To be able to benefit from the private equity approach, investors need to implement a value creation plan. Even if they have more involvement and control, directly investing institutions are constrained by this plan in the same way as fund managers. Funds structured as limited partnerships essentially protect the investment process by 'forcing' their LPs to stick with the value creation plan and thus provide a particularly appropriate framework to harvest an illiquidity risk premium private equity offers.[14] Funds assure commitment and counter the tendency not to invest during market downturns, where 'fearful hearts overwhelm logical heads'. As LPs are obliged to respond to capital calls, fund managers as intermediaries will continue to provide liquidity to portfolio companies that otherwise would be starved of capital or terminated inefficiently.

Meeting the laws of gravity

While some investors may be able to stay local, larger investment programmes are essentially forced to go international and are faced for their direct investments with the 'tyranny of distance' and diseconomies to amount of capital to be invested. Kaplan and Schoar (2005) found a concave relation between fund size and performance that suggests a decreasing return to scale of fund size (see **Figure 8.2**). On one hand there is a minimum feasible fund size, below which funds on average will generate losses. After achieving a peak at a certain size, average performance tends to fall with further increases.[15] Where these thresholds are will depend on the type of fund and geography and may not hold in all circumstances:

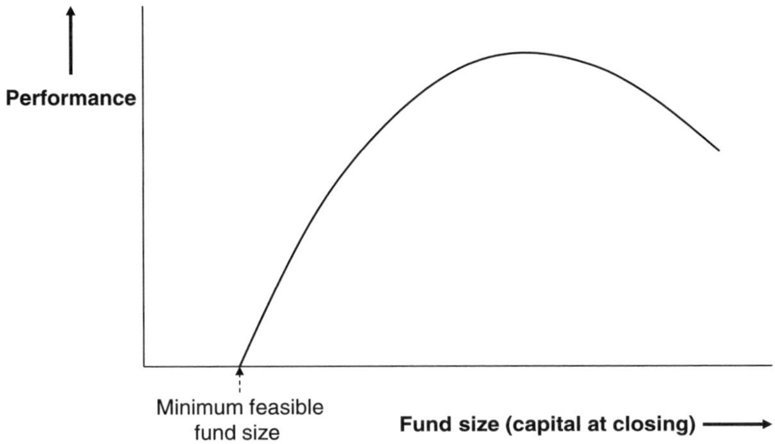

Figure 8.2 Concave relationship between fund size and performance

for instance, in the portfolio analysed by Phalippou and Gottschalg (2009) no such evidence was found.

However, in broad terms the result is widely accepted and plausible and also holds for portfolios of funds. Because of the size limitation for funds, increasing assets under management also lead to increases of the portfolio of funds' diversification. Also, overheads for staffing for investment management, research, back office, financial control, office space, IT (that when the number of funds exceeding certain levels also require staff increases), expenses for conducting due diligence, and travel expenses for monitoring funds in the portfolio need to be factored in. Another effect to be considered is the size of a portfolio (too many managers or too much capital) that imposes a limit on diversification benefits: there are only a few top-tier funds, and these most desirable funds have capped their capital under management.

Gabriel Robet developed a model that takes these factors into consideration and simulated portfolios of private equity funds.[16] The Sharpe ratio,[17] as a way to assess performance by adjusting for risks for such portfolios also shows a concave relationship. The results indicate that there is a threshold beyond which diversification is at best useless (see **Figure 8.3**).

The overheads diversification over this threshold is clearly harmful for smaller portfolios. Importantly, however, for larger amounts of capital it seems to be possible to add funds beyond their optimum without suffering from adverse diversification effects. We conclude that the main factor to consider is the amount to be invested

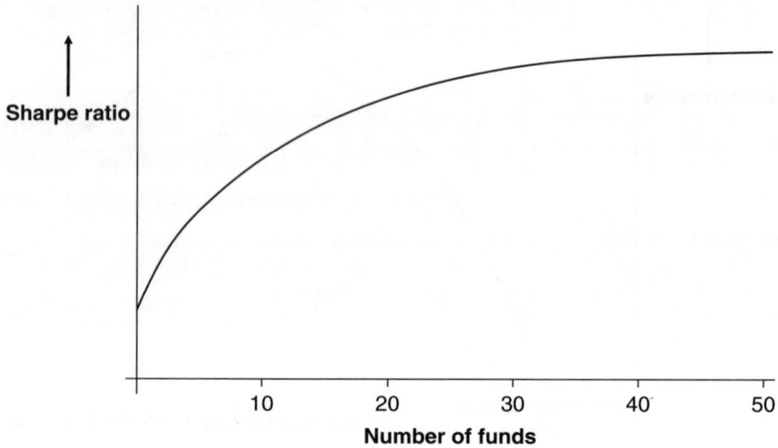

Figure 8.3 Concave relationship for portfolio of funds

in private equity. Direct investments will be more subject to size limitations than portfolios of funds.

For a small investment programme with focus on local and later-stage companies, investing directly will be advantageous. A medium-sized investment programme will require increasing the commitments to funds. For a large programme, the solo deals need to be more and more replaced by co-investments, with third-party fund managers supporting sourcing, monitoring and existing portfolio companies (see **Figure 8.4**).

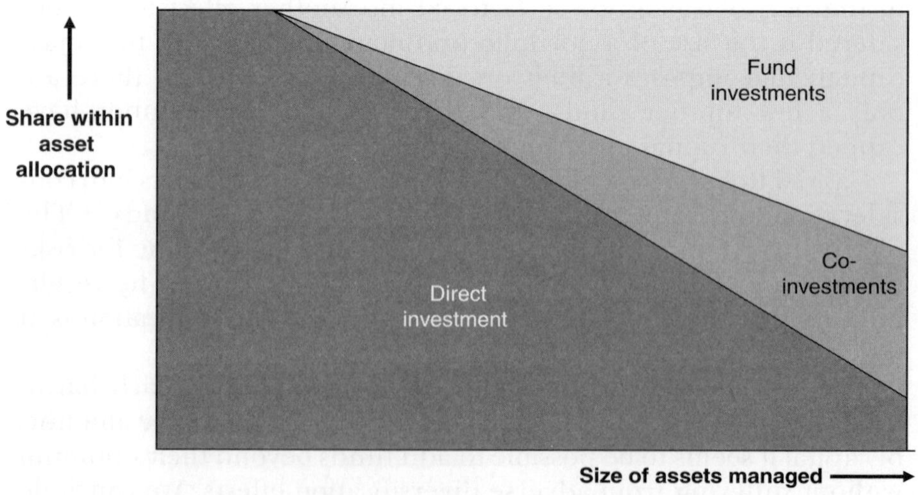

Figure 8.4 Direct investments vs. investments through funds

Funds-of-Funds

The so-called 'fund-of-funds' is probably the most common and relevant type of vehicle in the context of financial intermediation (see **Figure 8.1**). It pools a group of investors and uses the capital to assemble a diversified portfolio of private equity funds.[18] A fund-of-funds typically mirrors the private equity fund structure and is set up as a limited partnership, with a GP managing the day-to-day operations. Its LPs need to be committed for a period that will even exceed the usual private equity fund's lifetime, i.e., 10–15 years, in line with the investment horizon of the targeted funds, which are normally identified during a 3–4 year investment period. Also here to exit such a vehicle earlier, the investor must either sell its partnership interest at a discount on the secondary market, or default by ceasing to honour new capital calls and thus become subject to penalties.

Funds-of-funds are often also set up as listed vehicles specifically to attract smaller investors, such as high net worth individuals wanting to get access to the private equity asset class without going through the set-up of a dedicated programme and without being exposed to the illiquidity of unquoted investments. Such publicly quoted private equity funds-of-funds are based on familiar investment trust-like structures. They certainly can address the hurdles of regulatory requirements, tax efficiency and transparency but are still seen as less relevant for institutional investors.[19]

Benefits

Funds-of-funds manage several activities which tend to complement each other and require more technical skills and experience than the typical institutional investor has available in-house: primary investments in newly-formed limited partnerships, actively managing through buys and sells on the secondary markets, securitisations, or co-investments. As private equity is becoming an international asset class, investors are more and more faced with the tyrannies of time and distance when it comes, for instance, to monitoring and overcoming cultural gaps, language problems, taxation and legal issues. Often in-house resources are insufficient for covering a particular geography or industry sector.

Funds-of-funds are a solution for the sorting problem between 'good' and 'bad' private equity investments and address the information gap for investors not familiar with the asset class through their expertise in due diligence and monitoring. Securing access to top performing funds traditionally has been the fund-of-funds industry's major value proposition. Investors expect funds-of-funds to have access to successful, 'invitation only' funds, or to identify the future stars among the young and less known ones.

Funds-of-funds allow smaller investors to scale upwards, i.e., to invest in more funds. This is only to some degree to contribute to diversification but more by providing avenues to lower the cost of fund management.[20] Larger institutions can use funds-of-funds to scale downwards to invest larger amounts without being forced to consider many small investment proposals. Even sophisticated investors recognise the need to invest in smaller funds to gain exposure to niches such as emerging markets, less efficient private equity sectors because of their potential for greater returns, and also to defensively expand relationships with the 'star' fund managers of tomorrow. On the other hand, funds-of-funds are often criticised for just being 'index trackers', building on track record and access in order to avoid criticism and upsetting their investors, rather than being at the forefront of innovation and executing more risky and technologically challenging investment approaches.

Less extreme, less uncertainty, lower returns

Funds-of-funds are seen as 'safe havens' for investors in private equity as they allow for a reasonable downside protection through diversification. Not surprisingly, because of their diversification, funds-of-funds perform similarly to individual funds but with less pronounced extremes. However, just viewing them as 'pooled vehicles' like funds overlooks part of their business model. Fund-of-funds firms could be argued as 'selling off' their relationships with GPs to investors, for example, in the form of the separate accounts mentioned before. Consequently, just the financial track record delivered by a firm over its entire assets under management does not give the full picture. Just as relevant is the 'game strength' of a private equity firm managing funds-of-funds, i.e., the number, strengths and attractiveness of the relationships managed and its ability to segment and bundle these relationships into tailor-made mandates.

In the context of the limited partnership structure we argued that the 20 per cent carried interest is the fair compensation for successful investing under extreme uncertainty. For funds-of-funds launched between 1992 and 1999, Jo (2002) found that less than 50 per cent charged carried interest at all and that the average carried interest was 3.8 per cent.[21] At the end of the 1990s, 10 per cent carried interest was common; after 2000 the difficult market environment had brought that down to 5 per cent where it has stayed since. That funds-of-funds are unable to charge a higher level of carried interest underlines the argument: through building diversified portfolios of private equity funds they transform extreme uncertainty into quantifiable risk, for which 20 per cent are perceived to be excessive.

Costs

Fund-of-funds management fees are as hotly debated as those charged by funds. It is often argued that the fund-of-funds industry offers little value to investors. There is some performance component in the form of a carried interest, but the economics of a fund-of-funds are largely driven by the management fee where growing assets under management are the primary means to increase its profitability and firm value. The additional layer of management fees charged by funds-of-funds is often said to be too high and to outweigh their efficiency gains. In the line of argument, they would have to perform 0.7–3.4 per cent better to compensate for these 'fees-on-fees'. Comparing fund-of-funds returns with the underlying returns from private equity funds misses a number of points. The 'double layer of fees' is more a 'politically charged' argument than based on a rational assessment of the situation. The fact that a fund-of-funds will add a layer of fees on top of the fees for the funds under their management is certainly an issue, but investors should rather approach this as a decision whether to outsource parts of their investment value chain. In fact, the annual costs of an in-house team can be significant compared to that of a typical fund-of-funds. Due to the diseconomies of scale, the yearly costs of an internal team are estimated to be more than three times higher than the annual fees charged by a fund-of-funds.[22]

Outsourcing to funds-of-funds

A wholesale outsourcing to fund-of-funds managers can take various forms, and simplistically, there are three main structures: separate accounts, co-mingled accounts and pooled vehicles. A 'separate account' is a vehicle operating on behalf of a single institutional investor, for a fixed duration and with a structure established jointly with the fund-of-funds manager to meet specific legal, tax, strategic and other portfolio management needs. Such requirements can relate to the exclusion of investments in certain markets where the investor has an over-concentration or stronger allocation to other sectors. The agreement is only between the two parties and generally includes confidentiality provisions. From the investor's point of view, separate accounts are by far the most flexible approach but require some additional effort not only to identify the fund-of-funds manager to work with, but also to find a suitable structure. Nevertheless, investors tend to prefer separate accounts to other funds-of-funds' structures. The line between separate accounts and non-discretionary mandates is difficult to draw. Often two or more institutions have common objectives, such as a focus on a geographical region, or on venture capital, or on socially responsible investments and therefore share the same asset allocations in a 'commingled' account. With growing assets to be managed and a number of investors there comes a point where separate and commingled accounts become inefficient compared to a traditional large fund-of-funds with bundled services. Here institutional investors join a pool of other investors and the fund-of-funds managers tend to operate on a fully discretionary basis where they are given the authority to make investment decisions without first notifying their clients.

Speed Read

- Private equity is an expensive asset class. Economic and politically motivated concern has driven some large institutions to 'go solo'.
- There are clear limits for investing directly, and with increasing capital allocated to private equity, investors have no choice but to involve fund managers. As a rule of thumb, the right approach to a large degree depends on the size of the investment programme.
- For a small investment programme with a focus on local and later-stage companies investing directly will be advantageous. A medium-sized investment programme will require increasing the commitments to funds. For a large programme, the solo deals need to be more and more replaced by co-investments, with third-party fund managers supporting sourcing, monitoring and existing portfolio companies.

- The demise of the funds-of-funds industry has often been predicted, but they continue to fulfil an important role in bridging the private equity funds' world of uncertainty with the institutional investors' world of risk. Funds-of-funds also serve as an important stabiliser of the private equity market, immune as they are to the cyclical vagaries of other institutional investors. This gives them considerable negotiating power vis-à-vis GPs.
- Regardless of the approach chosen, the potential for cost savings will be less than widely expected and direct investing vs. funds-of-funds is rather a question of outsourcing the activity vs. doing this in-house.

Chapter 9

Economics of Private Equity Firms

The economics of a fund, which is to say how GPs can earn money from the services they provide, is commonly considered of crucial, if not supreme, importance to investor outcomes, because it has a major impact on the behaviour of fund managers. In fact, LP investment strategies should be influenced less by fund economics than by GP-relationship considerations.

General Fund Incentive Structure

The timing and manner in which a private equity fund makes distributions to its partners are provided for in the partnership agreement. These provisions are commonly referred to as the 'distribution waterfall' and are often the most complex parts of the agreement.[1] The expected GP compensation comprises fixed and variable components. The bulk of the fixed revenue comes through management fees whereas carried interest, transaction and monitoring fees are variable.

Annual management fee

Annual management fees are supposed to cover the basic costs of running and administering the fund and are paid throughout its contractual lifetime. Such fees are nearly always calculated as a percentage of capital the LPs commit to the fund, but generally taper off after the investment period,[2] or when a successor fund is formed. Some of the committed capital is used for these management fees and the remainder for making investments.[3]

The enduring nature of management fees lead some to criticise them as supporting failing funds and underperforming teams. However, alignment of interest is not necessarily equivalent to paying for performance. For GPs, survival as a firm is the overriding objective, and GPs are far more vulnerable to changes in the market than LPs, who can switch to other asset classes. Since it is impossible to determine in advance which GPs will succeed, rather than focus on the 'cost' of a particular fund, LPs would be better off managing the relationships with the 'winning firms' over the long term.

In principle the management fees should be a function of the fund size and the resources required to implement its strategy. Typically, they range from 2.5 per cent of committed capital for funds of less than €250 million to 1.5 per cent for the larger buyout funds. Having said this, the resources required for a €10m deal and a €10bn deal are not so different, creating potential for huge economies of scale and implicitly weakening the GP's incentives. However, over the years, as investor sophistication has increased, this has been counterbalanced by LPs resisting these fee levels and more stringent conditions under which these fees are provided.

Reuters reported that the mean management fee for buyout funds raised in 2010 and seeking $1 billion or more in commitments is 1.59 per cent, down 32 basis points from its peak for vintage 2008 funds of 1.91 per cent.[4] Nevertheless, industry norms are based on the precedents set by larger and more influential funds and it is a fair assumption that annual management fees of $15.9m are more than sufficient for operating a $1 billion fund. Jon Moulton, founder of Better Capital, estimated that the mega-funds are taking out about 80 per cent of their revenues in management fees, rather than carried interest.[5]

This contrasts with the situation at the other end of the spectrum: according to Maula and Murray (2003), specialist, early-stage technology funds probably need about 4–5 per cent of their commitments as management fees for covering the operating costs of their activities – a fee level that would be unacceptable to the vast majority of institutional investors or their advisers (see **Figure 9.1**).

It's interesting to note that while LPs are able to exercise significant power over the GPs as they can hold them up during next fund raising,[6] larger funds tend to lead to a larger, more diversified but also more fragmented LP basis, that weakens this control.

Carried interest

While management fees need to cover many expenses arising from actual investment work, including reasonable salaries for the investment managers at least during the five-year investment period, they are not intended to remain their primary source of income and their main incentive. Instead, LPs see the carried interest,

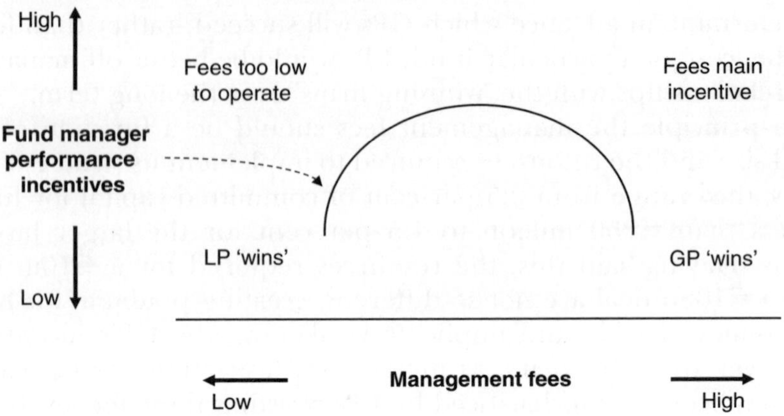

Figure 9.1 Incentive trade-off

that is to say the fund manager's share in the fund's net profits without contributing a corresponding share of its capital, as the most powerful incentive to create value.

Related to the carried interest is the question of the preferred return or hurdle rate, which is often misinterpreted as a compensation for the LP taking risk. This provision is intended to align the interests of the GP and the LPs by giving the fund managers an additional incentive to outperform a traditional investment benchmark. Hurdle rates were set at around 8 per cent during the private equity industry's infancy, when this was the level of returns generated by ten-year US treasuries. In fact its primary purpose is to incentivise deal flow screening in order to assure adherence to the targeted risk return profile. A hurdle that is set too high may cause fund managers to 'swing for the fences' and take on too much risk, whereas without a hurdle fund managers would be able go for low-risk deals that provide them with carried interest without delivering a return required for the private equity asset class.[7]

Transaction and monitoring fees

In the 1980s, it was common particularly for buyout funds to charge their portfolio companies fees for providing monitoring, consulting and investment banking-like services in putting together a transaction, such as an IPO or M&A. These fees provided a significant additional revenue stream and occasionally turned out to be quite large, although not easily visible to investors. Transaction fees are to a large degree a variable component of the GP's income as they are essentially driven by the number of portfolio companies

During the 1990s the pendulum swung back with LPs winning the right to share in such fee income and to make this activity less rewarding for the funds. The main motive behind this was the wish to discourage fund managers from participating in activities that come at the detriment of increasing the value of portfolio companies. Consequently, transaction fees are now either fully or partially 'offset' against future management fees.

Equity participation

An important incentive is the equity participation of the fund manager in the private equity fund. This investment of personal capital gives the fund managers not only an attractive upside but exposes them to a downside as well. Moreover, the fund managers can only sell their equity in the context of generating exits for the LPs which reduces the incentive to manipulate short-term performance.

This 'skin in the game' or 'hurt money' has become a standard instrument to assure the alignment of interests and should be a significant share of the fund managers' personal wealth. Two per cent of the commitment is seen as the norm, but for first-time teams and newer funds, where the fund management team has not yet accumulated sufficient personal means to invest this much, even smaller amounts can represent a significant percentage of each team member's net worth. Consequently, there is no formulaic answer: some more established firms appear to have put up between 5 per cent and 10 per cent of the commitment, even for multi-billion dollar funds.

Co-investments

When discussing the GP compensation, Cornelius (2011) also mentions co-investment opportunities that theoretically allow LPs to reduce their costs significantly. That no fees are charged on co-investments made alongside the funds is widely seen as the attraction of co-investments. However, by just focusing on (questionable) cost reduction, LPs overlook the major value creation component co-investments potentially offer.

Beyond Economics

The compensation of fund managers is an issue of continuing debate and investors in private equity funds remain concerned that income earned by GPs is excessive. In theory, it should not matter what the GP has earned with the portfolio companies but only what the LPs receive from the fund distribution's net-of-fees and carried interest. However, the public debate goes beyond economics and involves the much more complex considerations of equality, fairness and jarring parallels between fund managers and the pensioners whose money they invest.

Van den Burg and Rasmussen (2008), in their report to the European Parliament, described the payouts as 'extreme' and not market based. They saw the compensation structure neither as a 'law of nature' nor historically based, but as 'simply an unchallenged 'characteristic' of the industry'. Even experts close to the industry share this assessment: Phalippou (2011) in his study for the Ministry of Finance and the Norwegian Parliament described the fees in private equity as high 'by any standards'.

CalPERS Chief Investment Officer, Joseph Dear, captured this mood in his 2010 interview with Reuters: 'It just drives me nuts when I think about managers who are generating profits off the management fees.'[8] Indeed, management fees are paid regardless of the fund's performance and therefore fail to provide an incentive to work hard. Where they are high and quasi-guaranteed they stimulate tentative and risk-averse behaviour such as following the herd.

One solution for LPs is to ask for a budget in order to determine the necessary fees. This budget concept is widely seen as making most sense economically, but its implementation can be mechanically complex. Therefore, the simple, percentage-based model has still not gone out of favour, and essentially the fee structure is again dictated by supply and demand in the market. As a consequence, LPs should focus on the economics of the private equity firms that manage the funds.

For private equity funds, the managers' remuneration is structured in a way that expected returns are shared between managers and investors, but as a consequence the riskier product leads to more performance fees paid to the fund managers, which creates another point of friction with the typically more risk-averse cultures of LPs.

The Routes to Riches

Success in private equity is driven by performance-related incentives. While large management fees may give the impression that GPs are rewarded for no performance, fund managers only become wealthy on that basis if they manage to raise a succession of funds over long time period, and if they in parallel manage to increase the size of these funds – a situation that is conceivable only by the consistent demonstration of high performance.

Not just 'money for nothing'

The entry barriers into private equity fund management are significant: finding a critical mass of investors has always been difficult and for first-time funds can take much more than a year, if successful at all. Initially, funds are too small to make the team rich, even if they manage to deliver high performance. In fact, the implicit penalties for a failing GP that has just managed to raise one or two funds can be severe: the start-up expenses are lost, during this fund's lifetime team remuneration will be very low, for investment professionals there are not only significant opportunity costs but also the loss related to their equity participation, and finding attractive new employment after several years in private equity can also be problematic.

Typically a private equity firm will seek a new fund every three to five years.[9] Only if LPs become convinced that performance is explained by skills rather than luck, GPs will manage to raise their new funds faster and with more certainty and be able to increase the funds' size, possibly in combination with more rewarding terms and conditions. Successful GPs thus aim to build their personal wealth by managing fund groups, that is to say a series of funds raised quickly one after another and often even run in parallel.

Consider the GP's lifetime income

Capital under management can be obtained by raising more from existing investors or by seeking new classes of investors. The GP's lifetime income depends on the explicit compensation through management fees and carried interest and the implicit, market-based pay for performance caused by the relation between today's performance and subsequent fundraising.[10] For this purpose, GPs are faced with a number of trade-offs. If they go for short-term maximisation of management fees it may be a one-off as it jeopardises the relationship with their investors and their long-term prospects as a firm. Rapidly growing fund sizes can also increase management fees but at a certain point will result in underperformance with lower carried interest and also will make future fund raising more difficult. At the end of the day, for a GP success is being able to raise the next fund under the same or better conditions.

Chung et al. (2010) conclude that the total pay for performance in private equity is considerably larger, and exhibits much more cross-sectional variation, than implied by the carried interest alone. They estimate that for the typical first-time fund, the implicit pay for performance from expected future fundraising is of approximately the same order of magnitude as the explicit pay for performance received as carried interest in the current fund. However, this implicit pay for performance declines proportionately to the number of subsequent funds raised (see **Figure 9.2**).

While Metrick and Yasuda (2010) found that roughly two-thirds of the fund managers' compensation comes from fixed rather than variable components – thus echoing the concerns of many LPs – results put forward by Chung et al. (2010) suggest that these figures understate the GPs' total performance-based compensation which is larger, by a factor of about two, than previously thought.

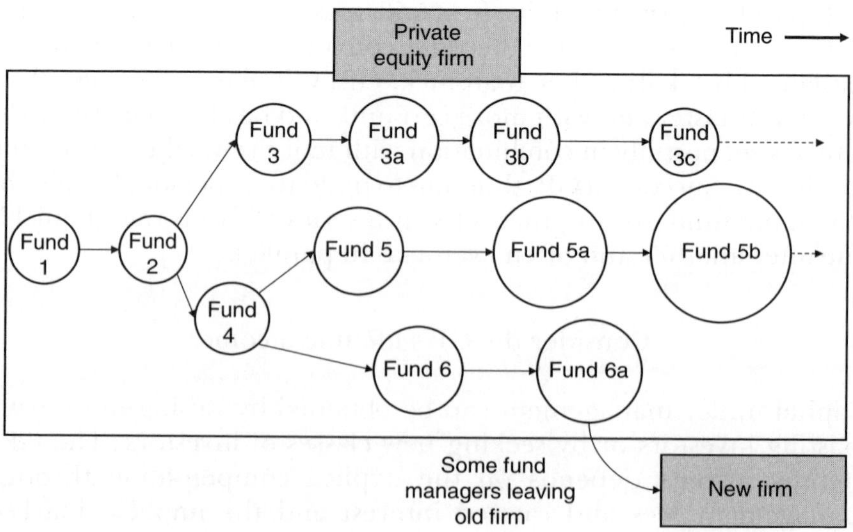

Figure 9.2 Subsequent funds drive private equity firm's economics

Reputation is critical and thus provides a significant performance incentive as it allows fund managers to earn fees on larger funds in the future. Moreover, based on their individual track records and the informal network built with the investor community, some fund managers strike out on their own and set up a new private equity firm, for instance, in situations where the old organisation has grown and the income needs to be shared with too many partners and staff.

Balancing growth vs. survival

GPs need to balance between 'growth' and 'survival' – two objectives that can be occasionally conflicting and thus not be fully aligned with those of their funds' LPs. While a fund's LPs provide carried interest as a, from their perspective, long-term, growth incentive, GPs need to assure their survival through short-term management fees and through long-term (in this case beyond one fund's lifetime) diversification – running several funds in parallel, geographical and sector diversification – that is diluting the GP's focus and his loyalty to just the present fund's LPs. In fact, LPs increasingly look at this aspect in their due diligence.

Incentives and penalties in private equity are designed to make GPs deliver high returns but GPs themselves may not be sure whether they are able to do this. For first-time funds there is a high probability of not raising the next fund because of underperformance compared to other GPs and fund managers, so they need to make the most out of the existing fund.

Applying LP Pressure

So how should limited partners approach the topic of fund economics? Firstly, it makes a difference whether the fund in question is large or small, managed by veterans or first-timers. The construction of terms and conditions is one of the few opportunities where LPs can anticipate and manage risk. Larger institutional investors – either directly or indirectly, through their gatekeepers – should, and do, exert continuous downward pressure on the fund's fee-based income. Fees are easier to challenge than the entire incentive structure, which would need to be agreed with other LPs and where the industry generally has shown to be resistant to change.

Strong investor pressure has resulted in the ILPA Principles that have had an impact on the waterfall arrangement for the performance-related remuneration, but investors have made less inroads regarding the non-performance-related fees.[11] This limited success is probably a function of the diversity of fund managers – on one hand there is a minimum level needed to cover the running costs of the fund, which limits the scope for negotiation for smaller funds. On the other hand, many LPs try to get access to the established players with a 'brand', who have no pressing need to give in to investor demands. It is fair to say, that LPs tend to negotiate where resistance is weak, not where negotiation is needed.

Rather than a one-size-fits-all optimal structure for all funds, we are looking at a trade-off that depends on a number of factors and needs to be looked at specifically. For GPs the ability to fend off those LPs that demand preferential terms depends to some degree on the assumption of performance persistence. GPs who have demonstrated skills and are in demand are better placed to withstand such pressures.

In fact, it is puzzling that despite apparent performance persistence, GPs seem unable to negotiate preferential terms themselves, for instance, by charging higher management fees. Hochberg et al. (2013) explain this as a result of the information asymmetries in private equity, i.e., the incumbent LPs hold bargaining power when negotiating follow-on investments with GPs. Should these LPs not agree to the GP's terms and conditions for the next fund and decide not to reinvest, this would be seen by potential new investors as a negative signal about the fund manager's skills. Moreover, these outside investors face a winner's curse: as the better-informed incumbent LPs will outbid them whenever the GP has skill, outsiders will withdraw from the market for follow-on funds.

Evolutionary Stasis

According to Phalippou (2011), there is already strong pressure especially from the large investors to modify compensation contracts. For instance, CalPERS was urged to move to a system in which 'nearly all' of a manager's compensation came from profit-sharing, rather than 'management or other fees'.[12] In his evaluation of the potential for Norwegian Government Pension Fund Global (GPFG) to invest in private equity, Phalippou (2011) suggested a mandate restricted to funds with low fixed fees and no portfolio company fees could be given.

Clearly, if investors of the size of CalPERS or the GPFG refuse certain types of fees, fee levels and terms and conditions, it is likely to influence the industry standards. The problem is that this implicitly favours large, established GPs which would create high entry barriers into the industry. Emerging GPs with just one or two funds under management require regular fees if they are to keep the lights on in the possibly many years prior to their first exits. On the other hand, it is not uncommon that established players, being in a much more comfortable position, are able to significantly reduce management fees or set-up side pockets to their funds where none are charged at all.[13]

For large funds, particularly mega-buyouts, economics are generally favourable for the GPs and alignment between them and their investors falls apart. Even significant equity participations cannot always assure the alignment. Before the beginning of the global financial crisis in 2008–2009 many banks wanted to get into the leverage loan business and were offering limited recourse or no-recourse loans to the staff of mega-funds to invest into their own funds.[14] Just focusing on fee levels leads to evolutionary stasis in an industry which depends on continuous innovation, ultimately to the detriment of most small- and medium-sized LPs.

Speed Read

- Judge the relationship, not the cost of the wedding. LPs should move beyond the myopic focus on a specific fund's compensation structure and look at the entire compensation over the lifetime of their relationship with a GP. LPs need to think about incentives not costs; paying high management fees for spectacular performance is better than paying no management fees for underperformance. When looking at investing in a series of funds with one GP there is certainly still great scope for creative structuring.
- Be flexible. This is a relationship. LPs should not attempt to apply one standard to all relationships but to tailor their requirements according to the specific situation. Mechanisms for alignment of interests and performance incentives work in a narrow area where funds are not too small and not too large – the industry has grown to a point where these mechanisms increasingly fail.

- Don't be over-awed by size. Size limitations of the industry weaken and remove alignment of interests; in the case of mega-buyouts, fees become excessive, but LPs want to get access to these 'safe' performers so that their negotiation power is too weak to change anything. In this case it may be the better option just to walk away and leave the 'comfort zone' of the 'brands'.

Chapter 10

Objectives

Perhaps it is surprising that so far we have not touched upon the question of objectives. For Clausewitz, the objective is the first principle of war as all else flows from it. The same is often considered to hold for investment strategies – identifying objectives, what one wants and, crucially, what one does not want, as well as any underlying constraints, such as tolerance of risk.[1] For investment managers, the objective defines the common purpose and gives direction to their activities. Guy Fraser-Sampson argues that objectives must be precisely laid down so that there can be no possible misunderstanding, as they are the yardstick success will be evaluated against. He goes on to criticise that answering this basic question was exactly what most of the world's investors neglected to do. The inability of decision makers to frame tangible and obtainable goals is often observed and viewed as a deep-seated strategy failure.

However, setting 'clear objectives' is an oversimplistic, even unrealistic, requirement, and one that has been attacked by several management thinkers, such as Henry Mintzberg, who has emphasised emergent strategy which arises informally. Nobel Prize winning economist, Herbert Simon, suggested that humans are not capable of optimisation and instead make choices that are merely satisfactory. In reality, we need to acknowledge that the various individuals and organisations involved have different priorities. Rather than formalising objectives, the private equity industry has relied on alignment of interests and powerful incentives instead of constraints. As such, it favours an arrangement in which all involved parties benefit from particular outcomes. It is an instrument to maximise the chances of an agreed outcome, but 'perfect alignment' is neither a realistic nor necessary goal.

True objectives and overpromises

Superficially at least, defining a clear investment objective seems straightforward: the risk adjusted long-term return targets – such as those calculated by a pension fund to meet its liabilities – to be achieved without external interference. However, there will frequently be other informal objectives or hidden agendas that can ultimately be of even greater importance than risk-adjusted returns to investors. These can range from idiosyncratic board preferences – a huge, developed world state pension fund once confided to the author they were terrified of the J-curve – to political and reputational considerations – such as the Norwegian Oil Funds' preference for 'socially-responsible' investment.

Moreover, there is no point in defining a strategy if its objective is impossible to reach within the given environment. In fact, for many pension funds in industrial countries with rapidly aging societies the target return required to meet liabilities is so high as to be impractical. Even in the case of war, Clausewitz argued that the military did have the right to decline technically unfeasible missions,[2] but the competition for getting access to capital poses a dilemma for fund managers. GPs need to make a strong case to investors, which often results in overpromising; for instance, to achieve a more challenging objective than competitors, to achieve it quicker, at lower costs, or being more likely to achieve it. In agreeing on return goals for alternative asset classes such as private equity where no, or no reliable, indices exist, there may be a moral dilemma: if a mandate is to be entrusted to asset managers, will they have the integrity to point out during the 'beauty parade' that overly ambitious investment return goals are unachievable even if it may cost them the mandate?

Likewise, the more ambitious LPs are, the more they are often convinced that they have picked the right fund manager. Alternatively, LPs shy away from the bold commitments that success seems to demand, choosing instead for themselves timid, uncontroversial strategies that are unlikely to meet their return target.

There is No Such Thing as Perfect Alignment

When dealing with finance, the tendency is to assume that objectives are either clearly defined or should be definable at least in theory. From this flows the idea of alignment of interests, which is a crucial concept in the private equity world. To insure the alignment of interests, objectives should be the same for investment managers and investors and should remain constant during the period of investing. This is implausible. Accepting this is crucial if one is to fully encompass motivations in a private equity context.

An invisible hierarchy of objectives?

First, fund managers as individuals are likely to be primarily concerned about their professional 'survival'. If things go drastically wrong and the firm is about to go under, their focus could be having sufficient time for looking for new employment. A behaviour consistent with this priority would be, for instance, to maintain management fees by refusing to alter the fund's terms and conditions, even if it is failing and LPs are pressing for changes.

The second likely priority is to assure the survival of the firm, as long as there is a chance that LPs can be swayed to maintain the relationship and back a future fund. Here the behaviour would rather be to forgo management fees, e.g., by giving back commitments if there are no promising opportunities, in order to preserve goodwill of investors and maintain the relationship for future fundraising.

Afterwards, GPs will put focus on their own growth, for example, by charging high management fees. Once a minimum return is achieved, finally the LPs' growth objectives take priority and are rewarded through, for example, the carried interest. Delivering a competitive profit is a constraint to assure the long-term survival of the GP. Only after this is assured, other internal and external stakeholder concerns – such as Environmental, Social and Governance (ESG) related issues – are likely to be endorsed by GPs and LPs, particularly as rarely any incentives are given for meeting such objectives.

A compromise for LPs

Objectives for a fund as a pooled vehicle are a compromise between various LPs: of course many consider high financial returns their only objective, but there are also investors who see portfolio diversification to be the main motivation for investing in private equity. Other LPs have to generate stable and consistent returns above a certain threshold in order to meet the liability schedule.

'Non-financial' investors – government agencies, for example – aim for a range of other objectives, such as job creation and economic growth. Public pension funds may face political pressure to support regional development and invest in local private equity opportunities. Corporate investors tend to put priority on access to technological developments that are relevant for their specific business, whereas banks may be willing to sacrifice on financial returns on private equity investments in order to get access to portfolio companies as future clients. Finally, learning how to invest in private equity with the objective of being perceived as sophisticated and increasing one's reputation is another reason for some investors to engage in this activity. These diverging priorities leave sufficient room for manoeuvre and any strategy shift or change of objectives is likely to be backed by at least some of the LPs.

And the World Keeps Spinning...

Incentives (of both 'carrot' and 'stick' varieties) are the preferred mechanism of aligning objectives, but all incentives are subject to trade-offs. As time passes and circumstances change, the balance of these trade-offs may also shift. And yet an illiquid portfolio cannot be so easily recalibrated, so deviations are a fact of life.

Everybody changes

LPs can often change their objectives and their associated priorities, for example from high returns over a long term to assuring liquidity over the short term. In the beginning of the Great Recession, LPs were struggling to meet capital called from the private equity funds. In this situation even large institutional investors like CalPERS were reported to have asked fund managers to delay capital calls.[3] To avoid being forced to exercise default remedies against their LPs and thus damaging their relationships, GPs were said to have agreed to a range of concessions, such as allowing LPs to reduce the size of their commitments, agreeing not to issue any capital calls until the LP's liquidity pressures ease, or facilitating the sale of the LP's interest in the fund.[4] Under these circumstances, however, it becomes more difficult for the GPs to manage towards originally agreed objectives and keep a prudent level of reserves. They may be forced to sell a company sooner for a potentially lower multiple in order to distribute to cash-strapped LPs or to recycle back into the fund to support their most valuable companies.

The Spiel

This scope for the interpretation of objectives also gives rise to complexity when it comes to assessing prospective managers for new commitments. The old industry adage that everyone is a 'top quartile' manager, is at least partly a function of the many different benchmarks that a manager can point – is it the (interim) IRR or (interim) multiple, which compares to peers in the private equity industry, or to, for instance, the public market equivalent which is a comparison to another asset class. Successfully raising a new fund can often come down to whether a manager can convincingly vary the strategic narrative.

Adjust Objectives and Strategies

Simpson (2013) argues that a strategy connects an operational approach to its ends, i.e., the objectives of policy. To insist on the maintenance of objectives that were established in the abstract ex-ante is to deny the possibility that the original aims are not attainable anymore. Instead, adjustments of objectives and strategies are necessary.[5] This, however, raises questions around delegation on one side and the so-called 'style-drift' on the other. How much and what type of flexibility LPs should allow fund managers is a strategic question of considerable importance.

Speed Read

- Agreeing and sticking with precise objectives is an unrealistic goal. Humans are not capable of optimisation and instead make choices that are merely satisfactory. Investors' formal and stated objectives are often not the most important ones.
- Investment managers may face a moral dilemma if return expectations are too high at the outset. Managers, like all groups of individuals, face multiple objectives – they should be expected to put their own professional survival first. Also LPs are not a homogenous mass – fund terms are a result of a compromise of their objectives.

- The passage of time can drastically change objectives for all parties. Rather than strive for 'perfect alignment of interests', parties should focus on instruments that maximise the chances of an agreed outcome. LPs need to allow some room for interpretation in order to give fund managers the flexibility needed to deal with uncertainty.

Chapter 11

Performance Persistence

The classic financial services caveat that 'past performance is not indicative of future returns', sits oddly with the wide consensus among investors that there is a link between prior fund returns and those in the future. What evidence there is seems to support such a link. For venture capital, Conner (2005) found that follow-on funds raised by fund managers whose prior fund's performance was in the top quartile had a 44 per cent chance of achieving a top-quartile IRR. Several other studies for private equity funds come to comparable results. If the distribution of returns across GPs were perfectly random and previous returns were irrelevant this figure would be 25 per cent.[1]

The various studies tend to agree that two successive funds have positively correlated returns, both for buyouts and venture capital. However, according to Chung (2010), the statistical significance is limited to a small number of large funds and the persistence does not have an economically large effect. He found persistence short-lived, with best and worst performing funds performing similarly in their second and third follow-on funds and performance converging across the GP's funds over time.

While the datasets underlying such findings are very limited,[2] the GP's track record remains one of the major decision criteria for LPs. Gatekeepers market their benchmarking services for checking and comparing the GP's performance and are able to sell access to the top fund managers. The fact that the performance persistence argument is neat, simple, intuitively sensible means any results that conflict with the hypothesis tend to be met with hostility. This is a pity, because on any close examination, performance persistence in private equity is an inadequate credo.

When You Can't Buy the Average . . .

It is debatable whether average private equity returns are sufficiently rewarding for LPs. Cornelius et al. (2013) reviewed the literature on risk-adjusted returns in private equity, based on which one might draw the 'sobering conclusion' that even on a risk-unadjusted basis, investments in private equity are rather unattractive, particularly when considering the high degree of illiquidity that investors need to accept.[3] As a consequence, there is no active versus passive debate in private equity. Fund selection, everyone agrees, is critical.

A fund's performance can be compared to a benchmark or performance hurdle or can be evaluated relative to its peers, i.e., in private equity typically to funds raised in the same vintage year. Even for buyouts – often viewed as a 'sure thing' – achieving competitive returns requires committing capital to funds that give a final performance in the 'first quartile' of their vintage year peer group. In the case of venture capital outperformance, Fraser-Sampson (2007) observed, that it is confined to the top decile.

And when you won't buy the mystery…

Investors who simply 'buy the private equity market portfolio' are unlikely to obtain competitive returns in the long-run. Buying the average is not a viable option open to LPs. Instead, the concept of 'performance persistence', whereby new funds raised by managers of the previous best funds will themselves be superior and show first quartile performance as well, has become private equity dogma, and a key principle behind the investment strategy of many LPs.

Implementing such an investment strategy seeks to identify a predecessor fund that has the characteristics of a top-quartile fund at the time when the LP needs to make the investment decision for the successor fund. As the successor fund usually is not fully liquidated and often is not even fully invested, this assessment is subject to significant uncertainty in itself. Obviously there are some difficulties applying the GP's performance persistence as guidance in practice. Moreover, as we will discuss later, this finding and its interpretation are far from assured. So why does the investment industry nevertheless embrace the performance persistence argument with considerable enthusiasm and rarely question it?

You have to buy the history

In the highly uncertain practice of making private equity commitments, anything that offers comfort or the feeling of certainty will always be welcomed. It gives purpose and direction to LPs' due diligence and offers a 'hard criterion' on which to base financial analysis of the predecessor funds. It is a kind of 'quant envy' born of a frustration that business school analytics are inadequate when faced with proposals for new funds as 'blind pools'. The rule 'only invest in a fund if its predecessor was top-quartile' has the attraction of being simple, at least.

Conscious of this 'top quartile' preoccupation, GPs frame the measurement of their past performance in any way that will demonstrate they are 'top fund managers'. As a consequence of being known to depend in their decision making on prior fund returns, LPs tend to only meet top quartile managers.[4] On the other hand, there is a roughly 40 per cent probability that managers with lower quartile funds do not come back to the market.[5] The high attrition rate with a combined repetition of upper performance seem to be the signature characteristics of the private equity asset class. This makes it difficult for investors to use top quartile performance as an effective screening criteria.

Don't shine a light on magic

The fact that the range of historical outcomes is wider for private equity than it is for other asset classes is one of the arguments put forward as evidence that performance persistence is caused by fund management skills. For private equity funds, the difference between a top-quartile return and a median return can be two or three times as much as in the case of mutual funds. But can we draw the conclusion from this observation, as many do, that in private equity, fund managers add significant value and that skills are the main explanation for the large, observed spread, i.e., the range between the best and the worst managers?

First of all, one cannot compare averages achieved by mutual funds, operating in public markets and forming a well defined and stable universe, with the private equity market with its fuzzy boundaries without formal restrictions to entry, where it is not possible to access every fund and the 'average' is difficult to define.

Irrespective of the fund managers' skills, a wide spread between the highest and the lowest return figures is likely to be observed if the asset class is volatile enough, preferably positively correlated, if the funds' portfolios are little diversified and if the observed population of funds is large. Mathonet and Meyer (2007) used a Monte Carlo simulation to investigate the relative impact of (a) diversification and (b) observable population on the expected observable performance range between the best and the worst managers for randomly selected funds. Based on this simulation the observed spread in the real fund dataset could still be consistent with randomness and with the hypothesis that the majority of published data on ex-post investment returns in private equity relates to skilled fund managers. Consequently, contrary to widely-held private equity industry belief, consistently picking above-average fund managers resists any simple formula and the recipe to 'go for the top quartile' is hopelessly oversimplistic. To weed out incompetent teams and unsuitable proposals is clearly necessary, but this alone is insufficient for generating outperformance.

A self-fulfilling prophecy?

Intuitively, performance persistence is a highly plausible assumption. The antithesis that underperforming GPs (if they were able to raise a follow-on fund) become top performers seems equally implausible. It therefore seems unlikely that one would go too far wrong by trying to base one's decision on the GP's track record. The main attraction of the performance persistence argument is its association with the claim that it is primarily caused by the GP's skills. That LPs prefer teams with a verifiable track record makes the market entry for new fund managers difficult. Established GPs are protected by having built up their reputations, thus gaining trust and access to LPs and through gaining the critical mass to successfully implement their own investment strategies.

In fact, such entry barriers may also contribute to the GP becoming a persistent performer, for instance by being able to raise larger funds: up to a certain point larger fund sizes allow them to do better deals. Having built a reputation and trust with its LPs, a GP is also able to raise a new fund faster, if promising investment opportunities are identified. New entrants without a track record will find it more difficult to attract investors, the fund raising will either fail or be more protracted and when they are able to start their investment activities, the opportunities will either have faded away or have been snatched up by the competition. Stronger LP support and a more diversified and divided LP base results in a higher degree of flexibility for the GP, which is also conducive to successful investing.

Performance Factors

Turning the supposed performance persistence into an investment strategy rests on the assumption that future top-quartile funds have characteristics that can be recognised ex-ante. This involves distinguishing skills from luck; added value from a rising tide. Performance may either depend on talented individuals or the processes and culture of the GP as an organisation. While it seems an accomplishment to be in the top quartile, in a thirty year career, assuming that the fund management team's composition does not change, a GP will have only a handful of opportunities to manage funds over their full lifetime. This is hardly enough data to estimate the impact of their skills with any confidence.[6]

Lucky Generals

Moreover, in recent years there has been increasing scepticism regarding private equity GPs having differential and proprietary skills.[7] While Conner (2005) found that first-time managers that raise follow-on funds tend to improve their performance in successive funds, this is insufficient as evidence for learning and increasing skills. As mentioned before, Kaplan and Schoar (2005) found a concave relation between fund size and performance: up to a certain point when their performance tends to decline again, larger funds also have higher returns. As first-time funds are usually smaller than the average, the performance improvement is more likely to be linked to the growth in fund size. This is consistent with the findings in Manninena et al. (2010) who demonstrated that the number of funds raised by a GP previously is insignificant for future returns and found no significant institutional learning for the GPs.

In situations where all participants make money at the same time like, for instance, in the VC market at the end of the 1990s, performance is likely to be driven by a secular trend and not by individual talent. This explanation is supported by the findings made in the study by Cornelius et al. (2009) already mentioned above. They found strong support for the hypothesis that fund performance is, among other factors, a function of industry selection. In particular top-quartile funds had chosen industries at a stage of a cycle that had a major positive impact on their subsequent performance. Chung (2010) comes to similar conclusions, i.e., that persistence is largely explained by common market conditions facing funds raised in succession and concluding that this result does not support the view that GPs have differential and proprietary skills.

In the case of buyouts with their large amount of leverage, the availability and pricing of debt financing has a significant impact on their performance. It is therefore no surprise that funds raised near to each other in time are affected by common macroeconomic conditions and that their performance shows higher correlations. Additionally, continuing opportunities and being able to ride on the previous funds' successes allow the GP to raise the next funds quicker. Having a higher number of funds exposed to favourable market conditions would clearly bias the GP's performance statistics favourably. Here it is rather the common market conditions facing successive funds that explain performance persistence.

Unlucky Generals

Equally as important in distinguishing luck from skill is distinguishing incompetence from misfortune. Lengthy fundraising processes and long fund lives mean a GP's chosen investment area, whether geography or sector, could be timed with a downturn or crisis that is out of their control. Cornelius et al. (2009) found funds with performance in the lower quartiles had chosen industries whose stage in the cycle had been less conducive to good returns. They concluded that acquiring assets in an industry at the wrong time of the cycle will make it considerably harder for the fund manager to achieve good returns. Indeed, good fund managers can also be unlucky, e.g., backing a good company where an exceptional CEO suddenly died or where the entire sector went into a protracted downturn.

Long-term exposure to market extremes can disproportionately favour one strategy over another, even if fund managers are equally competent. Likewise, Hendershott (2007) was able to calculate that for the best 250 of 1000 private equity funds, one would expect to find that 146 of them or 58.4 per cent were managed by top-quartile managers. That still leaves 41.6 per cent of the good funds managed by the 13.9 percent of ordinary managers who happened to be lucky. Faced with oversubscriptions or style drifts associated with growing fund sizes the false rejection error probability again becomes a factor. Consequently, there can be unlucky but skilful GPs who may be highly motivated but need to continue with small fund sizes, if they manage to raise a follow-on fund at all.

Performance persistence is short lived; investors might be better off looking for the funds run by good but unlucky managers who do not meet the strict screening criteria. On the other hand, could the LPs' skills in recognising good managers be a factor in the performance persistence story?

Skilful LPs Selecting the Best Funds?

Lerner et al. (2005) analysed investments in private equity funds over a 20-year period and found that the university endowments' annual returns were substantially and significantly larger than for any other large investor group. The results were seen as robust and not just explainable by luck or by history. They concluded that the private equity market is not efficient and that there are types of investors who can select funds that are better than average.

The explanations Lerner et al. (2005) put forward point towards LP skills: the successful investors pay competitive wages and give their professionals freedom in choosing investments. Otherwise there would be reduced effort, less qualified employees and high employee turnover. Private university endowments also enjoy greater flexibility to evaluate non-standard investment opportunities. Other institutions, particularly regulated ones, often are constrained by rigid decision criteria – for instance, not to invest in first-time teams – and are said to generally lack a sufficient understanding of private equity. Here the rank of employees within the organisation and their remuneration depend on how much cash they manage rather than how much return they generate, thus creating perverse incentives.

Not always . . .

Convincing as this narrative is, the results of Lerner et al. (2005) were not found to hold in general. According to Hobohm (2010) the superior performance of endowments is mostly confined to a few elite university endowments. He did an analysis comparable to that of Lerner et al. (2005) over longer time periods for private equity funds in general and found that differences in returns by investor type converge to the average. This finding would be consistent with all types of LPs gaining experience with private equity investing. Also in the case of buyouts during the decade after 2000, even inexperienced investors had access to successful and larger funds. Furthermore, Hobohm (2010) found little return differences for investors in different global regions. He still found that endowments stand out in VC fund investments, albeit with only weak statistical significance. His results suggest that the 'special VC expertise' for endowments was somewhat constrained to the period until 1999 and afterwards they may have still had some advantages, but those did not bear out. This, however, could also be a reflection of the generally depressed conditions in the VC markets following the burst of the Internet bubble or the fact that other classes of LPs increasingly learned about VC investing and thus levelled the playing field.[8]

One way of looking at the question of LP skills is by analysing their reinvestment decisions. In theory, LPs can gain much better 'hard' and 'soft' data through the monitoring of funds they have already invested in and thus should be able to make a much better informed decision when evaluating the next proposal put forward by the fund managers. Results put forward by Hochberg et al. (2013) suggest that LPs' reinvestment decisions are more sensitive to soft information than publicly available hard information – information not yet known to outsiders at the time of fundraising, e.g., ex-post IRRs, predicts returns on follow-on funds above and beyond hard information, such as interim IRRs, known at the time of fundraising.

Is it access rather than skills?

The question is, which is the more important driver of the LP's return: access – conceptually closer to having a favourable position in the market – or selection, which is closer to skills? According to Lerner and Schoar (2002) high performing GPs can often screen for 'deep-pocket' investors, those that have a low likelihood of facing a liquidity shock, as they can reduce the general partner's cost of capital in future fundraising. An LP not only needs to know about these GPs – which tend to stick with their existing investor base – he also needs to first gain access to some of their funds and then select the best available opportunities.

Manninena et al. (2010) used a sample of reinvestments made by large institutional investors and found that access is a more consequential explanation for return differences among LPs than selection skills. Their findings suggest that access is a key determinant of LP's investment returns and any initial investment decision has an 'echo' on the LP's successive investment returns that far outreaches the single fund's returns. Assuming that LPs have gained access to a GP with a top-quartile fund, does this also mean that re-upping is a successful strategy? Not quite, as Rouvinez (2006) pointed out: it 'definitely beats random investing, but still results in a one in three chance to end up with bottom half performance.' In other words, the impact may not be as strong as many expect.

The LP Uncertainty Principle

To turn the 'performance persistence' assumption into an investment strategy LPs must build up access to high-performing GPs and focus their due diligence on measuring and verifying historical performance and benchmarking it. Hendershott (2007) determined that when a manager has had three consecutive top-quartile private equity funds, potential investors can conclude with 80 per cent or greater confidence that the manager is exceptional. However, in practice investors will find it difficult to make meaningful use of these research findings: by the time there is sufficient evidence that a firm is really successful, the effect is likely to be gone.

Driving by looking in the rear mirror

The main problem is that all these analyses are based on data for mature funds close to the end of their lifetime. Only funds aged between at least six and eight years are sufficiently mature for drawing general conclusions regarding performance.[9] In the set of data used by Conner (2005), firms that raised a subsequent fund did so 2.9 years on average after raising the predecessor fund. Nearly half of these firms raised the subsequent funds in years two or three. In other words, top-quartile performance is not reliably visible before investors have to make their next commitment. Despite sophisticated in-depth quantitative analysis of the portfolio, companies and a team's resulting track record, for primary commitments investors are not buying the portfolio that they have so painstakingly analysed in their due diligence and that for the most recent portfolio they can only analyse the short-term development of immature investments.

Once a GP has had a string of clearly successful funds, everybody wants to jump on the bandwagon. That can result in oversubscription and investors who had been screening that market for such types of firms do not get access to their funds at the end. Alternatively, and in reality far more often, private equity capital chasing past performance leads to excessive fund growth. The increase in fund size reduces persistence even where fund managers have differential skills as this means moving away from the strategies that made a firm successful in the first place.

Fundamental limits to precision

How can we substantiate 'success' in private equity? As the approach to equity valuations is based on comparisons, the typical definition, as used above, is 'first-quartile' performance. While the quartiles' mathematical definition is clear, to what they refer is vague: the funds' internal rate of return or to their multiples, to their interim or their final returns, to gross returns or to returns net to LPs? In fact, to which peer group do the quartiles refer: private equity as a whole or differentiating between, say, buyouts and venture capital? In many cases it is even a problem to clearly allocate a fund to a vintage year that determines the peer group.[10]

If we base our definition of success on the quartile position in the benchmark, comparison should be made against funds that are subject to the same market conditions to assure that we are comparing apples with apples – that would be the vintage year cohort of the peer group. However, from vintage year to vintage year the composition of the peer group will change – rarely can two funds managed by the same management team be measured against the same peers. Private equity firms raise funds at irregular intervals, and therefore the firms that raised the funds that comprised the previous vintage year peer group may not be out looking for investors at the same time again. Drawing the conclusion that success is primarily caused by the GPs' skills assumes that all funds had equal starting positions and faced an identical market environment. As the peer group compositions will not remain constant, the persistence claim is difficult to verify.

Objects in a Rear View Mirror May Appear Larger

The inefficiency and opacity of the private equity market, and the LPs' ability to influence fundraising and negotiate terms and conditions are arguments supporting the assumption that LPs are able to recognise top funds and this is the main value driver of their investment strategy. Indeed, many gatekeepers argue that investing in top-quartile funds is not difficult if one is familiar with the asset class and is doing proper due diligence.[11] Assuming that it were so easy to identify top funds, private equity would essentially outperform all other asset classes.

Evaluate relationships, not past funds

As plausible as this sounds, why do we not observe more institutional investors boasting much higher returns stemming for their private equity activities? That not all institutional investors have much higher allocations to private equity could indicate widespread scepticism regarding this claim. There is anecdotal evidence that funds-of-funds' performance is usually rather unspectacular, despite the consistency of performance of private equity funds. As Demaira (2010) explains, the funds-of-funds' investment policies back the established names of private equity, despite mediocre results going forward. Performance persistence is a seductive argument, and presents a danger that LPs systematically overestimate the chance that strong performance of previous funds will persist even though, for instance, the targeted industry sector is in decline. As a consequence, LPs may not quickly enough cease or minimise the relationship with a GP or increase their commitments to other markets. Instead of driving a portfolio via the rear mirror, an LP needs to actively monitor and rebalance their portfolio of GP relationships.[12]

Disturbing questions

There has long been an argument and a sprawling literature – Tom Peters' and Robert Waterman's 1982 classic, *In Search of Excellence*, and Jim Collins' *Good to Great*, for instance – that some companies truly are better and will outperform through good times and bad times. But taken together and viewed over a longer time frame, the story the 'excellent company' books tell is not one of sustainable competitive advantage and enduring high performance.[13] Actually it is difficult to see why GPs should be exempt from the rule that all empires decline and fall and why they – in contrast to, say, hedge fund managers – should be able to sustain their excellence instead of being exposed to the dynamism of markets where all competitive advantages are temporary.

The belief in persistence is seductive and plays into the financial manager's preference to think about the here and now, use in-depth analysis upfront and move on to the next big thing – 'after committing there is nothing we can do'. But we should also consider the consequences of this strategy being at least partially false. In such circumstances, the strategy may not be 'wrong' but it will not address the issues and will miss the true value levers. This raises two questions: are there other ways to achieve outperformance without being able to select above-average funds? And alternatively (and probably more intriguingly), is it possible that the benchmark for outperformance is too high, i.e., that the risk of investing in private equity funds is overestimated?

Or is it simply that the impact of quartile criterion may well be overestimated, but that sophisticated LPs use a range of other quantitative and qualitative criteria as a basis of their investment decisions that are more able to make the difference? We will turn to this possibility in the next chapter.

Speed Read

- Performance persistence is based on the concept that GPs that are more skilful can apply their skills in various settings over time. It sounds plausible, but given the typical lifetime of funds, by the time good performance is manifest, the effect is likely to have passed.
- GPs being subject to luck and misfortune in terms of market timing and wider economic factors should be given greater weight in an investor's strategic considerations. Rather than being determined by the GP's skills, a fund's performance may be explained by outside factors, such as the performance of the targeted industry sector or the economy as a whole, over which individual fund managers have no control.
- Quartile comparisons are easy to manipulate in both metrics and peer groups. Therefore a due diligence that puts too much weight on a GP's past performance is deficient.

Chapter 12

Nobody Knows Anything

When investing in private equity funds, LPs typically aim to beat a target return, for example, set by a public equity index, or, importantly for funds-of-funds, outperform other LPs. The best 25 per cent of a vintage year's fund population have been shown to outperform most other types of assets. On the other hand, various reviews of research studies suggest that the private equity funds' average risk-adjusted returns have not been nearly as attractive as expected.[1] For primary investments in funds a pricing mechanism that could adjust for the risks incurred does not exist.[2] To compensate for this gap and the lack of risk-adjusted pricing, LPs must have strong selection skills.

The Quest for the 'Sure Thing'

The objective is clear: to identify the best. Studies that support performance persistence and point to selection criteria with apparently predictive power are in high demand. Due diligence is undertaken on fund managers' family life, golf handicap, hobbies (too risky, too much time spent on?), and, allegedly, even their horoscopes. Indeed, no halfway reasonable approach will fail to attract attention.

In fact, rare is the LP that does not appear – or pretends to be – absolutely convinced of his ability to pick 'top-quartile' funds. De Vany (2004) suggests that pervasive optimistic bias is based on unrealistic possible self-evaluations, an illusion of control and an unrealistic optimism about future developments. LPs are likely to be subject to all these factors. Related to optimism is overconfidence, i.e., believing that an outcome is more certain than facts would suggest. Before committing to a fund, LPs control what kind of information is requested and its level of detail. In an opaque environment some market players certainly have better insights than others. Decision-makers will evaluate just the data available and often assume that others may be less well informed than they are. The more pioneering and unfamiliar the market is, the more managers are likely to extrapolate in the wrong way and be overconfident in their judgment of uncertain events and their ability to pick winners. Actually this is what is needed to keep the private equity market dynamic and innovating, as Nassim Taleb observed: 'Natural and naturelike systems want overconfidence on the part of individual economic agents, i.e., the overestimation of their chances of success and underestimation of the risks of failure in their businesses, provided their failure does not impact others.'[3]

As discussed in the previous chapter, the performance persistence argument is strongly believed in, and track record is therefore an important pre-selection criterion, typically past 'top-quartile' performance gets extrapolated, leading to optimistic forecasts of the fund's potential. Assuming the worst case, i.e., that the fund fails and a significant share of the capital is lost, would rule out any investment. Therefore, internal discussions will be biased against the worst possible outcome, and fund proposals are likely to be selected where the most optimistic assessments tend to win the argument. That LPs have selection skills is occasionally questioned in academic studies but almost never in the industry.[4] The thought that previous successes were more due to luck than to skills are too uncomfortable to contemplate.

What is Due Diligence?

Due diligence is believed to be the key driver of a private equity programme's performance. While the importance of a proper due diligence is undeniable, it is a costly exercise, as on average it takes three months to do the work and compile a thorough report.[5] For alternative assets in general, the management of the due diligence activity has been commonly cited as a source of competitive advantage that can be approached as a distinct process and be made more efficient.[6]

It's who you know

Paraphrasing real estate, where it is 'location, location, location', in private equity it is 'people, people, people'. Institutional investors have to select fund managers mainly based on an assessment of the team, the GP's processes and its historical performance. As there are no assets held by the fund yet, the question is what the GP can do with the resources entrusted to him. A due diligence for primary investments in private equity funds is an assessment of a proposal before this fund's actual investment activity has commenced and therefore is predominantly based on qualitative criteria. This assessment comprises a formal checking of the fund proposal's compliance with best market practices and, more relevant for selecting superior investments, individual interviews, group interviews and reference calls.

Alternative assets firms gain no commercial advantage from transparency in the daily course of their business and – particularly in private equity – even have a legitimate need to maintain some confidential information. This, on the other hand, also allows the concealment of potentially embarrassing information, and prospective investors in funds raised by private equity firms need to conduct checks because no regulator will do this for them. Due diligence covers all activities associated with evaluating an investment proposal, and it is commonly defined as 'the process of investigation and evaluation, performed by investors, into the details of a potential investment, such as an examination of operations and management and the verification of material facts'.[7] It is a requirement and even a legal obligation for prudent investors, as well as complementing the information basis for better investment decisions.[8]

Due diligence addresses weaknesses

In this respect, due diligence is primarily a tool for information gathering and evaluation, not for decision-making. In practice, the distinction is seldom made: due diligence is used to weed out inferior funds and the remaining proposals will be invested in. However, the typical due diligence based on a 'tick box approach' will fail to identify superior investments. There is little differentiation between LPs in this respect and due diligence should be seen as of a defensive nature.

Some LPs argue that they, in fact, do not try to select the best funds but instead aim to weed out the worst. This cannot lead to above average returns, as due diligence is exactly aiming for this and has, when it comes to checking for a fund proposal's weaknesses, become nearly identical across institutional investors. In fact, as demonstrated in Mathonet and Meyer (2007), most funds with identifiable weaknesses will fail to close at all and thus will not become part of the population that forms the average (see **Figure 14.2**). As a consequence, available industry statistics by and large represent private equity funds – including some high-quality niche investments – that passed the rigorous due diligence of experienced investors. Due diligence leads to a 'qualified' population that is very close to the vintage year peer group composition and is thus insufficient for picking top-quartile. There are not weak and strong players coexisting in the market, but a core of established players with a steady stream of weak or unlucky entrants who take their turn, either perform at the margin and leave again or become established in their own right.

Selection and Due Diligence

The goal of 'selection' is to identify the best proposals and, harder still, to be better than other LPs. Selection is sequenced with proposals dropping out at each stage. As the average quality of the remaining set of proposals steadily increases, it becomes more and more difficult to differentiate between them: picking the ten best funds out of a hundred proposals in the first step is considerably easier than picking the best out of these ten in the steps that follow. With the reduction in numbers, the validity of the evaluation methods must increase and, as a consequence, the costs for applying a method increase. Also the methods used at the end of the process must be capable of making fine-grain distinctions between very good proposals.

Because due diligence is costly and time-consuming, a small percentage of the initial proposals make it to this stage.[9] According to Fraser-Sampson (2007), due diligence should only follow a decision in principle to invest. Particularly during the initial screening stages decision-making is far more judgmental and based on rather coarse criteria, as otherwise investors would not be able to cope with the flood of information they receive. Selection therefore may often be done on a quite weak information basis. Quite often due diligence data is compiled and reports are written not to arrive at a decision, but to justify a decision taken previously. The lengthy report is used as supporting evidence to seek approval for an investment where the decision-makers simply insist on a formal and documented process. The purpose of the analytical data is not to inform those who were uncertain whether to invest, but to give reassurance to those who had already decided to go ahead. The longer a due diligence takes and the more effort is spent, the greater the regret when rejecting a proposal and the more LPs tend to delude themselves and seek confirmation, monkeying around with comparisons until the result fits the original assumptions. The perception that 'every box had been ticked' creates the illusion that the fund is a 'sure-thing'.

While investors in private equity funds broadly agree on the basics of a due diligence process, there is a tendency to lump everything remotely related to analysis done before committing to a fund under the term 'due diligence'. Of course in reality due diligence cannot be executed step-by-step, but has to be an iterative process where several proposals are evaluated in parallel, where questions regarding one or more of the selected managers are followed up, other fund proposals are shortlisted, which then go through the same process. Due diligence and selection are connected and behavioural issues affect both: there will be regret, having spent so much effort and time, and having become close to the fund management team, to arrive at a 'no' as a conclusion.

Assessing equity investments is mainly based on comparisons and when trying to identify above-average funds the line between selection and due diligence is difficult to draw. Only thorough due diligence is likely to pick up the insight information that could give more confidence that of two otherwise similar proposals, one is better than the other.

Due diligence thus blurs with selection[10] and there are overlaps with other steps in the private equity investment process such as portfolio construction and market research. However, the former are two distinctive tasks that are often and erroneously equated, making a clearer distinction necessary. Despite all efforts, even the most valid due diligence methods are less good in predicting superior funds than funds that will definitely fail and thus should be excluded.

Limits of Effective Due Diligence

The dynamics of the private equity industry to a large extent follow an evolutionary process. In their selection, LPs must rely to a high degree on heuristics. It is not only costs and constraints such as lack of experienced staff or short deadlines that pose restrictions to an 'ideal' due diligence. This assumes that theoretically all factors are known and it is just lack of diligence that means LPs ignore them. In reality, it is more the 'unknown unknowns' and future events that cannot be known that determine the outcome and cannot be picked up by any due diligence. In alternative assets there cannot be a 'perfect fund' and investment managers are paid to make a judgment call. Spending twice as much effort on the due diligence does not make results twice as reliable.

Regularly at the end of boom periods, as in 2002 and 2009, institutional investors state that they will become stricter regarding their due diligence standards and industry research finds that 'in the future, only the best funds will be the recipients of [...] capital'.[11] However, is it really probable that in 'normal' periods investors would give 'basically anybody' their money? There are diminishing returns for analysis, but subconsciously or by virtue of education, training and career selection, decision-makers assume that extraordinary efforts ex-ante will result in extraordinary outcomes ex-post. If an investment goes wrong, rather than accepting the fact that uncertainty has led to this outcome, the typical allegation is that the due diligence had failed. It is always possible to identify a criterion that had been overlooked or a step that had not been followed. For decision-makers there may be an element of 'guilt' – not having been 'diligent enough', which therefore needs to be avoided in the future.

In many cases the due diligence performed has been criticised as ineffective and as looking at largely irrelevant criteria.[12] Even elements of 'superstitious reasoning' may be at work, i.e., confusing random chance with cause and effect, and overreacting to chance events. The escalation of due diligence duration and detail criticised by many industry insiders could be the result of a conditioning, such as observed by the behavioural scientist Skinner in his experiments with pigeons, where he argued that superstition would arise due to particular action patterns ex-ante and their subsequent, but causally unrelated, success.[13]

Many parts of a due diligence could also be seen as a 'courtship' where LPs and GPs select each other, with one partner initiating the courtship and the other choosing to go ahead or reject based on the demonstrated 'performance'. LPs most probably waste their time if they view due diligence as a tool to select superior funds. This exercise is more geared towards confirming the hypothesis of a decision essentially already made. The point is not that this effort is irrelevant, but it is the outcome of a maturing asset class that virtually every fund that attracts a critical mass of institutional investors will have a highly skilled management team.

Limits of Selection

The private equity industry has gradually but significantly shifted. There is a much higher share of experienced players and too much competition for opportunities at the margin. It is not simple any more to distinguish an average firm from a good one, and it is unlikely that a bad fund proposal will find a critical mass of LPs. There are no obvious duds left. Where there are weaknesses, they become apparent in hindsight only, after the environment has changed and turned against the GP's profile. In such an environment GPs beat their peers more because they were lucky or, as discussed in the chapter on performance persistence, because they were at the right place at the right time, and not, or to a much lesser degree as arguably in the industry's early years, because of their skills. Here there is no reliable way to identify the future top performers as even the clearly competent fund managers are influenced by chance, be it in the positive or negative way.

Intuition

During the early years of the private equity industry, with little competition and limited capital invested, getting the basics right made a huge difference. Meanwhile the composition of the LP and GP pool has changed significantly with most players now following comparable processes and employing experienced and competent investment professionals. In this respect, the limits to selection may also be an LP story. With increasing market allocation to private equity, returns fall and gradually investors again leave the private equity space and reduce allocations. It is likely that the less successful investors leave the market first, so after a number of repetitions the LPs know how to conduct due diligence and avoid mistakes. During the boom years of an emerging industry the narrative is dominated by those who won and boast their successes. Their voices drown out the mishaps of their less lucky peers, thus giving the picture of a market place where success is easy.

Humans believe that they are good at assessing other humans. In an asset class that so much relies on relationships and interactions between individuals, humans indeed may have great strengths when appraising teams.[14] Based on his own experience and various works he cites, Nobel laureate Daniel Kahneman concludes that intuition can lead to better results if the environment is sufficiently regular and the expert had a chance to learn its regularities. This, however, will not be the case for investments in private equity funds: firstly, the environment is changing continuously. Secondly, no investment manager will be able to evaluate a sufficiently large number of funds and see the outcome of his investment acumen after several decades to be able to learn from this and interpret all the factors that may have influenced the outcome. All lucky people believe that they are skilful, but do LPs have the skills to recognise top-performing funds?

Picking winners

On the back of an envelope, let's assume that we aim for the 'future top quartile' and that we can with 90 per cent accuracy say whether a fund falls into this category or not. From the proposals we screen, of the 25 per cent 'true top-quartile' performers we expect to identify 22.5 per cent correctly, but we will on average also erroneously reject 2.5 per cent. The majority of proposals we see are not 'future top quartile' but because we need to look at many we will also occasionally make a mistake and accept one of them. Out of the 75 per cent 'true non-top-quartile performers', we expect to be able to correctly reject 67.5 per cent but on average will also erroneously accept 7.5 per cent as 'top-quartile'. On average, a quarter of the funds identified as 'future top-quartile' will be incorrectly labelled. Now, to achieve 90 per cent accuracy is no mean feat, particularly when trying to predict outcomes over a period of ten years.

Many LPs view outperforming public equity as a minimum requirement to justify investments in private equity. To realise an acceptable outperformance, an LP should have the ability to allocate at least 50 per cent to top-quartile funds, 30 percent to 2nd quartile, 10 per cent to 3rd quartile and 10 per cent may fall in the 4th quartile.[15] To achieve this, our selection criterion would need to have an accuracy of 75 per cent to achieve 50 per cent top quartile in the portfolio. Moreover, this (or an additional) criterion needs to be able to identify above average funds with

80 per cent probability. To recall, by definition the average LP can select above-average funds only with 50 per cent probability. To be able to systematically beat public equity an LP needs to be significantly (and also sustainably) better in his selection than the average LP.

Tilting the odds

To some degree, how LPs select funds resembles Keynes' beauty contest, where if everybody finds it 'beautiful' the decision maker will not be blamed.[16] In fact, conservative investors such as pension funds and insurers are often blamed for being reluctant to innovate and for just following the lead of others. They use gatekeepers that are equally conservative.[17] Consultants are also reluctant to stick their necks out and tell their clients to invest in smaller GPs with less history that operate in emerging market spaces.[18] The desire to get into the established and therefore oversubscribed funds is a not uncommon response in an uncertain environment, to some degree comparable to the traditional axiom of purchasing agents that 'nobody ever got fired for buying IBM'. As a result most capital is allocated to GPs that manage oversubscribed funds and thus see no need to reduce their fees, but where the due diligence process is easy to conduct. Here selection is essentially just a due diligence based on a bureaucratic and standardised box-ticking. Such rigidity forms a self-imposed obstacle that stops conservative LPs from investing in less-established environments where paradoxically selection would have the strongest positive impact.[19]

If above-average selection were achieved as a result of skills, there would be a significant population of LPs who would be unable to identify 'top funds'. Taking into consideration that a fund has several LPs, no such formula would stay a secret for long. Once a criterion has been confirmed to be a reliable indicator for selecting superior investment it subsequently becomes the LP's due diligence criterion and gradually, and due to the idea diffusion in the industry unavoidably, becomes 'best practice'. Selection is an evolutionary arms race. Given that private equity players are often personally known to each other, rather than being anonymous economic agents, it is unrealistic to trust that systematic differences in the selection skills among LPs could exist over long periods of time. Selection in the sense of making better choices than one's peers only works either when the LP has an informational advantage in the same market space its peers are operating in, or when the LP is operating in a different market space with better opportunities than its peers and can pick funds there.

Speed Read

- Fund due diligence is a blunt sword, not a differentiator. As the industry matures and successful LPs are imitated, the pool of 'low hanging fruit' declines. Improvement in due diligence is counterbalanced by increased capital flows in private equity that increasingly accepted the asset class as reasonably 'safe'. Nowadays, due diligence processes followed by most LPs are broadly similar and cease to be a suitable selection tool.
- A fixation with due diligence has resulted in a misallocation of LP resources. Many LPs appear to put too much effort on due diligence at the expense of other aspects of investment management, such as portfolio management.
- Due diligence and selection should be treated differently. The delineation between due diligence and selection is unclear. Due diligence is more a check against standardised criteria, conducted in isolation and of a defensive nature, whereas selection also comprises a check of fit with intended strategy and thus needs to be conducted in a portfolio context. Due diligence is necessary but not sufficient to achieve high investment performance. It may be used to screen for standard funds without glaring weaknesses, but picking superior funds in this way is unlikely. Selection, on the other hand, is an evolutionary arms race where advantages are unsustainable.
- A fund investment is a probability distribution. Rather than looking for the 'best fund', selection needs to take the 'best fit' with a targeted portfolio structure into consideration: here it may make sense to give preference to a slightly weaker fund proposal if it leads to a better-balanced portfolio. In any case, systematically beating public markets requires sustainably superior selection skills that are not plausible and raises questions about private equity's risk and performance.

Chapter 13

Spreading Risks – Thinly and Thickly

According to Modern Portfolio Theory (MPT), the more diversified a portfolio and the more uncorrelated its components, the less the risk stems from each of its components. Diversification is a common thread in the investment approach of many institutional investors. This is supported by respected academics such as Benoit Mandelbrot, who recommended 'broad, very broad diversification with small equal allocations rather than what modern financial theory stipulates'.[1] At the LP's portfolio level, this can be achieved through different fund types, industries, geographies and vintage years, which is also seen as giving a considerable protection against adverse currency movements.

Impact of Diversification

A simulation based on private equity and VC funds in the latter part of the twentieth century is instructive. Looking at diversified portfolios of funds from vintage years between 1983 and 1998, Weidig and Mathonet (2004) concluded that venture capital and private equity should be a risky asset – they estimated a 90 per cent loss given default for a direct investment – but that the actual experience of investors is rather different. They analysed the risk profile of private equity and found that the distribution of multiples of a direct investment in venture capital is extremely skewed. For 30 per cent, all the capital invested is lost, but the distribution curve also shows a fat tail with extreme profits above a multiple of a hundred. Also the distribution of a fund's multiple shows a skew with a tail of strong profits above a multiple of ten. For a diversified portfolio of funds the multiple distribution of a fund-of-funds is nearly normally distributed with rapidly 'flattening' tails (see **Figure 13.1**).

The study is something of an anachronism now, given the travails of the VC sector since 2000, which prompts an important point: building wealth with a diversified portfolio only works if the entire market is growing and all the assets in the portfolio are performing

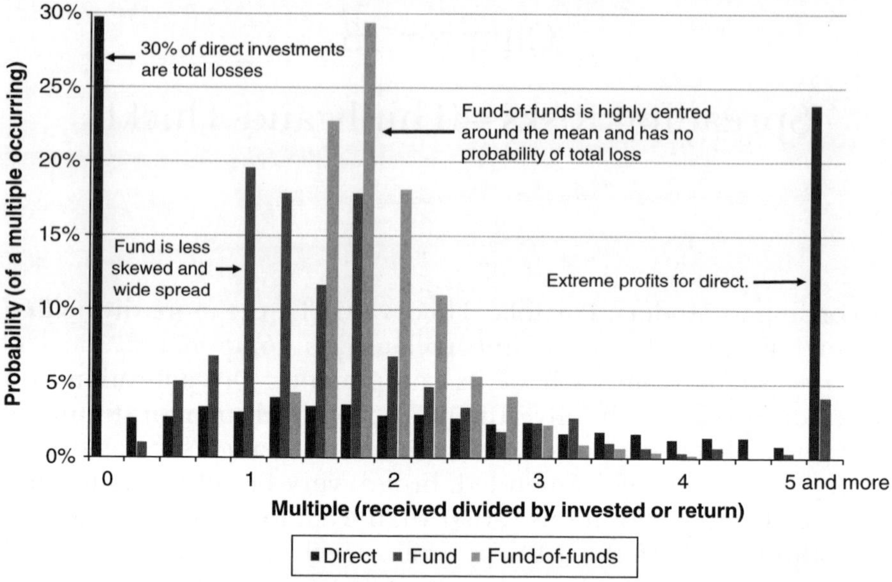

Figure 13.1 Risk profile of private equity
By Weidig and Mathonet 2003.
Sources: VentureXperts, Cochrane.

well. Even then, excessive diversification will limit the upside as the top performers will have little impact on the portfolio.

John Maynard Keynes said that '[a]s time goes on, I get more and more convinced that the right method in investment is to put fairly large sums into enterprises which one thinks one knows something about and in the management of which one thoroughly believes'. While diversification is a technique to protect the portfolio amid uncertainty and change, it does not seem compatible with achieving outperformance. As Warren Buffett confirms, wide diversification is only required when investors do not understand what they are doing. Investors use the principle of concentration to achieve growth but this requires superior knowledge of the market targeted.

The Limits of Diversification

'Selection' is said to be paramount in private equity investing but even the most confident investor would never invest in just one position. On the other hand, if we accept the idea that only the best funds provide a competitive return, diversification will eventually prove counterproductive. Diversification not only has the desirable effect of increasing an investor's protection against the downside, but it also has a detrimental impact on the portfolio's upside and, consequently, many private equity investors prefer to run concentrated portfolios. *The Economist* (2013) compared Clayton, Dubilier & Rice's concentrated portfolio comprising 17 companies to the Carlyle Group's highly diversified one with 210 companies. It allowed CD&R to put a lot of attention on each portfolio company, thus potentially being rewarded with a high payoff, but a few failures can also have a strong adverse impact on fund performance.

In addition, overdiversification is costly and can cause a vicious circle: within an increasing number of assets, the portfolio's return reverses to the average market performance and the upside is capped, as the probability to exceed a threshold declines.[2] Since the number of high quality assets in private equity is limited, the portfolio's average quality falls as the number of assets held rises. In addition, with a high number of proposals to assess, there are not only high costs associated with doing due diligence, structuring and monitoring but in all likelihood also decreasing rigour in the selection.

Overdiversification can also be an unwelcome consequence of the limited scalability of private equity assets in relation to very large assets under management. CalPERS at one time had investments in several hundred private equity funds. In 2006, it hired UBS Investment Bank to review its portfolio and subsequently sold off part of it in order to lessen the administrative burden and to optimise long-term performance.[3] Small institutions with less money to commit will find it easier to be selective than pension funds or insurers of CalPERS's size that need to put much larger amounts to work.

Where diversification helps to perform

If assets move in lockstep, diversification becomes an expensive but futile exercise. Conversely, the less correlated assets are, the more efficient and beneficial portfolio diversification becomes. Moreover, with growing diversification there is increasing stability of portfolio behaviour and notably more reliable cash flows, which support leverage as a way to manage a portfolio's risk profile.

Combining uncorrelated private equity assets

Due to their cyclical performance characteristics, distressed funds and secondary funds offer significant diversification benefits.[4]

Exposure to them can be increased in response to market signals indicating reduced commitments to buyout funds relative to the fundraising market.[5] Cornelius (2011) suggested combining the primary and secondary market. During economic downturns, secondary positions can be bought from more liquidity constrained LPs, whereas boom periods may even offer an opportunity to generate profits through selling off stakes on the secondary market. Phalippou (2011) added that this may also work between different segments in private equity, for instance, when there is strong demand for investments in infrastructure but little for venture capital, then an investor could buy VC funds on the secondary market and sell some of its infrastructure funds.

Occasionally, secondary transactions are suggested to accelerate the build-up of portfolios with an acceptable vintage year spread and to mitigate the portfolio's J-curve. As the competition for secondary investment opportunities is as cyclical as the private equity market as a whole, this may not always be a feasible option. A similar rationale underlies the idea of rebalancing the portfolio: reducing exposure to private equity by selling-off in booming markets may be beneficial, as mainly growing GPs are pruned and secondary markets tend to boom at the same time. For investors who do not have access to such opportunities, commitments to secondary funds-of-funds can be used as a hedge against a downturn in the primary fund market as well as in financial crises that affect institutional investors and lead to defaulting LPs.

Enabling leverage

Leverage in a portfolio of private equity funds manifests in various ways. It makes portfolios more vulnerable to rising interest rates and economic shocks. However, leverage is not always undesirable and, on a standalone basis, it is not a particularly useful measure of risk. It can be used to scale risk and return proportionally and therefore is one of the tools used to achieve a risk–return profile for the portfolio. Leverage can be seen as a technique to translate low but predictable returns into a high-return, high-risk investment. When using leverage, in the case of profits the shareholders are better off than bond holders, whereas in the case of losses these are magnified for the holders of equity before they affect the bond holders.

Securitisations are an avenue to invest in private equity using leverage.[6] Here notes are issued that give a predictable payoff for their holders, whereas the investors in their equity tranches are rewarded by much higher returns but incur significant risks. Assuring predictability implies a portfolio construction technique that is aiming for the underlying portfolio to be well balanced, that is, more designed than opportunistic. Securitisation is a good example of how financial engineering techniques can be used to help evaluate various risks and to influence their characteristics. The first and one of the main advantages of securitisations is that it changes the illiquid limited partnership interest of private equity funds into various groups of tradable assets; notably bonds, mezzanine and equity, which are usually listed on an exchange. This process transforms part of the illiquidity into a tradable asset and changes in appraisal-based valuations into market risk.

There are other portfolio management techniques that do not, or to a much lesser degree, depend on a predictable portfolio behaviour. For instance, so-called 'preferred equity' is essentially a way of splitting and timing of profits for different classes of shareholders and is another structure for an asymmetrical sharing of risks and rewards.

Market-Timing

When discussing diversification versus concentration, the question of market-timing is a specific case. Market-timing can be seen as part of an allocation strategy that aims to exploit market cyclicality. This is based on the observation that in private equity there are often marked differences in performance from one vintage year to another. Also, buyouts and venture capital participate in various ways from the economic environment.[7] Research findings suggest that market-timing skills matter in private equity not only from the viewpoint of the overall cycle but also with regard to individual industries.[8]

Feasibility of Market-Timing

The question is essentially the right level of reaction to external factors: at one extreme, all current information on the market is ignored, resulting in a sluggish adjustment of the portfolio to changes in the environment. For example, Cornelius (2011) points to indicators such as interest rates and spreads, valuations, fund inflows, investment volumes and defaults, which may flag a rising probability of an imminent market correction before it actually happens. At the other extreme, following the market too closely leads to continuous attempts to bring the private equity portfolio in line with these developments, which is too costly for an illiquid asset class.

Apparently, funds raised in vintage years where little capital is invested in private equity subsequently generate higher returns. Recession years are said to have produced the best vintages for private equity. Conversely, years with an abnormally high level of capital committed are believed to result in vintage years with lower returns.[9] During market exuberances, it is important to go for quality and be more restrictive than other investors, while during depressed market conditions it could make sense to be more flexible, as very often the overall vintage year quality can turn out to be attractive. Phalippou (2011) suggests investing relatively little in a boom – provided it can be recognised as such – and avoid the newly-formed, often low-quality, funds raised during these times. On the other hand, market downturns offer LPs very good opportunities to get access to newly-forming, high-quality GPs. In principle it therefore appears to be feasible to exploit such findings and try timing the market.

Limitations to LPs Timing the Market

Setting up a private equity programme and gaining a presence in this market requires a significant effort over several years. In this respect, it is virtually impossible to market-time the entry into, or the exit from, this asset class. Practically, LPs depend on the GPs coming back to the market to raise their next fund which, in combination with the time needed for due diligence, structuring the LPA and finding a critical mass of other LPs, severely limits the ability to increase the allocation in times where there is little money flowing into private equity. Also, drastically reducing allocations has practical limitations. LPs need to build up and maintain their network of established relationships with GPs, which restricts their ability to cut their commitments as this would jeopardise their future allocations to the asset class.

GPs are Timing the Market

The question of market-timing actually is conceptually close to the question of the so-called style drift, which will be discussed again later on in more detail. LPs are committing to blind pools and fund managers need flexibility regarding the companies targeted and the pacing of these investments. In other words, GPs are, at least in theory, in a better position to time the market.

According to Cornelius (2011), the fund manager's ability to time the industry cycle is of secondary importance for LPs compared with the GP's market-timing performance. As fund managers have the tendency to be cyclical and to shift their strategies, if LPs were to account for cyclicality as well, things would become messy. One important aspect of managing the LP's portfolio composition is therefore the degree of flexibility given to GPs.

Negative Impact of Market-Timing

In the eyes of many practitioners market-timing represents a losing strategy, as there is no evidence that large institutions would be consistently able to get in when the market is low and get out when it is high. While private equity performance appears to be cyclical, predicting these cycles and trying to forecast which vintage year will present the best opportunities for committing to funds with a ten-year lifetime is therefore generally not seen as possible.

By making concentrated bets against the adopted asset allocation, market-timers run the risk of inflicting serious damage by holding a portfolio inconsistent with the long-term objectives. Market-timing explicitly moves the portfolio away from long-term strategic targets, exposing the investor to avoidable risks. While there is a consensus in the industry that market-timing does not work, some investors believe that they can do it but there is anecdotal evidence that this usually ends in failure. Analysing the different fundraising and return cycles over the last 20 years makes one thing very clear: the perfect timing in an asset class which requires long-term commitment and does not offer daily liquidity is impossible. Instead, private equity requires a long-term approach with commitments through all market cycles.

Rules-Based Approach

Yale endowment's CIO, David Swensen, concludes that '[s]erious investors avoid timing markets'.[10] In order to get a good level of diversification, many investors have adopted what is variously referred to as 'controlled market-timing', 'cost-averaging' or 'rules-based' approach.[11] The proven modus operandi is to consistently invest a fixed amount throughout the vintage years, despite the progressive increase in perceived risk, as it essentially gives an anti-cyclical exposure to the ups and downs of the private equity market.

This approach leads to vintage year diversification and helps to alleviate overexposure to years with high valuations. The principle is to set an annual investment target for each private equity fund type, to avoid any inclination to try to time the cycles. When data and forecasts are not reliable, equal weighting is the theoretically optimal solution.[12] Therefore, rules-based diversification can be seen as applying this rule over time.[13] On the other hand, while behavioural biases like herd behaviour are avoided in this way, also potentially valuable information will be ignored.

Foreign Exchange

As private equity has developed into an international asset class, investors are exposed to currency movements in several dimensions: (1) from the LP's perspective 'upstream' towards their own sponsors and/or their liability schedule. For example, internationally diversified insurers have liabilities in different currencies which are not always matched by their private equity investments. (2) LPs may take foreign exchange (FX) exposure 'downstream' by committing to funds which are not denominated in the LP's base currency. As mentioned already, FX movements outside the LP's control can well result in an unintended overcommitment compared to the resources dedicated to the fund investments. (3) On the next intermediation level, fund managers often investing in portfolio companies that operate in a country with a different currency than that of the fund. (4) Finally, the portfolio companies themselves may be taking FX risk by doing business, say, in emerging markets.

Incorporating the Currency Decision

As a consequence, the currency decision needs to be explicitly incorporated in the investment process. This does not only relate to the liquidity and portfolio management on the LP's overall portfolio, but may also encompass incorporating special amendments to individual limited partnership agreements. Exchange rate fluctuations do not necessarily offset each other. For private equity funds, cash flows follow a specific pattern, e.g., investment periods with predominantly inflows and divestment periods with higher outflows. Here a long-term trend in exchange rate changes can have a significant negative as well as a positive impact. Consequently, investors in private equity – through funds and directly – are increasingly looking for solutions to understand risks and, if necessary, protect themselves against its possible adverse impact.

Trade-Offs and Rewards Stemming from Taking FX Risk

Let's consider the link between liquidity and capital risks and FX risk. For illustration: assume that an LP's main concern is liquidity risk, resulting from the need to honour capital calls in combination with the need to convert into a foreign currency on short notice at an unfavourable exchange rate. In theory, the limited partnership agreement could be structured so that all the fund's capital calls and repayments are in the LP's base currency and the FX risk is thus borne by the GP. However, this can well result in the fund either underperforming or failing altogether. In such a case the LP would trade off short-term liquidity risk (with impact on the cash flows between LP and GP) against long-term capital risk (with impact on the fund and its portfolio companies).

Risk-taking can be rewarded as well. For instance, if an LP believes that one foreign currency is overvalued, the commitments should be in this currency, and payments should be delayed as long as possible. In the case where the foreign currency is seen as undervalued compared to the LP's base currency, commitments should be made in the base currency and payments made as quickly as possible. For the long contractual lifetime of private equity funds, however, few LPs will hold strong enough beliefs to enter into such bets.

Essentially FX can be seen as one of several assets comprising the LP's portfolio. Depending on to what degree the timing of cash flows to and from the funds are correlated with FX movements, the impact of committing to funds in various currencies can actually be beneficial for the portfolio's risk and return as well as its liquidity profile.

Hedging as Solution?

The standard approach to deal with FX risk is through currency hedging with the help of financial instruments such as currency options. However, in the case of private equity there is uncertainty not only regarding the FX rate but also vis-à-vis the amount and the timing of the cash flows, all of which are unrelated. In theory, hedging instruments can be customised, but this is only possible for adequate costs if cash flows are predictable with a reasonable degree of confidence. This can, for instance, be the case where a relatively large position is held and also a rather short holding period is expected. Here, according to Cornelius (2011), hedging on a deal-by-deal basis can be cost-efficient and effective. Also an LP would be able to protect himself for reasonable costs against liquidity shortfalls caused by adverse FX movements by monitoring his cash-flow-at-risk over the relevant time horizon and then simply hedge for those periods where the resulting liquidity risk is highest.

By and large, however, the characteristics of private equity investments thus render traditional currency hedging strategies more or less redundant.[14] Whereas in many situations these 'tactical' measures and hedging via financial instruments can add value, attempts by LPs to systematically hedge against FX risks have rarely met with success and have generally been found to be prohibitively expensive. Cornelius (2011) found that FX hedging has remained largely absent in private equity and concludes that 'any currency hedging in private equity will remain imperfect, and the probably limited benefits for the LP have to be considered in light of the nontrivial costs of such strategies.'

Natural hedges

Unlike FX hedging through derivatives, a so-called 'natural hedge' does not require the use of a sophisticated financial instrument. A natural hedge is a technique to lessen risk in one investment by making an investment that offsets, at least to some degree, the original one. This is opposed to hedging achieved by making two contrasting investments on the same asset, which will usually not work for private equity. It is important to understand that natural hedging requires that the private equity portfolio is engineered ex-ante by modelling its cash flow characteristics and by trying to achieve a targeted risk profile. Although it does not eliminate risk completely, a natural hedge allows investors in private equity to lessen their FX risk.

For an LP's liabilities (i.e., insurance, pensions, or borrowings in the case of securitisations) the obvious natural hedge is to match the commitments and their timing correspondingly, which works only to a limited extent because it heavily constrains the geographies in which it can be invested. A sizeable and properly diversified portfolio of private equity funds to some degree mitigates the impact of FX risk, as FX denominated capital calls are often, at least partially, offset by repayments in the same currency. Clearly, these cash flows will rarely coincide, which therefore requires modelling of their timing and their amounts. Such a pooling works also on the portfolio companies themselves and allows many institutional investors to work with 'currency overlays', where a basket of currencies reflects the risk exposure against individual companies.

Managing independency

Taking FX exposure as a portfolio management tool is only meaningful if the exchange rate movements show little correlation with cash flows or the value development. Consequently, an important component of natural hedging is managing this independency. In the case of funds, FX movements can have a significant impact on the fund managers' carried interest and thus can accelerate and also delay exits. The terms and conditions set under the limited partnership agreement can to some degree influence this. The limited partnership agreement can set out that FX is a criterion taken into account during the screening for deals and define currency diversification limits. LPs can also agree with fund managers not to invest in companies with specific currency mismatches between income and expenditure or that such risks will be monitored.

This raises the question of the fund managers' incentives. If carried interest is calculated based on the investor's currency only, it poses an agency problem, as it keeps the principal fully exposed to the currency risk, while the manager can only benefit from it. For example, in addition to the hurdle and carry calculation in the fund's currency, investors could ask for a carried interest calculation on the underlying investments' currencies, to strip off the effect of exchange rates. This argument put forward, for example, in Meyer and Mathonet (2005) is that no carry should be paid on the 'profits' attributable to currency appreciation, since this would not be due to the manager's skill. Incorporating a schedule for foreign exchange movements into the carried interest calculation and other covenants could mitigate this. However, one could also argue that differentiating between luck and skill for FX related impacts is hardly possible and would not make not much sense for protecting the LPs. Ultimately the fund managers have to search for an opportunity; this search alone requires skills. To a huge degree a fund's success or failure is also driven by industry developments and not only by skills, so it begs the question why do this only in the case of exposure to foreign currencies. For this reason perhaps, at least to date, limited partnership agreements rarely address FX issues.

How to Achieve Diversification

Even where the broad approach to diversification appears to be clarified, there remain a number of questions regarding the practical implementation. Private equity portfolios are usually constructed either top-down or bottom-up, but neither method can be applied in its extremes. Naive diversification is not as 'naive' as it appears and there are questions regarding the optimal level of diversification and the impact of cash flows.

Top-down vs. bottom-up

A top-down approach is based on a construction of the overall portfolio, determining allocation ranges and then searching for opportunities that fit these allocations. It gives priority to the choice of sectors, countries, trends and vintage years as opposed to the selection of individual assets. It could be argued that investors that follow a top-down approach put a stronger emphasis on managing the strategy, the asset allocation and the diversification of their portfolio. Others doubt whether a top-down approach is meaningful and high-growth markets equate to high-return private equity markets. Apart from the questions associated with determining the weight of the allocations, the major shortcoming of a top-down approach is that a strict adherence to these ranges is not possible in reality. In case of investments in funds, in practice it may be difficult to find and access a sufficient number of superior managers to fill in each predetermined subclass allocation. Indeed, often only one or two superior managers operate in a particular sector, and they raise capital only every three to four years.

Essentially, the bottom-up approach is focused on screening all investment opportunities with their quality being the overriding criterion, irrespective of portfolio considerations such as sector or geographical diversification which here are assumed to have a lesser impact. The starting point is the identification of suitable investments, followed by an intensive analysis and due diligence in order to rank opportunities by their attractiveness. The bottom-up approach has several attractive features and arguably is the most widely used: it appeals to intuition, is simple, easy to understand and robust as it depends solely on ranking. However, it is not without problems and, because it is very opportunistic, it can lead to an unbalanced portfolio, carrying considerably more risk than expected.

In practice the bottom-up and top-down approaches are typically used in tandem, with most investors following a combined approach. Neither would investors consider assets that are not of a minimum quality just to fulfil a targeted allocation. Likewise, even investors that are convinced of their selection skills are conscious of the importance of effective diversification.

Naive diversification

Naive diversification, where portfolios comprise a number of assets with an equal size of investment, in practice are found to be not significantly inferior and close to some point on the efficient frontier. In fact, naive diversification is the optimal strategy when there is no information that allows differentiation between assets.[15] For instance, investors who believe in a specific market segment without being able to form an opinion on individual opportunities should put the same amount in several investments in this market. However, for portfolios of private equity funds this is only workable within a range where size of commitment and fund size can be assumed as independent. Committing the same amount to every fund in the portfolio introduces a bias as it is implicitly a bet that smaller funds will perform better than larger ones. Also, trying to track the market by taking the same percentage in every fund is problematic, as LPs incur high fixed costs for smaller funds while committing too much for very large funds that tend to show lower performance. Such an approach, in fact, leads to the worst outcome, as it creates overexposure to fundraising booms that tend, as discussed before, to be followed by busts.[16]

In practice, investors will of course rather try to keep their allocations within a band, trying to pursue a slightly countercyclical strategy and bearing in mind their capacity constraints. Investing the same amount of capital in each vintage year requires a sufficient number of attractive and accessible funds. One factor, as already mentioned, is that LPs cannot commit independently from other LPs and during market downturns even high-quality GPs will find it difficult to raise funds. Consequently, small investors are in a better position to adhere to the rules than LPs that have to allocate very large amounts in each part of the cycle that may not always be matched by a sufficient number of high-quality opportunities. Particularly large institutional investors in practice need to a follow a combination of rules-based and discretionary allocations.

Optimum level of diversification

Answering the question of what level of diversification is 'optimal' is not straightforward. For portfolios of private equity funds, Weidig and Mathonet (2004) found that the maximum diversification benefit is achieved with just twenty to thirty positions. The question of how much to diversify depends on an assessment of an investor's selection skills and the returns targeted for the overall private equity portfolio. Investors that are convinced of their skills in identifying and accessing opportunities with returns above the targeted return may find it more meaningful to go for very concentrated portfolios just comprising the best opportunities (see **Figure 13.2 A**).

If investors cannot assume that their selection skills will be decisive, but are optimistic about the asset class and have reasons to believe that the universe of available opportunities promises an

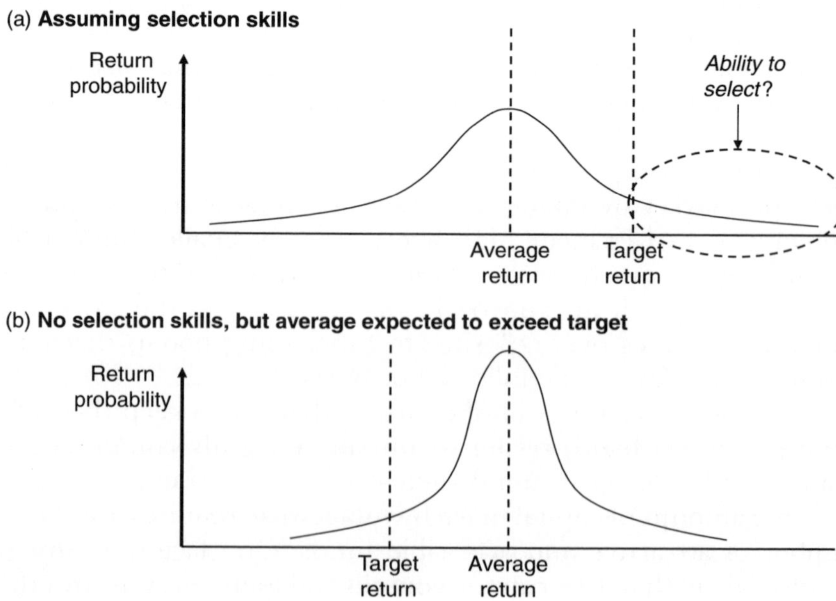

Figure 13.2 How much diversification?

average return above the targeted return – which can well be the case, at least temporarily, in some booming market niches – a highly diversified portfolio would be advisable to protect against a performance below the target (see **Figure 13.2 B**).

In many situations, however, neither one nor the other can be assumed. How can we deal with a situation of high uncertainty where we are not confident in our ability to identify winners and average returns may be insufficient? This situation describes, for example, the VC market in many countries. Such a diversified portfolio will typically be too expensive, therefore we need to look at how to amplify a positive impact, such as through 'real options', which we will discuss later.

Cash flows

Committing evenly to achieve vintage year diversification is also important for mitigating commitment risk. When adding illiquid funds to a portfolio of assets, they interplay not in terms of price movements but in terms of liquidity streams. Evergreen funds, that is to say, funds that do not mature but instead have an indefinite lifetime, only allow limited diversification over time as there are no constraints regarding the investment period and capital calls are clustered at the same time.

By fixing the investment periods to a few vintage years, the limited partnership structure allows investors to stagger capital calls over time (see **Figure 13.3**) and make them less correlated.

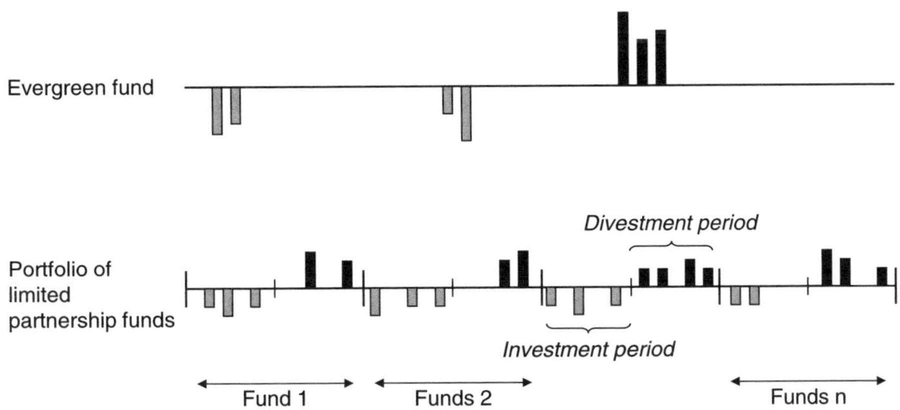

Figure 13.3 Diversification of capital calls (schematic)

Speed Read

- While diversification is a technique to protect the portfolio amid uncertainty and change, with an increasing number of assets the portfolio's return reverses to the average market performance. Investors use the principle of concentration to achieve growth.
- On the other hand, with growing diversification there is increasing stability of portfolio behaviour and notably more reliable cash flows, which support leverage as a way to manage a portfolio's risk profile.
- In the eyes of many practitioners, market-timing represents a losing strategy. The proven modus operandi is to consistently invest a fixed amount throughout the vintage years, despite the progressive increase in perceived risk, as it essentially gives an anti-cyclical exposure to the ups and downs of the private equity market.
- FX can be seen as one of several assets comprising the LP's portfolio. The impact of committing to funds in various currencies can actually be beneficial for the portfolio's risk and return as well as its liquidity profile. Investors in private equity mainly rely on natural hedges against FX risk. Here portfolios are engineered ex-ante by modelling cash flow characteristics and by trying to achieve a targeted risk profile.
- The question of how much to diversify depends on the achievable average returns, an assessment of an investor's selection skills and the returns targeted for the overall private equity portfolio.
- In situations of high uncertainty, where investors are not confident of their ability to identify winners and average returns may be insufficient, diversification needs to be looked at in the context of portfolios of real options.

Chapter 14

Private Equity Risk

It seems obvious and intuitive that the greater the potential return one might seek, the greater the risk that one generally needs to assume. There is a widespread belief that private equity by virtue of being more – or rather being perceived to be more – risky than other asset classes it will, almost by definition, also show strong outperformance. However, if risk was automatically rewarded, it would not be called risk. In fact, the claim of outperformance by the private equity asset class is far less clear than conventional wisdom might suggest.

This chapter is not about private equity risk from the perspective of risk avoidance or operational risks, such as legal, reputation and ESG-related issues. There is of course an interdependence between these risks, but financial risk exists even if operationally everything is in hand. Risk management techniques for private equity are in their early days and many aspects are still misunderstood and even controversial. Nevertheless, refining our understanding of this subject is critical in order to design an effective investment strategy. There are several points that require reflection particularly in the context of private equity funds as the main modus operandi of institutional investing in this asset class: what is the value of the fund? This is the starting point for risk measurement. What is the exposure to and the risk of a fund which, in fact, initially holds no assets and how can we model it?

An Empty Set

When talking about 'risk' in the context of private equity, we are mainly looking at situations of 'uncertainty' in the definition of University of Chicago economist, Frank Knight, where there is no valid basis for classifying instances.[1] Outcomes are so unique or so infrequent that it is meaningless to tabulate experience as a measure of their probability. Consequently, probabilities need to be estimated and the universe of possible or likely outcomes to be inferred.

Quite different from a priori and statistical probabilities this is a 'probability judgment'.

Managing risks is not just about assessing and quantifying all that could go wrong, but understanding all the things that need to go right for the investment strategy to be successful.[2] The measurement of risks should be an input for investment decision-making, not just for reporting of risks ex-post. To achieve this, risk measurement needs to be able to capture the economic reality. For private equity, more than for conventional asset classes, this poses a dilemma: any forward looking assessment will be highly judgmental and needs to factor in intangibles, whereas financial managers are trained to base their decisions on hard evidence, which will only be available in the form of historical and thus largely irrelevant data.

In parallel to the 'Golden Age' of private equity until 2007, there were huge advances in financial risk management. However, risk measurement for private equity is still in its infancy, and as Bongaerts and Charlier (2006) found, 'the academic literature on the intersection of the two is very close to an empty set'. While there is an abundance of papers on banking regulation, there was 'curiously enough', hardly any on the treatment of private equity under the Basel II Capital Accord for the banking industry. At the time of writing, the situation has not significantly changed. Some early steps to becoming more systematic about risk measurement were undertaken recently,[3] but private equity risks are usually still modelled in an overly-simplistic and thus often misleading fashion.

What is Value?

A correct valuation is the basis for risk measurement and, as a consequence, also for the development of an investment strategy. 'Correct' does not necessarily mean 'precise', but rather that it captures the economic reality of an asset without systematic biases and distortions. In this respect, private equity poses a challenge.

In a fair value world the value of portfolio companies must be reflected in a calculated equivalent of a market price. Private equity valuations are drawn up according to standards such as the 'International Private Equity and Venture Capital Valuation Guidelines'.[4] One line of argument is to look at the mechanics of the valuation process and simply criticise the method of deriving the fair market value.[5] Valuations are subjective by definition whereas prices are objective as they can be transacted upon. Markets are viewed as crucial for risk management as they in theory provide liquidity to investors who can correct an investment error by selling the asset back to the market. Much confusion regarding valuations in private equity comes from the way that value and price are habitually mixed up in the discussion. Valuations change only when substantial new information exists that would influence long-run expectations.[6]

The way that accounting values are determined and, following from this, risks are looked at, has been repeatedly criticised.[7] Industry valuation standards for private equity are essentially conventions endorsed by accountants and regulators. The attraction of these valuations are their relative simplicity with apparently limited scope for creativity, giving the appearance of tangibility. Such a valuation is a high-quality piece of information and to some degree believed to be verifiable as it is audited. It is, however, in many cases an incomplete picture of the economic reality as it leaves critical intangibles out and has limitations incorporating crucial judgment. Demaira (2010) suggested that the fair market value rule's promoters 'decided to adopt a rule which would free them from very difficult issues, despite the fact that it does not make any economic or financial sense'.[8] For private equity this rule is problematic as, for instance, it does not take the intended time horizon, in line with the 'intervention phase', for holding the asset into consideration.[9] In fact, the fair value regime may not have helped to make the asset class more transparent. Previous standards – based on the lower cost and the latest valuation round – may even have provided investors with more meaningful disclosure, because their reduced volatility made valuations simple and trends easier to detect and understand.

Investments in funds

For investments in private equity funds this is becoming even more difficult. First of all, initially funds are 'blind pools', i.e., they hold no quantifiable assets yet, but they still from day one constitute a risk for their LPs. Moreover, the limited partnership is structurally illiquid: in contrast to asset classes that may become illiquid, thanks to financial turmoil and heightened risk aversion, investors in asset classes such as private equity are aware ex-ante of the risk they take. In addition to the questionable attempt to mark such assets to market mentioned already, the common avenues to value private equity funds and to measure their risks are:

- Use secondary transactions of fund stakes to measure market risk.
- Model a 'fair market transaction' of fund stakes based on the fund's present value.[10]

The latter approach acknowledges that the secondary market for private equity assets is too opaque and not deep enough, transactions are too infrequent, and often sellers are acting under compulsion. Consequently, the secondary market is not suitable as a reference point for fair value and a rather impractical approach.

According to EVCA 'Risk Measurement Guidelines', the relevant unit for risk assessment is the LP's share in the private equity fund.[11] Unfortunately, there remains confusion about what the LP partnership interest is. Often no differentiation between funds and investments directly held is made. For instance, the 'look-through approach' under Basel requires banks to risk weight the underlying exposures of a fund as if the exposures were directly held.[12] Researchers such as Sørensen et al. (2013), on the other hand, make a distinction, albeit not a material one. They view the LP's partnership interest to be the LP's claim on the fund, including the obligation to pay the remaining management fees and the right to the eventual proceeds from the sale of the fund's asset, net of the GP's carried interest. Here the LP's partnership interest is valued as an illiquid claim on the fund's underlying assets.

However, from this perspective the value of a fund prior to its first investment would be zero, as the fund does not hold any asset yet – or even negative, as the valuation needs to factor in the future management fees. One major problem obviously lies in the conventions of how funds are modelled.[13]

Role of undrawn commitments

When looking at the limited partnership the crucial question relates to the undrawn commitments: do they 'belong' to the fund and are thus part of the allocation to private equity or not? A number of LPs faced serious problems during the recent financial crisis because of their undrawn commitments.[14] Their experience has increased the interest of practitioners and academics alike in what has been coined 'commitment risk' or 'funding risk'.

The valuation of the fund's underlying assets is only reconcilable with a present value perspective for the fund if the LP is not following an overcommitment strategy. Overcommitting investors commit more to funds than they have available as resources. This can also be unintentional, for instance due to FX rate changes with an adverse impact on the resources available to respond to capital calls. In the case of overcommitments, future distributions from one fund are needed to honour the capital calls for another fund. In the case where these distributions are insufficient the LP is taking on 'commitment risk' as he may become a defaulting investor.

Many LPs view their undrawn commitments essentially as irrelevant from a liquidity standpoint, given their relatively small allocations to illiquid partnerships compared with their holdings of public equity and bonds. Investors also believe that they can avoid commitment risk by not overcommitting and by holding liquidity in risk-free and extremely liquid instruments, such as treasury bills. The question is whether there are opportunity costs associated with the undrawn commitments locked up in liquid assets. According to finance's standard model, assets are valued by breaking them into different components.[15] From this perspective, treasury bills are zero-NPV investments, with low returns reflecting the absence of risk – so there should be no opportunity costs. But why, for instance, do LPs investing in a fund-of-funds allow it to overcommit? This would in the standard model's logic add no value and, in fact, just gives the fund-of-funds' GP more carried interest.

We are not questioning financial theory, but the flaw appears to relate to the method of breaking down a fund into its components. Investments in funds are occasionally modelled as loans with the LPs acting as lenders. Cornelius et al. (2013) suggest the opposite view: economically the situation is as if the GP called the entire amount of commitments on the first day of the fund's lifetime and lends the undrawn capital back to the LPs. While this may seem counterintuitive, this approach is motivated by the observation that it is actually the GP who holds the power over the use of the undrawn commitments. As for an ordinary loan, the GP can restructure the relationship with the LP if the latter defaults. In this situation the LP may lose the paid-in capital or suffer other penalties, with the GP holding the paid-in capital as collateral. There is also a clearly specified time period during which the capital needs to be paid by the LP (i.e., the investment period).

Note that from this new perspective the value of a fund at the point of its first capital call would be the commitment size. The fund's value is the aggregate of its equity (represented by its assets held) and debt (i.e., the undrawn commitments 'lent' to the LPs). Here the GP is the 'owner' of the undrawn capital and it should not matter to whom the GP 'lends' it. While the LPs happily, but probably mistakenly, accept a treasury return for the undrawn capital they hold themselves they would certainly not be willing to do this if the GP were to lend this to a third party. In this explanation the pieces of the puzzle fall into place: funds-of-funds who as LPs overcommit aim to compensate for these opportunity costs and essentially take on leverage. However, academic research into commitment risk is still in its infancy, so this view has not found general acceptance yet.[16]

Modelling Private Equity Risk

The availability of undrawn capital is a great risk mitigator in the world of private equity investing, as access to cash in case of crisis is the only effective hedge against extreme uncertainty.[17] If there is no obligation to sell, for a given target return and probability to exceed this target, volatility can be transformed into time or a contractual lifetime.

Are we on course?

Volatility is not a meaningful measure of risk for assets that follow a lifecycle, such as the J-curve. Investors without time constraints are not exposed to volatility. Guy Fraser-Sampson compared the question of achieving a return target for a fund with taking a train to an important meeting one cannot miss.[18] Rather than being worried about the speed, one would rather care about the fact that the train should arrive on time at the end of the journey. Taking this analogy, the impact of valuation changes needs to be put in context: if the train stops for five minutes just before its scheduled arrival time, one would clearly miss one's meeting. If, however, the train is running five minutes behind schedule two hours before the planned arrival, there is a fair chance to catch up.[19]

The essence of private equity investing is a bet on a future environment and focusing on managing the convergence towards this future. Here we differentiate between the 'intervention phase' where investors are actively involved and apply private equity techniques for operational improvements and the 'exit phase' after this invention has ended and investors sell off the portfolio company or hold on to it just passively.

Convergence model

For funds, this intervention phase is contractually fixed. For direct investments we know the planned time for the 'intervention period' and there is a set of expectations and an agreement between the managers, creditors and sponsors as to what the company intends to achieve over this time frame. For private equity type investments, leverage is part of the value creation process. As Baker and Smith (1998) pointed out, leverage can be usefully reemployed to stimulate improvements in operating performance. Part of a transaction is an agreement between the managers, creditors and sponsors as to what the company intended to achieve over the intervention phase.[20]

The debt/equity ratio at the early stages of the buyout process is not comparable to the debt/equity ratio of the company's peers in the market. Therefore, leveraging – even if higher compared to normal firms – is not a problem per se during the intervention phase. It only becomes a problem if milestones are not met, debt is not retired and the company is not deleveraged quickly enough. All other things being equal, leverage for an investment only constitutes higher risk if the degree of leverage is higher than that of other private-equity-held companies in a similar stage in the intervention phase. In fact, we are faced with an issue that is to some degree comparable to that of the J-curve for funds, where early write-offs cannot be seen as indicative for the fund's final performance. During the intervention period interim figures do not reflect the final outcome. Over time portfolio companies become increasingly independent, as with decreasing leverage the private equity financer's control over their management weakens. Consequently, when looking at risks, we model this as a convergence towards a target peer group during the intervention phase.

Convergence adjusted multiple approach

Detailed financial models, for example based on Discounted Cash Flows (DCF), can capture excess leverage and deleveraging of private equity investing. However, these techniques may require an excessive workload which make them unsuitable for continuous monitoring of risks. An alternative is what we term a 'convergence adjusted multiple approach'. This is conceptually close to the venture capitalists' method for valuing start-ups, based on what value can be expected for a given number of years in the future.

The starting point for modelling risks for a private-equity-held asset is its 'historical peer group', e.g., companies or funds that can be considered as similar and where their financial returns can be taken as a reasonably realistic point of reference. Moreover, we need to consider the asset's 'current peer group', such as other private-equity-held portfolio companies or funds that were launched in the same vintage year and are thus subject to the same market environment. Other private equity assets are arguably a better basis for comparison, but in many situations their data will be difficult to compile. Alternatively, publicly quoted assets representing the future exit environment and for which more consistent data is available can, after adjusting for their lower probability of failure, be a suitable current peer group.

First we project developments in the relevant market environment with the aim of determining where the current peer group will be at the end of the intervention phase. In principle we model the convergence of a historical peer group's returns and the current peer group's returns to derive the probability distribution for the current peer group's returns. Then we project the position of the asset within its current peer group. These two steps allow us to determine where an asset will be relative to its peer group at the end of the invention phase, and come up with the probability distribution for the asset's returns that we need to measure its risk. Caution should be taken to avoid giving undue weight to the latest data during the early years as it tends to be a too unreliable estimate of the final return. The projections converge towards one another and towards the true outcome with more evidence over time (see **Figure 14.1**).

What risk-taking is rewarded?

There are several mechanisms to reward the taking of risks with excess financial returns. For traditional asset classes this is typically through risk-adjusted pricing, meaning that the higher the risk, the higher the premium required by the investor. The typical limited partnership structure, however, does not allow for risk-adjusted pricing. All primary positions are bought at par (i.e., without

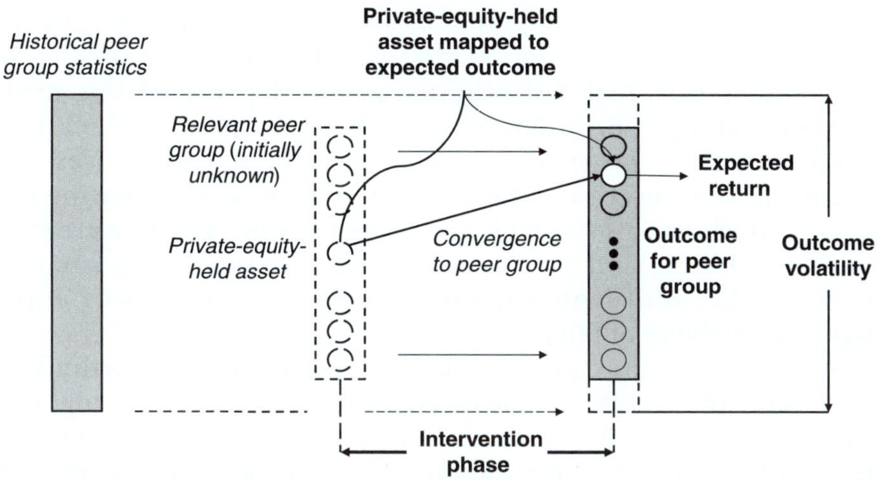

Figure 14.1 Private equity risk model

premium or discount) and there is no predefined coupon payment but only an uncertain performance and a predefined cost structure. Reducing fees, particularly for smaller funds has limits and cannot compensate for risks.[21] Instead, pricing comes in the form of reduced LP demand, leading to a lower size in combination with a lower probability of closing the fund (see **Figure 14.2**).

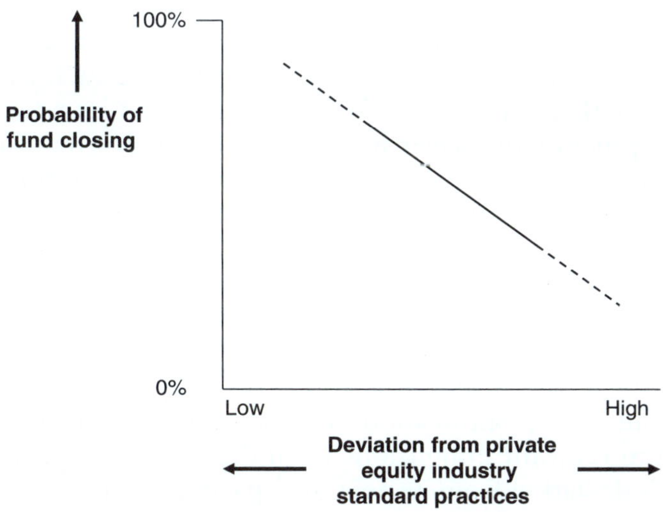

Figure 14.2 Probability of fund closing depending on deviations from standard practices[22]

So in the absence of quantifiable risk and risk-adjusted pricing for funds, what risk-seeking is rewarded for private equity? Here the ability to earn high risk-adjusted profits depends on systematically innovating by proprietary research, moving into new markets where expertise and skills do not need to be too strong yet and to learn how to succeed in them. In alternative assets, behaving too conservatively can also result in deviating from markets that are continuously shifting and thus actually creates risks. Moving towards market niches with higher uncertainty does not necessarily imply higher probability of failure.[23]

In this context the cause of risk and the associated opportunity is doing something different or doing things differently. 'Doing' can refer to action as well as inaction. Increased risk is taken when one deviates from the practices followed by the majority of the market participants, a concept which is close to the idea of 'mutations' in biological systems.

'Similarity' to peer group

We may not know everything from private equity statistics, but this does not mean that we know nothing. While it cannot be assumed that statistics will remain stable in the future, its broad features, such as the high volatility and the skewness, are certain to last and these offer help when looking at risks. Probability distributions describe 'baskets' of similar assets, i.e., a 'peer group'. Risk is caused by deviations from its peer group or through trade-offs, such as leverage that can go either way.

For the purpose of measuring risks we break down available historical data into classes and determine how similar these classes are to the private-equity-held asset. As the private equity market evolves over time, such historical data can of course only offer an indication of what is possible in the future. The concept behind a 'class similarity score' is that risk-taking is doing something different. Against this background, we suggest focusing on the degree of similarity of the asset with respect to its peer group as a reference point for quantification. The scoring aims to measure the deviation in relevant dimensions from this peer group. A portfolio company's deviation from its peer group can come in various forms: different products and services, different corporate or capital structure, different client base, few strong customers or many weaker customers and so on. Pre-investment, the degree of deviation can be measured by a qualitative scoring, along the lines proposed in Meyer and Mathonet (2005), who use what is often referred to as 'institutional quality' funds as the reference point for measuring deviations. There is no generally accepted definition of which funds are 'institutional quality' and which funds fall out of this category.[24] Ultimately, this can simply be a grand way of referring to funds managed by established GPs but rather than being guarantors of high investment performance they should be seen as the benchmark population for quantifying risks.

Limitations to Modelling Private Equity Risk

Regardless of how detailed a risk model is and how much effort is put into it, we need to accept, as Karl Popper argued, the impossibility of prediction in human affairs. This objection can be overcome for a stable and repetitive universe in which rational actors make efficient use of available information and where the 'unknown unknowns' disappear to be replaced by measurable risk. This, however, cannot be assumed for private equity. Any predictive capability of a model decays rapidly with changes in the financial markets and the economy. A model needs to run often and consistently to be useful for investment decision making. Here any risk model is just part of a control loop of measurements and actions that steer the portfolio. Particularly in an environment of uncertainty, simpler methods for projections often work better than complicated ones and allow effective decision-making despite limited data and computing power.[25] As Keynes, probably apocryphally, observed, it is better to be roughly right than precisely wrong. Simple models with few and broadly categorised parameters may deliver less precision but can be more often within relevant tolerances and be quicker to execute.

Regarding limited partnership funds there remain even ambiguities regarding the definition of exposure – including or excluding undrawn commitments? This raises the question how we can measure the financial return of portfolios of funds, a subject we will turn to in the following chapter.

Speed Read

- Despite their wide acceptance, prevailing approaches for valuing private equity assets and, as a consequence, measuring their risks are deficient. Any approach must accept the challenge of working with little and low-quality data.

- There is a vicious circle: private equity is perceived to be very risky, resulting in negligible allocations to this asset class. As a consequence, little effort is put into modelling risks and those employed tend to be simple but misleading, further reinforcing a sense of riskiness.
- The perception that risk for private equity is 'very high' may be true for individual investments, but for well selected and diversified portfolios, gains tend to more than compensate for these losses.
- Correct – but not necessarily precise – valuation is the cornerstone of effective risk modelling. Notably the role of the funds' undrawn commitments so far is not fully understood. Academic research into commitment risk is still in its infancy.
- In context of private equity assets without a functioning market, the cause of risk and the associated opportunity is doing something different or doing things differently. Increased risk is taken when one deviates from the practices followed by the majority of the market participants.
- Risks associated with investments in limited partnership funds need to be modelled based on qualitative as well as quantitative data. In this environment characterised by extreme uncertainty, simpler methods often work better than complicated ones.

Chapter 15

Performance Measurement

There is a rich academic literature on the performance of private-equity-held assets compared to other asset classes, but the question how much money institutional investors can earn through investments in a fund has been barely touched upon. Factors such as the LP's individual selection skills and how the specific portfolio of funds is built and managed make generalisations difficult. If we accept that undrawn commitments are part of the LP's exposure, different treasury returns, among other factors, need to be taken into consideration as well.

Measuring private equity performance

There are a confusing number of different perspectives on private equity performance. GPs report gross as well as net returns to their LPs. Industry statistics generally present fund performance data net-of-fees and carried interest. As we saw in the previous chapter, there is even uncertainty on how to value funds in the first place and whether or not to consider the impact of the undrawn commitments.

Fund performance

The well known J-curve pattern of a fund's annual returns contributes to the confusion. It tends to be negative in early years, giving the impression that a fund's performance is 'disastrous'. Once the trend reverses, valuation of portfolio companies go up and after some exits are done, it gives a picture of 'stellar' annual returns before levelling off again towards the end of the fund's lifetime. The 'true' performance, however, is usually steadier but also less spectacular.

The Total Value to Paid-In (TVPI), also called the 'money multiple' is one way of looking at a fund's performance. The TVPI's limitation is that it does not provide information on the investment period's duration. A fund's Internal Rate of Return (IRR) is the most commonly used performance measure, but it has a number of well known shortcomings. Phalippou (2009) suggested the Modified Internal Rate of Return (MIRR) as a way to overcome the IRR's limitations. The MIRR considers the external cost of capital as well as the external reinvestment and thus also captures the fund's undrawn capital, at least simplistically.[1]

Performance of portfolios of funds

Performance for portfolios of funds is measured, for instance, as a 'pooled IRR' or as 'commitment-weighted IRR'. The pooled IRR is a measure that attempts to capture investment timing and scale. It is calculated by treating all funds as if they were one composite fund. This composite fund's cash flow series is then used to calculate the pooled IRR. The advantage of this measure is that it does take the scale and timing of cash flows into account and therefore also reflects the LP's skills to time the market. The disadvantage is that larger cash flows will be given more weight, so in a composite portfolio of small early-stage funds and large later-stage or buyout funds, the larger funds will distort the picture.

The commitment-weighted IRR is an average calculated by weighting the rates of return by commitment. The commitment-weighted IRR does not capture the actual investment and timing as the commitment is static. It is a useful measure for the LP's skill to select and allocate the right amount to funds. If the funds invested all their capital during the first takedown, the pooled return and commitment weighted return would be identical. However, neither the pooled nor the commitment-weighted IRR reflect how the LP manages the capital which is dedicated to investments in private equity but not called by the funds.

Dedicated resources

Resources are dedicated to investments in private equity to seed what we term here as a 'programme'. It is assumed that the programme should be of a long-term nature, spanning several decades or even on an evergreen basis. As a consequence, distributions from private equity funds remain in the programme and will, for instance, be allocated to commitments to other funds in the future. Usually there will be a target for the programme, above which

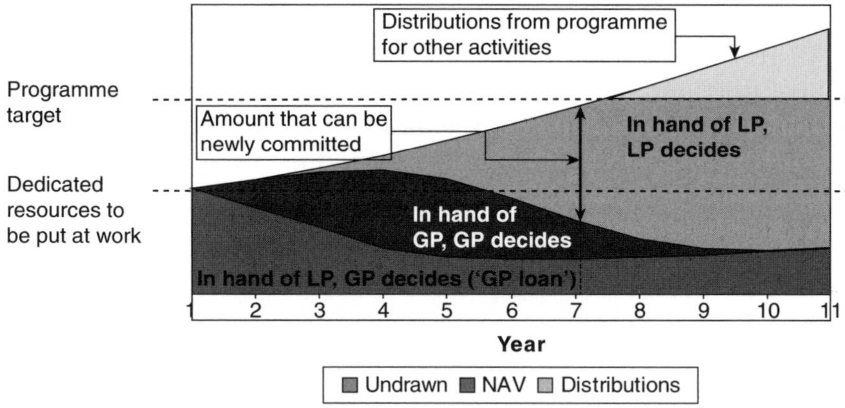

Figure 15.1 Development of dedicated resources

distributions will not be further committed to private equity and returned to the programme's sponsor where it can be used for other activities, such as to be allocated to other asset classes to keep a balanced portfolio or to pay down liabilities. **Figure 15.1** gives a simplified view on how the dedicated resources are developing.

Development of dedicated resources

Resources dedicated to private equity comprise uncommitted capital, undrawn capital and capital invested by the funds. The capital moves through several stages. Initially, the dedicated resources are uncommitted as no funds have been identified yet but the programme's objective is to create a portfolio comprising a series of funds. Once the LP has committed to a fund, this amount becomes undrawn capital but remains in the hands of the LP. However, as discussed before, in substance during the investment period the GP has at any time the right to call this capital and the LP has the obligation to honour all capital calls.

The differences between a fund's commitments and investments need to be kept in mind. The commitments are only indicative of the LP's portfolio composition whereas investments represent the real allocation of capital to private equity and are reflected in the NAV. The available commitments will not be needed at once but are drawn down and invested over time, typically several years. The GP starts to look for attractive investments, closes deals and then calls the undrawn capital. Once called and invested by the GP, the LP has no right to interfere in the management. The timing of realisations and distributions to the LP are exclusively under the GP's control.

Once portfolio companies have been exited, the GP distributes the proceeds to the fund's LPs again. These distributions can again be used as uncommitted capital, returned to the sponsor who provided the dedicated resources, or can be allocated to the capital yet undrawn by other funds the LP has already committed to. The use of this capital and the timing of its use is fully under the LP's control.

Reaching a targeted allocation to private equity

Murphy (2007) sees the invested value (on an unrealised cost basis) as the appropriate metric for sizing and managing commitments to private equity and suggests that a target allocation can be reached in roughly 10 years by annually committing amounts between 14 per cent and 22 per cent of the target allocation amount. Large initial commitments can help to reach the target allocation earlier but can lead to unbalanced and thus riskier portfolios with concentration of funds in some vintage years.[2]

Many institutional investors plan to shorten the time to reach their target exposure by acquiring fund positions on the secondary market. Since access to such opportunities requires, in fact, a high level of sophistication as an investor in private equity, this is not feasible for newcomers to the asset class. An alternative is committing to funds raised by secondary players who specialise in this activity, but there are also practical limitations. Firstly, LPs may occasionally need to sell off stakes in funds because they suddenly have an unanticipated need for liquidity, although this is a situation mostly restricted to market downturns when very few institutional investors think about launching a private equity investment programme in any case. Secondly, the size of the secondary market is an immaterial fraction of the amounts committed to primary stakes in funds and therefore it will be difficult to significantly accelerate the build-up of the portfolio.

Various institutional investors try to invest the uncommitted and undrawn capital in publicly quoted private equity to keep the dedicated resources as fully exposed to the asset class as possible.[3] However, such attempts are questionable for a number of reasons. Publicly quoted private equity ultimately follows the dynamics of quoted equity and cannot be seen as a proxy for private equity funds structured as LPs. Moreover, publicly quoted vehicles can only rarely access the capital markets for additional funding and therefore need to hold more cash than an LP. Therefore the LP's problem of how to invest cash is just transferred to players who are even less well placed to make use of it.[4] Practical experience suggests that investing in small cap quoted equity offers the best trade-off between liquidity and returns reasonably close to private equity.[5] Alternatively, dedicated resources can be minimised by overcommitments.

Return on dedicated resources

Cash-rich institutional investors delude themselves if they do not consider dedicated resources in their entirety. If uncommitted and undrawn capital is invested in other asset classes it is essentially 'lent' to them but it does not go away. Looking at the return on dedicated resources, including the uncommitted and undrawn capital, gives LPs a more reliable picture of the economic reality. The effective rate of return on dedicated resources that investors experience is different from, for instance, the pooled IRR of the portfolio of funds. This difference has implications regarding the structuring of incentives for the LP's investment professionals. One simple way of measuring the return on dedicated resources is looking at the ratio of the difference of resources at the beginning and the end of the period related to the respective time period.[6]

Considering returns on dedicated resources is in line with the concept of the Economic Value Added (EVA), that is, the profit earned by an activity less the costs of providing capital for this activity. Value is created when the return on the activity is greater than the cost of capital.[7] A negative EVA suggests that, in the words of the late Peter Drucker, resources are 'devoured' without providing a commensurate return for their use. The key feature of EVA is that it incorporates a charge for the use of capital. It incentivises managerial behaviour by explicitly identifying and incorporating the cost of capital. As a consequence, EVA raises the bar and promotes more efficient allocation of capital.[8]

Relation to MIRR

To some degree, this way of looking at the performance of a programme can be compared to that proposed by Phalippou (2009) as an alternative way of incentivising GPs. He suggested basing the GP's incentives on the MIRR, where the full amount of capital committed is put on a separate and fictitious account at inception to earn a hurdle rate.[9] When the fund calls capital for investments or as management fees, it is as if it drew from this account.[10] Phalippou argues that this gives the right incentives: funds decrease the MIRR if the called capital cannot be put at work at the hurdle rate and penalises 'good' funds for not calling capital.

However, just looking at the dimension of GP incentives is not likely to make a big difference. Already current industry practices work against GPs calling capital that could not be invested to reach the hurdle rate. Certainly higher management fees associated with a larger portfolio are a factor, but they would not be eliminated through this new incentive structure. Also it is difficult to see why a 'good' fund would not call capital given investment opportunities with an expected return above the hurdle exist and, while in theory having a significant impact, in practice the scope for 'gaming the IRR' appears to be rather limited. This way of looking at fund performance goes in the right direction, but it assumes that LPs exert little control over their resources dedicated to private equity. Instead, LPs in many ways are better placed to manage their exposure, for example, through the amount and the timing of their new commitments and through overcommitments.

Impact of uncommitted and undrawn capital

For illustration, let us look at two extreme cases. In the first case the commitment drawn in full at the fund's time of inception and invested in private equity right away. All portfolio companies are exited and the proceeds are repaid to the LP at the end of the fund's lifetime. In this case the return on dedicated resources would be equivalent to the private equity return. This is a theoretical case as no deal pipeline could be strong enough, so that a portfolio of companies could be built up at once and neither could their exits be timed to occur at the same time. In the second case, commitments are not drawn at all and remain invested in treasury. In this case the fund's lifetime ends with the investment period as it will be stopped then. Also, this case is unrealistic, as LPs would 'pull the plug' at a much earlier time. In the first case, all other things being equal, the LP would show outperformance on a dedicated resource level vis-à-vis an average LP, while in the second case, underperformance. Measuring a fund's return exclusively on the basis of actual capital flows and ignoring the undrawn commitments thus provides the upper boundary for the fund's performance. This observation motivates so-called 'overcommitment strategies' for minimising uncommitted and undrawn capital, which assumes, as already touched upon in the previous chapter, that there are indeed opportunity costs for this capital.

Overcommitments

On average only 20–40 per cent of an LP's commitments are invested per year. It generally takes three to six years for a fund to call most of the capital from its investors, depending on the attractiveness of the investment opportunities. On the other hand, funds will start to exit portfolio companies and to return money to the LPs before all the capital has been invested. In practice, often these repayments are netted against capital calls for a fund's new and follow-on investments. As a consequence, the resources available are never completely invested in private equity funds and historically, the average exposure ranges from 60 to 70 per cent.[11] When overcommitting, an LP commits more capital in aggregate than is actually available as dedicated resources, with the gap expected to be filled by future distributions from the existing portfolio of funds. Another but equivalent way of looking at this is that an overcommitting LP commits to a new fund before an old one has fully exited its portfolio and distributed everything to the LP.

Not only LPs overcommit

There are two angles to consider when discussing overcommitments. Firstly, overcommitments aim to reduce the 'cash drag' resulting from the uncommitted and undrawn commitments, a situation from which particularly publicly quoted private equity funds-of-funds suffer. Here, shareholders essentially pay in all their capital at once and it needs to be quickly put to work as otherwise only low returns are generated with negative effect on the total return. Secondly, overcommitments are necessary because of the long lead times caused, for example, through sourcing opportunities, conducting due diligence, or negotiating the limited partnership agreements.

Overcommitments by LPs need to be distinguished from what is sometimes also labelled overcommitments by individual funds. GPs usually draw down only between 80–95 per cent of the capital they have raised, with proceeds from exited investments sometimes being reinvested. This recycling within a fund is different from an LP's overcommitment because the GP has no obligation to continue to finance a portfolio company or to reinvest the proceeds by acquiring new assets, whereas an LP is contractually obliged to honour the capital calls.

The question here is who is better placed to put this amount to work in private equity? If the GP is 'good' with strong deal flow or promising portfolio companies that need additional funding then it makes more sense to allow the GP to reinvest. If this is not the case, and the LP is advanced in his due diligence with other stronger GPs, this amount would probably be better allocated to new commitments.

What level of overcommitment?

An overcommitment ratio (OCR) of less than 100 per cent suggests an inefficient use of resources, given the long lead times associated with the due diligence process and the negotiations of the limited partnership agreements. A ratio of greater than 100 per cent, on the other hand, signals increased commitment risk in the sense that the investors might not have the required cash to respond to unpredictable capital calls when they occur. Views differ as to the degree of overcommitment that would still be seen as prudent. Arguably, an investor only becomes 'really' overcommitted at OCRs above 105 per cent to 110 per cent, with OCRs of 125 per cent and even more found to be relatively common.[12]

It is clear that one cannot sign for more than one expects to get as returns from the existing portfolio. Consequently, the long-term average return of an asset class puts a ceiling on overcommitting. In the case of buyout funds, average returns are higher than those for VC funds where returns also tend to be more volatile and where liquidity often 'dries up' over protracted periods. For VC-focused programmes overcommitment ratios would be significantly lower than in the case of later-stage private equity.

What are the risks related to overcommitments?

A number of LPs faced serious problems during the recent financial crisis because of the significant undrawn commitments they had made in their alternative investment portfolios. Their experience has increased the interest of practitioners and academics alike in what has been coined 'commitment risk' or 'funding risk', as already mentioned. Commitment risk in all likelihood will vary significantly across investors and appears to depend, for example, on the investors' ability and/or willingness to diversify their portfolios across vintage years and, within vintage years, between funds.[13]

There seems to be merit in treating overcommitments as leverage from the point of view of measuring and managing risk.[14] Although overcommitments may not involve debt, they are motivated by similar considerations and entail similar risks that need to be monitored and managed carefully. Overcommitting is essentially 'leveraging over time' as it has the same magnifying effect on returns and also – as a result of forced sell-offs – on losses. Generally, the combination of leverage and an illiquid market is highly dangerous, so without overcommitments one never gets into the problem of realising assets. LPs who are not overcommitted do not run out of liquidity and cannot be forced to sell – for them the lack of private equity's liquidity is irrelevant.[15] But an overcommitted LP may be forced to sell, which because of the contractual illiquidity, the thin market for such assets and the negotiation under time-pressure will nearly always result in prices to the seller's disadvantage.

Diversifying a portfolio of funds has not only a trade-off of risks versus returns but also is interrelated with the management of uncommitted and undrawn capital. Contributions and distributions are stochastic, and consequently LPs manoeuvre between the Scylla of being undercommitted and thus running opportunity costs and the Charybdis of becoming extensively overcommitted. Through a high level of diversification essentially the portfolio's returns are capped but, on the other hand, cash flows become smoother and thus allow better investing of the undrawn capital.

It's an LP Thing

LPs measure and criticise fund managers' performance, but what are the drivers of the LP's investment performance? Very little is known about incentives for investment managers within LP organisations such as pension funds and insurance companies. The majority of these professionals are salaried managers and anecdotal evidence suggests that the task of these investment managers is mainly to select the right funds and monitor them, and less the portfolio management and the management of uncommitted and undrawn capital. Clearly LPs need to be properly incentivised.

Attempts to look at alternative performance measures for funds, such as the MIRR, are certainly improvements on the IRR. They may provide a more accurate picture of a fund's performance but they still fail to give an incentive to LPs to critically look at their own investment strategy. It does not make sense to obsess over incentives for GPs in situations where an LP is better placed to improve his performance. When looking at the return on dedicated resources, we are actually measuring what could be seen as the MIRR on the level of the portfolio of funds. As a result, LP incentives should relate to the management of the dedicated resources level because there are significant differences and implications compared to the portfolio of funds. There are a number of drivers of the dedicated resources' performance, such as selection of funds, minimising undrawn capital through overcommitments, and portfolio strategy. LPs have a number of constraints and trade-offs to manage and this cannot be treated just by 'kicking down the can' to the GPs in their portfolio.

The question remains why 'return on dedicated resources' (RoDR) is not the industry standard for measuring the LP's private equity performance. One aspect, already touched upon as relevant for the discussion on risk, are the accounting conventions LPs follow for their investments in private equity funds. Accounting rules must strike a compromise between potentially conflicting objectives. For private equity funds the conflict lies between reliability, verifiability, and simplicity of valuation standards on one side and of capturing the economic substance of long-term investments and their future growth on the other side. The numbers reported by fund managers to their LPs are often inconsistent with the objective of measuring economic performance and therefore require adjustments. From a risk and performance measurement perspective an accounting presentation without the right adjustments leads to significant under-allocation to private equity. To eliminate this perverse incentive, all economic assets, such as uncommitted capital, and liabilities such as undrawn commitments should be recognised, in order to obtain a better reflection of economic reality and to motivate the right managerial behaviour.[16] Distortions such as conservative bias and the unwillingness to recognise intangibles should be addressed, but such adjustments are often looked at with suspicion and rejected by the institutional investors' community, particularly as they are not in line with current industry practices.

Moreover, looking at the performance of a private equity programme from this perspective raises a number of 'disturbing' questions: if private equity performance, already controversial now, is diluted further by considering uncommitted and undrawn capital, why bother with this asset class in the first place? One answer lies, as discussed already, in how risk is measured. While investors often measure private equity risk and performance incorrectly, they may be approximately right about the relationship between these figures.

Speed Read

- LPs manage those resources they have dedicated to private equity investments and their performance should be measured on this basis, regardless of whether or not they have sufficient liquidity at any given point in time.
- Performance measurement for a portfolio of funds cannot ignore undrawn commitments as this gives an incomplete picture of the return on dedicated resources. We advocate a performance measurement of a private equity investment programme that is taking the dedicated resources as a reference point.
- Managing on the basis of dedicated resources employs a number of levers. This not only relies on selection of funds but also on portfolio management such as minimising undrawn capital through implicitly overcommitting.

Chapter 16
The Galapagos Islands of Finance

The signature pattern of the markets in which alternative investors operate in consists of fleeting opportunities with limited lifetimes, fuzzy boundaries and overlaps with other asset classes, lack of public data, reliance on qualitative judgment and, as a consequence, great scope for a cult of personalities with investment managers sometimes behaving like prima donnas not much different from artists and actors. There is a convergence between private equity, hedge funds and other forms of alternative investing, rendering clear classifications impossible.[1] Modern Portfolio Theory (MPT) provides the theoretical basis for investors' acceptance of alternative assets in general. Adding non-correlated assets, such as private equity, to a portfolio of publicly quoted securities can improve the portfolio's risk and return characteristics. However, private equity does not sit well within the world of efficient markets, where an asset can be traded over the short term and prices are on average close to its true economic value.

To apply MPT, investors should be able to evaluate returns, risk – as measured by the standard deviation of returns – and correlations for all considered assets to determine an efficient asset allocation. Attempts to use appraisal-based valuations as proxies for prices and to calculate these figures in order to apply the framework of MPT to private equity have met with little success. In fact, based on the interviews conducted by Browne (2006) none of the investors used MPT to design their private equity portfolios. Instead and as discussed before, LPs tend to rely on simple techniques such as naive diversification. The so-called Adaptive Market Hypothesis (AMH) offers an opportunity to present an integrated theory. Essentially it does not conflict with the Efficient Market Hypothesis (EMH), but explains that investors make markets more efficient by looking for inefficiencies and profiting from them until they disappear, or at least, until they get so small that further search is not worth the costs any longer. While for the EMH the notion of equilibrium is central, albeit never realised in practice, in the AMH markets are explained as in continuous flux and undergoing an evolutionary process.

The Adaptive Market Hypothesis – Motivation and Background

The AMH assumes that market participants make mistakes but they also learn. Competition drives adaptation and innovation, natural selection shapes market ecology, and evolution determines market dynamics. Speculative opportunities do exist in the market, but appear and disappear over time, so innovation in the form of continuous search for new opportunities is the key to survival. Unsuccessful investors, the ones who continue to make maladaptive decisions, are eventually eliminated from the population.

AMH originated in the hedge fund world in order to reconcile the raison d'être of many hedge funds – doing arbitrage – with the EMH which assumes that no arbitrage is possible. The AMH understands the market inefficiencies that hedge funds exploit as fleeting opportunities. Some hedge funds may be the first to spot them and have a time window during which they can profit, but eventually the inefficiency is detected by others as well and finally disappears. To stay ahead in the game, hedge fund managers need to continuously look out for new inefficiencies. But even an excellent track record does not guarantee that the manager can find comparable opportunities again, and indeed many fail as they cannot find any.

AMH is a relatively recent framework – Andrew Lo, a professor at the MIT Sloan School of Management, put it forward in a 2004 paper – but the application of evolutionary ideas to economic behaviour is not new.[2] Students of the history of economic thought will recall that Thomas Malthus used biological arguments to project rather dire economic consequences. In fact, there apparently was a lot of cross fertilisation, as the evolutionary biologists Charles Darwin and Alfred Russel Wallace were strongly influenced by Malthus. Also, Schumpeter's notions of 'creative destruction' and 'burst of entrepreneurial activity' seem to be very much inspired by the concept of evolution.

Andrew Lo admitted that the practical implementation of his theory would be more difficult than investing under the EMH framework.[3] His arguments were mainly put forward in the context of hedge funds, which he viewed as the 'Galapagos Islands' of the financial globe but are closer to markets that are viewed as efficient and where academia is struggling with a reconciliation of the various theoretical frameworks.[4]

Private equity, however, offers a better area for practical applications. The underlying dynamics are more difficult to sense as the pace of evolution is much slower than in the hedge fund world, but the observable structures clearly support Lo's hypothesis. Investors in private equity may have difficulties viewing their portfolio management as an arms race against other market participants with a similar capacity for evolutionary improvement. According to Richard Dawkins, evolution 'has equipped our brains with a subjective consciousness of risk and improbability suitable for creatures with a lifetime of less than a century.'[5] But arms races are run in evolutionary time, rather than on the short time horizon most investors perceive to be relevant. When taking a long-term perspective, and looking at players like endowments or family offices, we see indications for evolutionary processes. The industry is experimenting with other structures, terms and conditions – not always successfully, but what is 'best practice' today can well be outdated tomorrow. This is certainly not in the extraordinary speed of the hedge fund industry. In private equity, things move at a more 'glacial' speed and in almost 'geological' time, but the same dynamics appear to be at work.

Non-Linear Behaviour of Private Equity Markets

The private equity market can be viewed as a complex adaptive system that is made up of multiple interconnected components interacting with each other. A set of rules forces these components to examine and respond to each other's behaviour. This leads to improvements in their own behaviour and, as a consequence, the behaviour of the system they comprise.[6] Such systems are adaptive in the sense that they have the capacity to change and learn from experience. This process does not necessarily happen rapidly.

Self-organisation occurs when a system in a steady state is exposed to an environment that can destabilise it and forces it to take up a new steady state where it is working more efficiently. In nature, systems are always on the borderline of stability in order to be easily tipped into a new, possible better, steady state. There can be 'islands of stability' behaving in a predictable way and being relatively unaffected by small changes. In some areas of the private equity market, firms grow to such a size that they almost lead, as in the case of dinosaurs, to an evolutionary standstill or to a crossing over to other areas of the financial system, such as hedge funds or merchant banking. Regularly, however, parts of the private equity markets are faced with substantial changes regarding their players and their competitive situation. Temporarily this will result in an unpredictable behaviour until the environment has again adjusted to the new situation. In a networked environment, like the private equity market, uncertainty is especially unsettling since its origins and its effects are connected in a non-linear manner. To allow self-organisation, systems need mechanisms that will prevent them from staying in a new steady state if it becomes less efficient. The self-liquidation of limited partnership funds and the resulting need to go fundraising at regular intervals could be interpreted as such a mechanism.

Linear systems, where the whole is equal to the sum of its parts, and where small causes produce small effects and large causes generate large effects, are straightforward to model. The problem can be broken up into smaller parts, which can be solved individually and added back in order to obtain the solution to the original problem.[7] The dynamics of private equity investing do not, at least not always, allow this approach. There are positive as well as negative feedback loops with time-lags, which distinctly involve nonlinearities. For instance, competitive track records of GPs or booming industry sectors attract investors until the supply of attractive investments cannot meet the demand for such opportunities any longer. Indeed, private equity commitments are cyclical, moving in line with the performance of other asset classes.[8] Moreover, a period of two or three years of success or failure determines how much capital goes into the area or is withdrawn.[9] The private equity market may be better off with a smaller number of players attracting steady funding but due to its high illiquidity and long-term investment horizon, it allows participants to fail slowly, so no efficient correction is taking place.

The landscape in which investors are operating changes its character in ways that cannot be analytically predicted. This is discomforting for financial managers who rather favour theoretical justifications for idealised systems with linear behaviour under which outcomes may be guaranteed. The discussion around performance persistence may serve as one example. As Beyerchen (1992) observed, the predominance of 'linear intuition' is endemic and in private equity it has often too much influence on value judgments and choices, with negative consequences for investors. This is not to say that linearity is nowhere valid in this landscape, characterised as it is by competing and interactive factors, but we are faced with a messy mix of order and unpredictability. There may be times where the private equity market appears to be stable, but such periods do not last long.

Living systems successfully cope with a world where benevolent environments gradually become hostile and where in previously hostile environments new opportunities arise. It therefore makes sense to view a portfolio as such a 'living system' – an appropriate analogy as such systems can cope with uncertainty without being able to predict. They are continuously directed towards the dual objectives of survival in a hostile environment and growth under favourable conditions.

Economics and the Biological Metaphor

To investment managers, who put emphasis on analysis, planning and control, an analogy to biological systems – coming into being without planning, having an innate ability to self-organise and being able to create order out of disorder – may seem odd. Economists, however, often base their reasoning on allegories from fields such as physics and, increasingly, biology. In the biological metaphor, the degree of market efficiency is related to environmental factors characterising market ecology, such as the number of competitors in the market, the magnitude of profit opportunities available, and the adaptability of the market participants.

Species of finance

With 'species' we mean the distinct groups of market participants each behaving in a common manner.[10] For example, pension funds may be considered one species, or banks or endowments are others. Lo (2008) also considers retail investors, market-makers and hedge funds as distinct species. If they are competing for rather scarce resources within a single part of the private equity market, there will be more information on this part but returns will go down as well. We assume that the decline of profitability is driven by the growing popularity of a niche and as a direct consequence of the influx of funding into 'proven performers' and 'top teams'. For example, if we assume that innovation 'grows organically' (like a shoal of cod), the VC market may become 'overfished' as too many funds go after deals that are not 'mature' enough – fishermen as a 'species' may die out.

The same evolutionary process applies to institutional investors in alternative assets. Practices of successful LPs start to spread and become market practice. For instance, the so-called Harvard or Yale endowment model with its high allocation to illiquid assets has been very influential for some time, but has been looked at more critically since the beginning of the Great Recession in 2008, with fewer institutions copying it.[11]

As nobody has full knowledge of the market and its future, market participants always look for improvements and experiment. Newly emerging fund managers need to 'mutate' to differentiate themselves from the mainstream and offer a unique selling point to prospective investors. Without change in the private equity market, such 'mutations' usually will not work out, unless the fund managers are simply lucky. Highly successful new rules will be rare, few may work out 'big', but the majority of mutations fail. What is a successful rule on the other hand quickly becomes best practice. As a consequence the set of rules undergoes an evolutionary process, with the bottom-performing rules being eliminated and new rules engineered to fill their place.

Finding one's fit

The private equity landscape is not just in flux like all other parts of the economy, its entire raison d'être is to instil change and thrive under it. The lifeblood of this asset class are inefficiencies, organisational changes, succession, strategy shifts in general, and restructuring of entire industries, changes in economies, industry structures and regulation or technical innovations that give rise to entrepreneurial opportunities.

Unsuccessful market participants that have suffered high losses or that do not attract further investments are eventually eliminated from the population and replaced by new groups with little or different experience. LPs are regularly exiting the market due to lack of success or because other asset classes appear to offer more attractive returns. Some investors may also be forced out of private equity due to, for instance, new regulation. Ferguson (2008) reflected on the evolution of financial services and concluded that 'animals' eating one another is not the main factor. He rather saw the process of speciation where entirely new types of firms are created as the driving force behind the evolutionary arms race.[12]

While GPs need to reduce their activities in certain niches or even fail entirely, comparable teams may reappear a few years later after enough investors and managers have moved on to greener pastures. The need to regularly raise a follow-on fund forces a response to changed market conditions. The fund raising process is a check and balance that ensures that only the best possible follow-on funds materialise and assures quick adaptation and improvements compared with the old fund generation. The 'mortality' associated with a failed fundraising process assures that GPs do their best.

Also for the relationship between GPs and LPs we can draw a parallel to nature, where the successful organisms manage to mate and reproduce, to pass a mixture of their successful genes on to the next generation. GPs pass on their 'DNA'[13] in the forms of strategy, expertise and experience to the successor funds. Markets change very quickly, but the need to regularly fundraise forces fund managers as well as their investors to adapt this 'genetic code' to each other's needs and requirements – the description of the fundraising as 'mating ritual' is not farfetched. The spawning off of new funds into emerging teams occupies attractive market niches. These dynamics are well suited for dealing with discontinuities that require constant exploration and the generation of options.

Structures used in the private equity industry, while often viewed as inefficient, are able to deal with continuous adaptation to changing market conditions. In evolutionary biology the set of all possible genotypes – the specific genetic makeup of an individual in the form of DNA – their degree of similarity, and their related fitness values is called a 'fitness landscape'.

Fitness Landscapes

Such fitness landscapes, also called 'adaptive landscapes', use 'height' and 'distance' to visualise the fitness, i.e., the reproductive success, and the relationship between genotypes. 'Height' describes the fitness of a genotype, whereas 'distance' indicates how similar or different they are. Since the 1930s, biologists have pictured nature as a fitness landscape with a series of hills and valleys of different heights and depths and describe fitness as the ability to successfully search such landscapes to survive and compete.[14] Species adapt through a process similar to 'hill climbing' where mutations from one generation to the next generation result in a move within the landscape. Natural selection and survival of the fittest will push a population of species towards a peak of high fitness in the landscape.

Fitness landscapes associated with evolutionary systems tend to be roughly correlated, so there is neither a completely random 'zigzag' nor one symmetrical single peak. Nor are they static but change over time. Uncertainty relates to how the landscape is structured – one can see neither the hills nor the valleys – and where, how, and how quickly it is changing. When significant changes happen, well adapted species are more likely to loose than to gain. For mutations that are not well adapted, however, one can assume that the change in the environment does not worsen their chance more than for well adapted species, but it may occasionally improve their position.

In a smooth fitness landscape, neighbouring positions are correlated. Flexibility could be interpreted as enabling local search, i.e., 'short jumps', aiming at short-term results and improvements in order to incrementally align to a static or slowly changing environment. Exploration can also make 'long jumps' that are needed to search within a volatile and rugged fitness landscape, where neighbouring positions are uncorrelated. In such an environment a small step is just as dangerous and can lead as much to unpredictable results as a long jump. Hostile environments and the strategic dependency on the environment increase searching. Here search processes are more ad hoc and improvisational. However, long jumps lead to new knowledge necessary for competing in emerging markets and generate a menu of options in order too protect against environmental shifts and to reduce the likelihood of failure. While long jumps may generate superior paybacks they are expensive. Most become failed experiments and land in the bottom of an even lower valley of the fitness landscape and die out.

Occupying positions

The organisms are defined through a series of parameters that can be continuously changed and can be visualised as being positioned on a fitness landscape. Committing to a fund is essentially irreversible and like taking a position in the private equity market's fitness landscape. If the environment or their competition changes, they either move by changing the parameters to another position in the landscape where they have a better fit again or they will be faced with an increased probability of becoming extinct. As Small (2003) observed, this kind of selection process also takes intangibles such as motivation and team spirit into account: for example, the success of a fund management team will not only depend on the individuals but also on how well they work together and how their skills and experiences complement each other. Private equity firms look for niches in which they could more easily exploit their specific strengths,[15] and such niches even grow in developed markets, for instance, in the form of turnarounds.[16] Certain types of investments have a better fit at other positions in the private equity landscape. Growth equity may be a niche in developed markets, but it is mainstream in emerging economies.[17] Distressed situations or secondary transactions are opportunistic and niche investments, but done under relative certainty. Investing in emerging markets or emerging teams, on the other hand, is done under considerable uncertainty. It therefore makes sense to look for 'emerging spaces' independently from geographic considerations and not just associate exploration with emerging markets. While there are apparently always profitable niches, the problem is finding them.

Positions need to be continuously adjusted in order to keep abreast of the shifting fitness landscape. An example of taking positions is 'thematic investing' which aims to identify themes that may shape the future and then think about ways that certain companies will benefit from them. This approach can be shown to generate considerable excess returns but requires the identification of trends that offer sustainable opportunities.[18] For instance, the aging of society belongs to such long-term trends.

Private equity associations, LAVCA for instance, publish an annual scorecard for countries, rating them on a wide range of factors spanning the regulatory and judicial, fiscal and cultural factors. Investors trying to enter emerging markets may be faced with entrepreneurs reluctant or unwilling to accept private equity funding, competition by local banks or adverse political reaction. Over time, however, significant changes can be observed in various countries and a large part of the world appears to offer exciting prospects medium to long term.[19] Private equity houses are said to turn away from low-growth buyout deals in Europe and North America and, for illustration, are looking to Africa's rising middle class, drawn by a youthful and booming population that is estimated to almost double to two billion by 2050.[20]

There can be several promising niches that may or may not change over the investment period. A specialist GP may be best adapted to a given niche and perform better in static environments, whereas a generalist, while sub-optimal, can better adjust to changes in the environment. A market niche gradually becomes exhausted, resulting in a period of underperformance and investors leaving the niche. Eventually, with increasing scarcity of funding and a revival of opportunities the niche may become attractive again, but market participants are slow to react as they often rely on data relating to recent history which do not support resumed investments.

What risk-taking is rewarded?

The aim of coming up with a 'perfect ranking' leading to clearly identifiable 'best funds' is illusive. Even if we were able to rank national economies and industry sectors by attractiveness, teams by their competences, or funds according to their terms and conditions, it is not possible to derive a single collective ranking from a set of rankings of different criteria. In fact, such a ranking cannot exist, a classical paradox in social choice theory as shown by Condorcet and Arrow.[21]

The idea that there is a 'best' fund to invest in also implicitly assumes a static environment, which is clearly not the case. Instead, investors need to ask two questions: (1) is the targeted 'ecological niche' promising and (2) does the 'species' have the best fit, i.e., is it well adapted to the 'niche'? In the context of the evolutionary analogy, if individuals deviate from the mainstream of their species they either get eatcn morc quickly or cat morc – although positive mutations are rarer than mutations that are detrimental to an individual's survival. 'Potential' and 'novelty' form a relationship similar to return and risk.

This links to the definition of risk put forward in a previous chapter, i.e., where the cause of risk and the associated opportunity is viewed as doing something different or doing things differently. In the context of the AMH this could, for instance, be deviating from standard industry practices, such as codified in the ILPA Principles. For LPs looking for the 'best' funds this does not appear to make sense. However, many potentially interesting funds deviate in several dimensions from ILPA Principles, but investing would make sense under the AMH.

It should be noted that 'mainstream' relates to the perception of risk. Whether these risks will materialise or not is irrelevant, as the perceptions and the resulting best practices reflect the aggregate experiences of the market. Sometimes these best practices are just based on anecdotal evidence as they reflect actual opinions held in the industry. As an example, many institutional investors would usually not be willing to commit to the typical first-time fund. Typically such funds market themselves as specialists, in other words, they try to operate in an 'ecological niche' and are less adapted to the general environment. Moreover, these fledgling fund management teams usually lack the resources to switch strategy or to ride out a longer market downturn. Being less adapted and less flexible the first-time fund depends on things going according to plan – which often is not the case, and therefore the pessimistic view that such funds may suffer a higher mortality is understandable.

Venturing out in new attractive market niches very often involves backing new teams. This needs to be managed on a portfolio level, balancing between exploiting mature relationships and exploring new ones. It may be a mistake to categorically reject first-time funds and just consider GPs with track record. In fact, LPs could often even be better protected by avoiding overcrowded and oversubscribed funds and by deviating from the standard behaviour of other investors and by exploring the boundaries of financial markets.[22] Private equity investors who are first movers in geographical regions are faced with the 'tyrannies of distance, language and experience'.[23] While they initially cannot rely on reliable data, this risk-taking is compensated by gaining privileged access to high quality teams and arbitrage opportunities.

Intelligent Design

The idea of interpreting the private equity market as evolutionary and looking for parallels in nature could be challenged. Clearly there are many important differences between biological and economic evolution. Evolution is nature's 'killer application' and works essentially unplanned and uncoordinated, whereas humans clearly have the ability to prepare for future developments, plan and influence outcomes. Financial structures do not emerge randomly but are subject to deliberate design and choice. Rather than genetically produced, they are transmitted across time culturally through a variety of legal, social and psychological mechanisms that are hard to change. There is also a diffusion of successful practices as professionals get recruited by other institutions and thus spread their knowledge. On the other hand, no structure can stand on its own and new ones depend on the interaction with other players, which will be largely unpredictable and result in many failed experiments. Indeed, the private equity industry provides a rich medium for financial speciation.[24] Like in all evolutionary systems, to stop experimenting and moving is a recipe for extinction. Such systems can benefit from changes and stresses in the environment but only up to a point; they remain vulnerable to revolutionary and catastrophic changes, caused, for instance, by crashes in the financial markets or regulation altering the rules of the game.

Speed Read

- The Adaptive Market Hypothesis (AMH), originally conceived to reconcile the Efficient Market Hypothesis with the existence of hedge funds, can most fittingly be applied to the private equity market.
- The AMH embraces biological principles, a metaphor that can be usefully applied to private equity, for which change and adaptation is not just a fact of life, but its raison d'être. In this circumstance, investors search for arbitrage opportunities in 'pockets of inefficiencies'.
- An investment strategy for private equity should model evolutionary systems, striking a balance between stability and experimenting. Rules for investing undergo an evolutionary process, with the bottom-performing rules being eliminated and new rules engineered to fill their place.
- The private equity industry provides a rich medium for financial speciation. Like in all evolutionary systems, to stop experimenting and moving is a recipe for extinction.

Chapter 17

The Locust and the Deep Blue Sea

Managing private equity portfolios appears to fit well into the framework of the Adaptive Market Hypothesis (AMH). In this framework competition drives adaptation and innovation and natural selection shapes the market's dynamics. Contrary to the Efficient Market Hypothesis, in the AMH world arbitrage opportunities exist and this is particularly the case with private equity.

To assure their survival market participants need to keep their eye on newly emerging arbitrage opportunities. Chances to outperform exist but only temporarily and cannot necessarily be identified based on historic data. When rich data becomes available, opportunities will often have passed already. Investors in private equity need to actively search for these opportunities; they are known only to a few market participants and will only exist for a limited time. Innovation and adaptation to changing market conditions is needed to maintain a high level of financial returns and thus is the key to survival as well as to growth. Decreasing returns in a market niche leads to investors either failing or exiting this niche. Niches may fall out of favour and be overlooked for a while, but when renewed potential is identified and returns grow, it will lead to entries again.

In the AMH framework any relationship between risk and return is difficult to reliably quantify and unlikely to be stable. To a large degree it is determined by the relative sizes and preferences of the various populations of participants in the market. The measure for risk introduced for this purpose is the fit with the landscape: the closer the fit, the lower the risk. To achieve a consistent level of expected returns and risks it is necessary to experiment, i.e., to consciously seek a lower fit with the current private equity landscape and adapt and flexibly react to changing market conditions.

Oil, Oceans and Bees

In the early twentieth century, limited partnerships were used to raise capital for prospecting new oil fields and private equity firms follow a similar lifecycle: when they go out fundraising for the first time they are seen as 'unknowns' and will find it difficult to attract enough investors. Expert investors, however, often find such opportunities worth the gamble and have some allocation to 'emerging teams'. Such investors behave like oil companies that explore new oil fields. Research and selection skills may help to decide where to 'drill', but explorations often fail and therefore cannot be profitable on their own. In the case where the LP hits an 'oil field' and an emerging team becomes a success, the relationship can be exploited over a series of funds. But like oil-fields that get depleted, GPs can also go into decline, as their funds grow too large, their teams unwieldy, they become complacent or simply retire and close shop. And of course success attracts competition.

One solution is well explained by another metaphor – 'Blue Ocean Strategy' – developed by INSEAD professors, W. Chan Kim and Renée Mauborgne.[1] They argue that competition should be neutralised by seeking out uncontested market spaces that offer opportunities for highly profitable growth. They refer to these spaces as 'blue oceans' and contrast them to 'red oceans' where there are clear boundaries and cut-throat competition turns the water bloody. The professors explain that the dominant focus of traditional strategy work has been on competition-based strategies and that 'creating blue oceans has remained wishful thinking that is seen as too risky for managers to pursue'. Indeed, corporate strategy is heavily influenced by its root in military strategy with its focus on limited terrain and the need to beat an enemy to succeed. Certainly, this perspective remains highly relevant for investment strategies where the ability to attract capital largely depends on outperforming competing investors. Nevertheless, in a constantly changing market environment investors in private equity can draw distinctive strength by discovering niches that are uncontested and offer strong opportunities for arbitrage.

Unfortunately, 'blue oceans' by definition are largely uncharted and investors lack data to guide them in their decision-making. This takes us to our third and final metaphor. How a fund manager can discover sustainable opportunities in a large landscape is embodied in the foraging behaviour of bees that coordinate their activities and engage in concurrent searches. The bulk of the bees exploit existing sources of nectar that are likely to be exhausted sooner or later, while a few scout bees take real flyers and search quite far. Certainly this strategy will inevitably have many unsuccessful and exhausting searches, but it will also have a greater likelihood of finding new and better sources without getting stuck in a depleted area. Concurrent search activities simply increase the chances of discovery (of course locusts operate in the same way, but that would be one metaphor too many).

Discovering Niches and Occupying Them

So far we have assumed a trade-off between the ease of discovering niches and return potential. One vital choice affecting investor performance is related to entry order, i.e., whether to be a pioneer or a follower into hitherto unexploited market space.[2] A pioneer that possesses the skills and the resources can occupy a superior position in the market space, exploit its opportunities and enjoy several competitive advantages. By establishing a recognition and reputation, a pioneer can raise the entry barriers for late comers. LPs that are early backers of an emerging and successful GP can essentially block the access for other LPs by, for instance, committing quickly to its next fund and by being secretive about its return potential.

Subsequent funds are often closed to new investors because the fund manager simply does not want to go fundraising with new investors again and has no problem raising follow-on funds with the existing pool of LPs. It may not even be known to other investors that such GPs are in fundraising mode.

While it is obvious that GPs greatly benefit from a loyal and reliable investor community, long-term relationships can also be advantageous for LPs. Initial selection of funds based on due diligence is more error-prone than information obtained as an existing fund investor. This is consistent with various research findings that suggest that successful investors in funds proactively use the information they gain as inside investors.[3] In the opaque private equity market, the search for and due diligence of funds is a costly exercise, and by and large LPs prefer familiar GPs to unknown faces. They are therefore more likely to reinvest in follow-on funds raised by private equity firms than LPs that do not appear to build on such information. Consequently, the relationship between fund managers and their investors can be relatively stable over a protracted time period. Through their monitoring, existing LPs can more reliably judge competencies than it is possible to do in due diligence of unknown fund management teams.

For an LP, it is especially desirable to hold on to good fund managers, as the best teams will have an established investor base and therefore will no longer be out for fundraising, especially during their growth stage where investors would be most able to exploit the benefits of this relationship. A more stable investor base also enables better planning, as LPs early on indicate among themselves whether they will back a follow-on fund. As LPs form a network, even if they do not have the means to continue, they often refer other investors to a good team. A predictable closing puts money at work more efficiently. Once a niche has been identified and occupied, discretion (or secrecy) may be a sensible policy to protect it from competition among other LPs.

Growth vs. Survival

The highest priority of a market participant as a 'species' is survival, but once it is assured, the main objective becomes growth. Assuring survival is costly and for an entire portfolio unsustainable in the long run. We associate the growth mode with confirmed opportunities for arbitrage, typically caused by changes in the market or 'bubbles' in market niches, and knowledge about these market niches and their dynamics. Investors need to switch into the survival mode when pockets of inefficiencies are exhausted and no new opportunities have been identified.

Which of these approaches are to be employed and how much priority is given to them depends mainly on the objectives to be met by the investor. Survival can be achieved, for example, through careful screening of deals, a high degree of diversification or hedging of foreign exchange risks. While due to the overall lower failure rate the downside is limited, such protection is very costly and not sustainable over the long term. The objective 'growth' requires superior picking skills, which as discussed already are rather doubtful, or the ability to amplify upside, for example through employing leverage, which requires slack resources to absorb a higher failure rate of experiments.

Threats rather than opportunities, uncertainty caused by chaotic changes or recessions, are indicators for the need to switch into the survival mode. Switching from growth to survival can be through suspending new commitments and waiting, cutting external services, maintaining one's reputation and relationship with one's own backers, and, in the extreme, triaging the portfolio and selling off stakes in the secondary market.

On the other hand, switching from survival to growth requires financial reserves – for instance from backers with whom strong relationships were maintained – for executing and amplifying successful experiments and reducing diversification and focusing the portfolio again. Switching from one mode into another is very inefficient for private equity as due to its illiquidity a rebalancing is not possible, at least not for acceptable costs.

Exploration vs. Exploitation

The search for knowledge and opportunities is a fundamental concept in explanations of economic evolution. Finding exploitable opportunities that allow a meaningful allocation of resources requires exploration. Instead of basing the portfolio composition on a reliable evaluation and rich data, the underlying concept is experimentation, i.e., trial and error. From this perspective, each commitment to a fund is an experiment in the private equity landscape. Some of these experiments succeed and need to be amplified, while others fail and gradually disappear.

The key to successful private equity investing is identifying the practical potential for arbitrage and its economic significance. As Janeway (2012) argues, at a 'deep level, this double task is no different from what [the French historian] Braudel described as the evaluation in parallel of the capabilities of maritime navigation and the forecast conditions of demand for and supply of pepper 500 years ago'. The classical case of arbitrage is long-distance trade where price differences between two markets were steep and supply and demand in complete ignorance of each other. This allowed middlemen to earn super profits, but over time competition became unavoidable. While one commodity's super-profits vanished, at that time it was still possible to find new routes to other commodities and earn super-profits again.[4]

When exploring, investors are operating in niches with no or little history, data or transparency (see **Figure 17.1**). The potential for returns are high and – because there is little competition – risks can actually be far lower than perceived by outsiders. In fact, we assume a link between the 'hit rate', i.e., selecting a good investment, and the payoff, i.e., getting a high return out of this investment, depending on the competition and the crowding within an area. During the exploration the probability of a 'hit' is low, but the payoff can be very high. Exceptional winners are so rare that there are no meaningful statistics that would allow a reliable quantification. The success is tied to the extreme events, not the average.

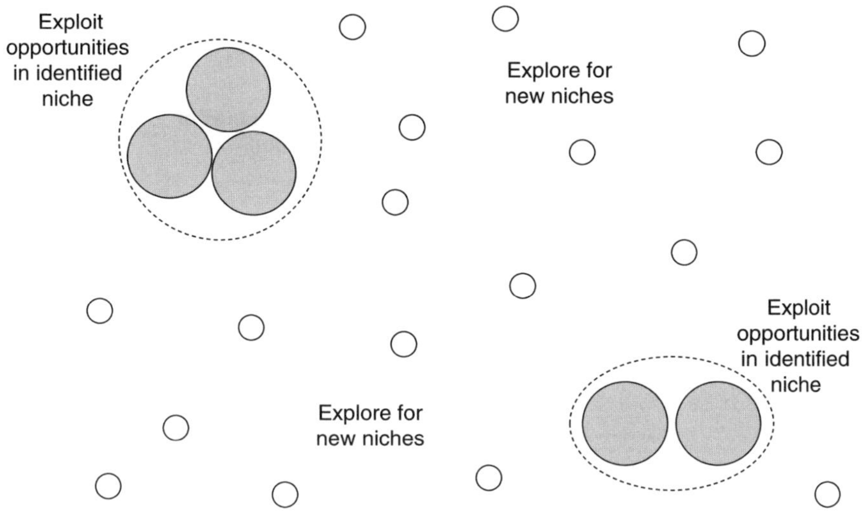

Figure 17.1 Taking positions in the fitness landscape

When exploiting, investors are operating in areas with high transparency and, for example, in relationships with funds of 'institutional quality'. The perceived risk may be low but due to increasing competition also the potential for returns is rather average. During exploitation the probability of a 'hit' is high, but the payoff is gradually declining. In situations of established markets, more detailed analysis is necessary to identify pockets of inefficiencies and opportunities for entrepreneurship arbitrage. In emerging market spaces such analysis often does not make sense. Instead, a budget for experimentation needs to be put aside. The portfolio management aims to maximise the probability of hits and of their aggregated payoff.

Investors explore through diversification and exploit through building concentrated portfolios or increasing their allocations to niches with identified potential (see **Figure 17.2**). It cannot be guaranteed that exploration will lead to a result and will thus increase volatility of outcomes. On the other hand, opportunities in identified niches can become 'islands of stability' that allow the engineering of portfolios with quantifiable statistical characteristics. But how long can a niche be profitably exploited?

Opportunities for profit in any given market could be compared to the amount of food and water in a particular local ecology.[5] Many such opportunities may be too small and therefore not exploitable for larger investors. Also, dwindling food supplies or an increase in

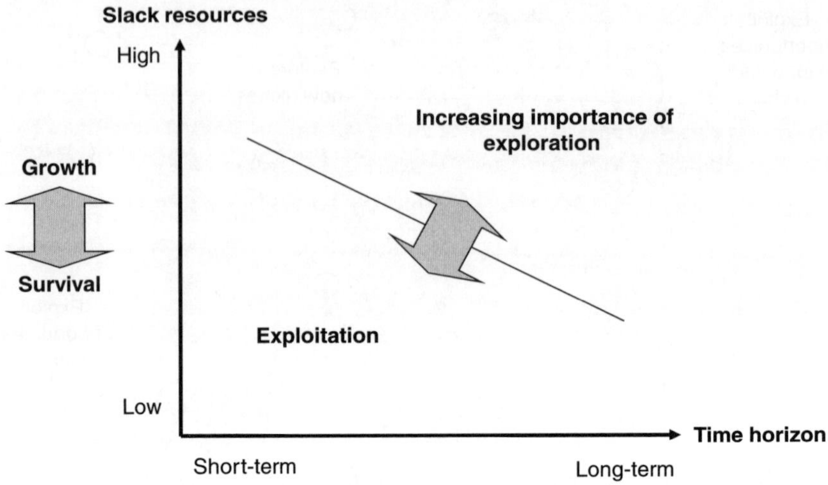

Figure 17.2 Managing the balance between growth, survival / exploration, exploitation / time horizon and slack resources[6]

the animal population lead to depleting resources and fiercer competition. The resulting decline in populations decreases the level of competition and starts the cycle again. In extreme situations, where food sources are permanently exhausted or environmental conditions shift dramatically, certain species become extinct. Andrew Lo views economic profits as the ultimate food source on which participants in financial markets depend for their survival. From this model the dynamics of market interactions and financial innovation can be readily derived.

Exploration and exploitation and survival and growth are related but not identical. Exploration does not make sense in an environment which is growing as a 'tide lifts many boats' and it is difficult to have an edge here. Exploration also takes too long and, because of the many failures, is too expensive to assure survival. Ideally investors should be able to exploit a growth environment, which, however, will not be able to assure survival over the long term.

Long-Term vs. Short-Term

Search and experimentation today builds the basis for 'exploiting' future opportunities. However, investors are also faced with constraints related to their investment horizon and their slack resources that can force them to make sub-optimal choices. A too short-term oriented investment horizon, such as the 10 to 15 years of a typical fund-of-funds, essentially restricts the choices an LP has available. For example, the implicit option inherent in the investment into a newly emerging team only has value if the investor is following a time horizon beyond one fund commitment.

Exploiting existing knowledge tends to be short-term oriented and exploring new knowledge requires longer time horizons. Exploration is the price to be paid to assure long-term survival whereas exploitation is exposed to short-term shocks. Exploration is required for growth but is an expensive strategy for two reasons. Firstly, many experiments pursued in the course of exploration fail. Secondly, if experiments turn out to be successful, resources are required to take larger stakes in order to exploit the successes. Therefore, for an investor exploration is only a feasible strategy if there are also sufficient slack resources available. Monitoring will not create much value unless opportunities can be turned into adjustments of the portfolio. Otherwise exploration has to be put aside and the short-term survival of the portfolio has to be assured through exploitation of identified opportunities.

Over the long term, and with other investors following and niches becoming crowded, the potential for superior investment returns diminishes. Private equity investors who continuously outperform the market are unlikely to exist. Successful investment strategies have to balance exploitation and exploration as well as short-term and long-term orientation (see **Figure 17.2**). To survive, they must adapt to the changing environment and explore for new spaces in the market. Exploration to the exclusion of exploitation incurs high costs without being sufficiently compensated by successful experiments and results in many underdeveloped opportunities.[7] Conversely, exploitation without exploration can result in failure to adapt to the changing competitive conditions and investors being left behind their peers.

Real Options

Investment decisions are rarely of a 'take it or leave it' type, and flexibility, i.e., opportunities to make decisions over the life of the investment that affect its outcome, is valuable. In situations of extreme uncertainty, it is meaningful to be flexible and also to bet on many horses, which certainly comes at a significant price. All growth-oriented investment approaches need to be active, whereas the 'survival mode' can only help to preserve resources in times of extreme uncertainty and during downturns.

With private equity being highly illiquid and commitment in practice irreversible, how can we switch from an investment approach that increases the likelihood for survival, albeit at significant costs, to growth-oriented investing? One answer is real options that allow value creation within changing and emerging market spaces, such as first-time funds, technology-oriented investing, emerging markets, and offer a way to amplify successful experiments as well as to deal with uncertainty. A real option can be defined as the right, but not the obligation, to take an action at a predetermined cost, for a predetermined period of time. Real options carry implicit costs on one side but have a value in situations where changes are unpredictable.

'Betting on many horses' establishes a link to 'nature's strategy' of evolution that, with mutations and the associated trial-and-error, uses a comparable mechanism for creating real options. In essence evolution says 'I will try lots of things and see what works and do more of what works and less of what doesn't.'[8] Evolution is a search algorithm that automatically strikes the right balance between exploration, exploitation, growth and survival. The approach is to explore, observe and select, amplify, and repeat this continuously (see **Figure 17.3**). Stopping failed experiments is as important as amplifying positive outcomes. Exiting a depleted niche early

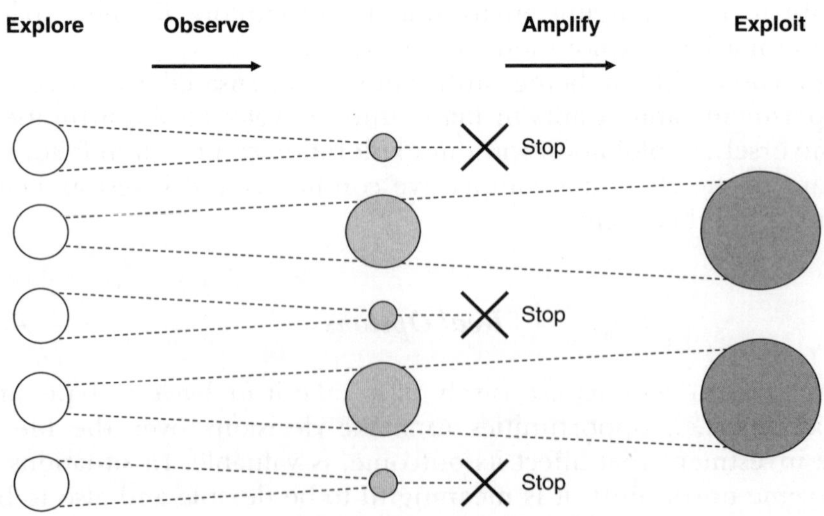

Figure 17.3 Explore, observe, amplify and exploit

enough and moving on to less contested ones helps to avoid losses. The entire VC industry is organised to follow the successful firms and shed the losers quickly. In dying industries, no investment will be able to turn the trend. Indeed the performance persistence argument may be dangerous if it stops investors from leaving a market in a timely enough manner. Investors need to avoid or exit areas in the market where too many of their peers go. There may be low uncertainty as there is a long history with much data, but due to the overcrowding, returns decline and risk actually increases.

Speed Read

- Investors in private equity need to keep their eye on newly emerging entrepreneurship-arbitrage opportunities. Chances to outperform exist, but only temporarily and cannot necessarily be identified based on historic data. When rich data becomes available, opportunities will often have passed already.
- The measure for risk is the fit with the private equity landscape: the closer the fit, the lower the risk. To achieve a consistent level of expected returns and risks it is necessary to experiment, i.e., to consciously seek a lower fit with the current landscape and adapt and flexibly react to changing market conditions.
- Investors explore through diversification and exploit through building concentrated portfolios or increasing their allocations to niches with identified potential. It cannot be guaranteed that exploration will lead to a result and will thus increase volatility of outcomes.
- Evolution is a search algorithm that automatically strikes the right balance between exploration, exploitation, growth and survival. The approach is to explore, observe and select, amplify, and repeat this continuously.
- As in the case of living systems, speed of reaction is decisive, which is why real options, apart from providing flexibility, are an important tool for survival and growth.

Chapter 18
Don't Confuse Transparency with Intelligence

In an age of 'big data' the availability of perfect information is almost seen as a given, and many financial market participants feel negligent unless their decision is based on complete analysis backed up by reliable figures. It sounds like a good idea, but in private equity, at least, it is not. As inefficiencies in financial markets become exploited and saturated, investors must continuously explore new under-researched but potentially profitable niches in order to stay ahead of the game.

At first glance, the more information we have, the better our decisions should become. Professional training has conditioned financial analysts to rely on high-quality – complete, timely, correct and precise – data. However, while historically investment decision-making was enabled 'through' information, managers now appear to be condemned to fight more 'for' information before any decision can be made.[1] 'Success is repeatable' has become a dogma which is rarely challenged. Spending a huge effort on the analysis of historical data plays into most institutions' culture, which is based on striving for perfect information and the avoidance of uncertainty.

The Quest for Certainty in Numbers

It is a source of some confusion among those that view private equity as secretive and opaque that the information provided by private equity fund managers to their LPs is often better than public companies can provide to their shareholders.[2] However, real opacity, the kind that cannot be resolved by better efforts, occurs outside of this portfolio company/GP/LP relationship.

Limits to data quality

For instance, private equity data made available by service providers, such as Thomson VentureXpert, Cambridge Associates or Preqin, is likely to have gaps, as market participants are not all known. Not all firms contribute data, and underperforming fund managers often withhold negative information and drop out. Therefore it is difficult to assess how complete a picture of the market is provided. Data is also expected to be error prone, as in fact relatively few parties work with the data, funds and portfolio companies are usually not accessible for investment purposes anyway and therefore there is only a limited degree of peer review as a check and balance. Finally, data can be stale, as it is often only updated after significant events. Moreover, reporting of financial statements can be delayed, often significantly. As some databases also cover funds-of-funds, their data could result in double counting. It is a general characteristic of an ever-changing, alternative market space that innovations and emerging market spaces are initially not recognised as such and wrongly categorised or are simply ignored entirely.[3] As a consequence, all databases will cover high-quality as well as low-quality data.

Public markets digest all available information and judgments essentially in real time and turn them into financial figures that can be instantaneously used for investment decisions. Contrast this with the situation in private equity, where the analysts would need to sift through literally tons of raw data which is incomplete, irrelevant, outdated, contradictory or outright incomprehensible. In fact, the more data is available, the longer the time needed for understanding it and the more difficult it becomes to distinguish the relevant from the useless.

Economics of data markets

Producing good private equity statistics is particularly hard and many underestimate the degree of difficulty. Lack of private equity data and its deficiencies in quality have been lamented within and outside the industry and repeatedly even provoked calls for regulatory action. However, there are limitations that result from the voluntary participation, the fact that proprietary information is critical for investment success, and, as a result, from the economics of the market for external data providers.

GPs and LPs have a limited incentive to report internal proprietary data to external data service providers, as they can free-ride on data already contributed by others. Transparency is only acceptable to a degree where others cannot create a competitive advantage.

Therefore no party will provide data of higher quality than one is expected to receive from the data service provider, as this would create advantages for others and disadvantages for oneself. Parties that do not need data or are not put under pressure from their investors – or maybe in future by regulators – to participate in surveys are therefore unlikely to voluntarily provide information.

'AMH' Market Intelligence

Private equity market intelligence is the capacity to acquire and apply knowledge to achieve the set investment objectives for the purpose of strategy development, decision-making, and benchmarking. Private equity investors need to tackle two questions: first, how to find a profitable niche and, second, how to protect it – for instance, by keeping it secret. Imitating other LPs is to some degree a response to a situation where an investor lacks knowledge. One may not be familiar with a market or a GP, but many assume that others know something one does not know. Research takes here the characteristics of espionage.

Uncertainty as opportunity

In efficient markets there is little differentiation between risk and uncertainty, as uncertainty is practically the same for all participants. In private markets, according to the AMH, decision-makers usually face situations that are unique and unprecedented, and where alternatives are not really all known or understood.[4] Especially in venture capital with fast moving technological changes, newly evolving business models, short boom-to-bust-periods, and long investment periods, it is highly difficult, or even impossible, to systematically collect data that allows establishing patterns with any statistical significance.

Investors will not know whether information exists or is relevant, and in many cases information does not exist at all. All of this implies a very high probability of making investment errors even if all available information is taken into account. In these situations, mathematical probability assignments usually cannot be made and managers should be warned of the false sense of mathematical precision. On the other hand, less data and high 'fuzziness' of information may even be indicative of better opportunities. As the Yale Investment Office's David Swensen observed, 'you outperform by finding inefficiencies most of the market has not yet uncovered'.[5]

Institutional investors who rely on outside advice rather than deciding based on their own market intelligence cannot perform better than their peers, as consultants make money by giving advice to as many people as possible. Rather than trying to eliminate uncertainty, private equity investors create value by continuously operating in an opaque environment and pushing into pockets of uncertainty, as this is where inefficiencies and opportunities for arbitrage are most likely to be found. They finance new ideas and inventions before others have realised their potential.

It is a common fallacy to confuse absence of data with higher risk. In fact, the more that is known about an opportunity and the longer it exists, the lower the potential usually is. Rich data implies consensus and, as an extreme consequence, herding. For example, when there is a verifiable track record ranging over several predecessor funds, it often is too late as the fund may be oversubscribed, the terms and conditions unattractive or the fund manager becoming complacent.

Proprietary information as competitive advantage

The trade-off is between information that is kept proprietary and information that is shared with others. Unlike in the case of publicly quoted securities, the private equity manager can legally employ inside information, such as management projections, in its investment process. Consequently, superior strategies are based on – compared to the funds' competitors – better knowledge and understanding of the environment. With a reasonable portfolio size, investors have access to up-to-date and rich information in the area they are active in and therefore is likely to concern them most. There are thus diminishing returns of scale, as one can also work with imperfect information and fill gaps applying one's own judgment.

Many institutional investors therefore create and maintain their own databases on industry statistics. They have privileged access to data on the funds they have invested in and are not constrained by the standard format and detail of data made available by external providers. These investors can therefore develop their own methodologies, and their reporting formats can go beyond what is required under industry standard reporting guidelines and even include portfolio company information. The quality of internal data is generally better but may often be biased according to the specific investment style.

From rutter to gutter

Data follows a lifecycle driven by the associated costs (see **Figure 18.1**): initially nobody has sufficient knowledge on a new market segment, which carries too much risk of wrong decisions due to the high uncertainty. Proprietary research into this market segment reduces this uncertainty and gives private knowledge for superior investment decisions. From an outside perspective, this research may produce poor-quality data with no or little consensus on its interpretation but it is highly valuable for the owner of this research.

While perfect information is out of reach, it is sufficient to have better intelligence and to make use of it quicker than competing investors. To keep with the analogy of the trade voyages, we may compare this proprietary research to the 'rutters' (the Portuguese 'roteiros') compiled by pilots on the highly risky, exploratory voyages during medieval times. These rutters carefully documented the progress of each expedition providing a step-by-step chronicle,

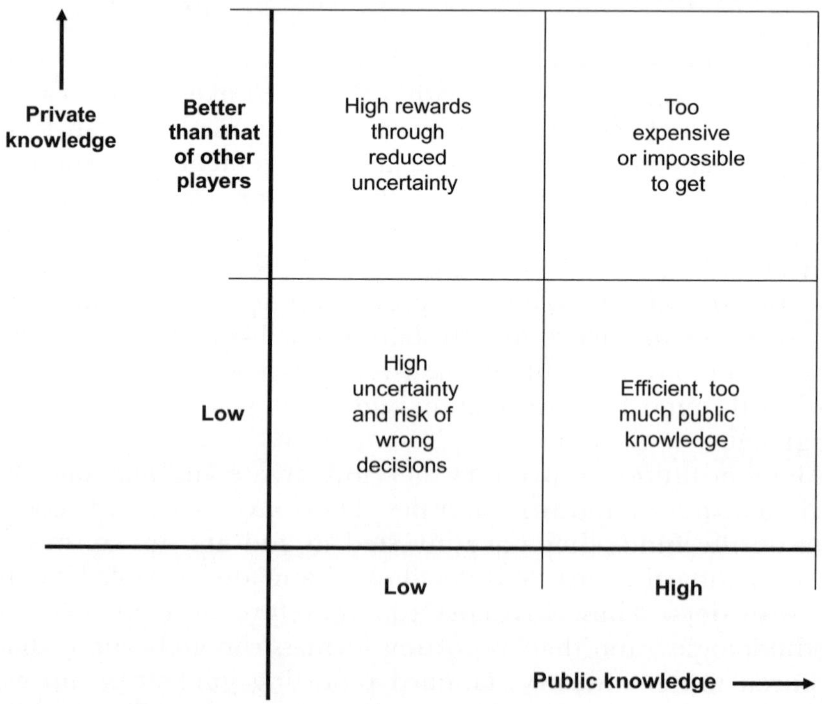

Figure 18.1 Cost of data for superior decision-making

providing information such as the colour of the water, which was useful for navigating the journey out and the journey back. They were regarded as too precious to publish and, in fact, were often declared to be state secrets with betrayal punishable by death.[6] With increasingly detailed maps, however, these trade routes could not be kept confidential any longer and competitors eventually took all excess profits away.

Over time, and with increasing success, it becomes ever more difficult to keep the knowledge about a profitable market segment secret and more and more data reaches the public domain, attracting competing investors. With data and increasing consensus, market intelligence ceases to be a differentiator. Finally it becomes next to impossible to keep an edge over what is already widely known – which is also an indication for investors to move on. In fact, the more data that is available on a specific segment of the market and the higher its quality, the more money has already gone into it and the less return potential remains for future investing.

The Need for Judgment

According to *The Economist*, 'In financial markets, the word transparency is nearly always equated with information disclosure.'[7] Being able to sift through external low-quality data and link it with internal high-quality data to produce research or to run proprietary models often gives an edge. For outside observers, the intransparency and confidentiality of the industry is difficult to accept, but it is the combination of skills, experience and proprietary research, in the absence of published data that defines successful private equity investing. Here, incomplete and inaccurate but timely and proprietary information has more value than detailed and highly accurate but outdated data available to the public.

The behaviour that is considered to be prudent in public markets is likely to lead to underperformance in alternative assets. We can associate more and better data with reduced return potential and thus with a higher risk of not meeting set objectives for financial returns. Too much data implies too little experimentation. Successful investors profit by exploiting market inefficiencies. Scarce capital and few rivals imply better prices, more opportunities and result in high returns. Unfortunately, successes also attract capital and competition and lead to a scarcity of profitable opportunities. From the LP perspective, it is not only absence of data which is an issue.

In many cases, available data is irrelevant, not only because it cannot be properly interpreted, but also because LPs usually cannot act upon its insights.

Another trade-off is between detail and intelligence. With growing assets under management, a number of companies in the portfolio and wider geographic spread, the operational tempo increases and in parallel reduces the time available for analysing and interpreting data in order to see the big picture. Moreover, as more information is dug up, the number of additional inquiries increases, as many managers want to get a synopsis of all possible opportunities in all dimensions. With additional data, further unknowns come up and challenge findings that were already regarded as certain. As a consequence, decisions are delayed in expectance of the latest findings, which allows time to drill into new areas. What often is perceived as aversion to risk would more aptly be described as 'decision aversion'. Eventually the decision will be made by a competing but quicker investor, a situation that occurs actually quite often. Spending too much time on irrelevant data is akin to losing the race against time. Investors need to focus on the essential. Short-term developments that deviate from the expected long term may also be signals that other scenarios are evolving. The short term therefore cannot be ignored entirely, but likewise it is dangerous to pursue any opportunity that comes up. This opportunity may well signal changes in the environment, but equally could be 'noise' that is not representative and may lead to failure.

Trust, not Transparency

Despite all the criticisms, more progress has been made in regards to transparency than is often acknowledged, which creates another problem: easily available information invites micromanagement and interference by LPs who simply 'know too much' and thus take away precisely the initiative and flexibility the GPs need to become successful. In private equity, much information is potentially available, but it needs to be analysed and understood. This can only be done locally as changes are too quick for centralised institutional investors to react. Flexibility also means the ability to make something out of the information as it is collected and new things are learned about an environment. According to Desportes (2007), the basic principle is to give actors room for initiative while setting a framework for collective action that preserves meaning and purpose.

Going against the grain is only possible for investment professionals who are trusted by their sponsors. The ever louder calls for transparency in the financial industry to a large degree reflect a crisis of trust. In fact, this is another size limitation of the private equity industry. Trust is not scalable and the supply of trusted GPs could not keep up with the demand for such firms. Even if all data is put on the table, its assessment and interpretation ultimately relies on professional opinion. As much as LPs, the public and regulators entertain this idea, trust cannot be replaced through disclosure.

Speed Read

- Investment strategies are to a large degree based on an informational advantage. A lack of widely available data in private equity markets is an advantage to those who can merge information from various sources and apply judgment to their interpretation.
- Private equity operates in markets that are neither efficient nor regulated. Here intelligence and networks form the basis of an investment strategy; the opacity of this market makes approaches based on secrecy and proprietary insights feasible.
- In private equity, the investment strategy also has to answer the question how to search for opportunities and identify the best proposals and do this ahead of competing investors.
- The more data is available on a specific segment of the market and the higher its quality, the more money has already gone into it and the less return potential remains for future investing.

Chapter 19

Spreading Risks – Part II

The challenge of portfolio management in private equity is unusual because it takes place within an unknown and changing landscape – the primary job is to search for pockets of opportunity. The role of diversification is also idiosyncratic – we employ it because we do not know where exactly to search for opportunities and whether our search will be successful.

Immediately, investors in private equity are faced with a challenge, since managers tend to refer to investment strategies in terms of classifications such as, for example, leveraged buyouts, venture capital, mezzanine debt, distressed investing, special situations investing and growth capital.[1] Such classifications may serve as a rejection criterion, i.e., the proposal 'does not meet our strategy' or to define restrictions, such as 'we do not invest in first-time funds'. However, private equity is an extremely heterogeneous asset class which is very difficult to classify. Rather than seeing them as 'strategies', these classifications describe types of private equity investments with very different characteristics. They help investors who need to understand the different performance drivers in order to make informed decisions about diversification, or for a risk factor allocation approach that seeks to exploit diversification gains from uncorrelated investment risks.[2]

Diversification as Search

Diversification aims to reduce risks and depends on correlations between the various assets held. To achieve a good degree of protection for assuring survival, portfolios should comprise assets that perform independently from each other or are even negatively correlated. Investing through funds allows coverage of larger geographical areas, but incurs the danger of overdiversification, where the potential upside is diversified away as well. Stacking a portfolio with too many similar investments will lead to a regression of the mean. Does an investor really need several firms from the same category in his portfolio? Because figures on correlation are unreliable, unstable or not available at all, portfolio construction rather aims to assure a high degree of independence between various targets.

In the context of the Adaptive Market Hypothesis (AMH), the lack of correlation – important for diversification – therefore takes on another meaning. Diversification is not only relevant as an instrument for managing risk but also part of a search algorithm, employing a cycle of trial and error before scaling up what works. Searching in 'uncorrelated' market segments assures that costs are minimised by avoiding searching in the same area or searching there twice. A very high level of diversification is even beneficial when pursued within a real option strategy, but too expensive without it. Investors who either do not recognise the value of optionality or let the options essentially expire as they lack the process to exercise them, tend to suffer from adverse effects associated with overdiversification.

Dimensions

For long-term illiquid assets such as private equity funds – for which no correlation data is available or considered to be reliable – diversification over various dimensions needs to be specifically managed. Investors see the stage focus, the vintage year, the broad industry sector (such as ICT, life science, generalists), the geographical region (such as the US, Asia, Western Europe, Eastern Europe, emerging markets), the currency and the agent or counterparty concentration, i.e., the exposure to a specific fund manager, as the main dimensions of private equity portfolio diversification.[3] Some are specific to private equity, such as the stage focus and the vintage year; others are also applicable for standard asset classes, such as the industry sector, the geography, the currency or the agent concentration.

In principle, the higher the resolution for each dimension, the more we will be able to differentiate between funds, but definitions can only be very fuzzy. For example, the investment focus is mainly based on the self-declaration of the managers, and drifts in strategy are common. Does 'geography' relate to the fund or to the portfolio companies? Probably the fund's location is the 'best guess', but some are operating in several countries. For such questions certainly rules can be drawn up, but it can become quite complex and we also have to ask ourselves the question of how we can manage this. In reality, for most of these dimensions, only a 'low resolution' will be practical. In any case, such a classification can only be very general and quite coarse. We limit this discussion to a classification according to type of intermediation, focus of the intermediary, the intervention approach, the type of the targeted investment and the market.

Intermediation

The number of GPs, with their specific management 'style' and their specialised expertise in a particular segment of the market, is one of the key dimensions to consider when building a portfolio.

Agent concentration

Maintaining a relationship with the same GP extending over several funds reduces the need for screening and pre-investment due diligence work and thus saves the investors time and money. However, during the normally ten plus two years lifetime of a fund, it is quite likely that a fund management team will go through a crisis situation, such as tensions among the team members, the departure of a key person, or the spin-out of part of the team. Having relationships with several GPs mitigates the potential over-reliance upon a few key investment professionals.

Delegation

In an environment of high opacity and uncertainty, success depends to a large degree on subsidiarity, where things are handled by the smallest possible unit that can manage them with efficacy. In many situations, delegating investment authority to intermediaries, such as funds, and giving them freedom of decision-making can be more conducive to success than micromanaging by directly investing. Fund-of-funds investing in itself can be argued to allow for diversification as the portfolio of funds is spread across various set-ups, sectors and geographies. Co-investing could be seen as a hybrid standing between direct investments and involving an intermediary.

Focus

Intermediaries fall in two broad categories: specialists focusing, for instance, on country, sector or type of transaction, while generalist funds do different types of deals across many industry sectors and countries. Typically, high technology risk leads to favouring specialist over generalist funds that often lack deep expertise in, for example, sectors such as telecom, IT, biotech and life sciences, or specific private equity stages, including seed capital and early-stage ventures. Managers who have devoted their careers to building an industry-specific knowledge base and developing unique business relationships, should be best positioned to invest successfully in a given sector. Their unique skill sets and their ability to identify good deals and screen out bad ones are expected to lead to attractive returns.

Interventionist approach

Depending on the type of intermediary intervention, and whether the investment is more efficiency- or entrepreneurially-oriented, approaches can be markedly different in regards to value creation, financial instruments used and control applied.

Investors in private equity can create value through financial, operational, strategic or restructuring expertise. Financial engineering is typically used to increase the leverage at a portfolio company and depends on the availability of credit. Increasing the earnings of a portfolio company will create value in all circumstances but is more difficult.

Another dimension to consider is the instrument used – equity and/or debt. Equity theoretically has an unlimited upside and thus becomes more important the longer the investment horizon. On the other hand, selling equity, particularly controlling stakes, requires more skills and effort than liquidating debt. Investors with deep sector expertise are better placed to identify the right buyers and present the sale in the most compelling light. Under normal circumstances, debt is self-liquidating but in the case where the company defaults on the loan, the lender has the right to convert into its equity. In between is mezzanine, which is typically used to finance the expansion of existing companies. It is actually closer to equity, as it is generally subordinated to debt provided by senior lenders.

Investors in venture capital typically use no debt and gain control of a company over time through a series of equity investments. Return stems from building companies and from managing growth. Buyout funds typically use debt financing with significant leverage to purchase all, or substantially all, of a company's equity. Assets of the acquired company are used as collateral for the debt, and the cash flow of the company is used to pay it off.

Control

One aspect of control is the trade-off with intermediation. Clearly, the fund-of-funds route leads to a certain loss of control for an institutional investor. It is also related to the approach to value creation. Control-oriented investing makes sense in situations where active operational and managerial interventions are beneficial, or where – for instance, through high leverage – investors are exposed to increased risks. Where, on the other hand, a competent company management is in place, a non-controlling minority stake may be more motivating. Investors can also reserve some degree of negative control by being granted the right to veto certain decisions, such as those relating to capital expenditure, dividends and executive remuneration.

Target

Investments can be broadly classified by the targeted size and stage focus, reflecting their maturity.

Size of target company

The size of the targeted investment is one classification dimension and needs to be in line with the investment objectives, as various factors such as management resources or number of potential opportunities implicitly set a maximum size for the capital to be put at work. What is considered 'small', 'medium' or 'large' depends on the type of investment: a small buyout would, in terms of commitment, dwarf a typical VC deal.

For buyout investments, on the other hand, there are generally few limitations to investment size, as there is a high number of stable-growth and mature companies that can be targeted and opportunities to employ large amounts of capital in these transactions. For funds, their size has implications for the management fees. Too small fund sizes are uneconomical whereas for funds that are too large, the alignment of interests between fund managers and LPs becomes weaker.

Stage focus

Another way to classify private equity investments is by stage. Stage focus categories are arguably easier to define for venture capital, where seed stage, early stage and later stage can be clearly identified. For buyouts, typically focusing on companies that are mature or even in decline, this rarely makes sense. Spreading investments across companies at various stages of maturity also leads to a staggered pace of realisations and thus less dependence upon market conditions at particular points in time.

Finally, a problem that makes a classification by stage focus difficult is that portfolio companies grow over the portfolio build-up. Indeed, seed investments are expected to germinate and allow the business to start. After these early stages, these investments, when successful, will expand and develop during their later stages to end up, finally and hopefully, in fruitful exits. This implies that after several years, the risk profile of a fund will change with the evolution of its portfolio companies. To take this into account, investors can either adjust the stage focus of their funds with the evolution of their portfolio companies or, more simply, take the vintage year as one of the diversification dimensions.

Market Environment

A broad categorisation of the market environment is by industry sectors, geographies and, related to geographies, macroeconomic factors such as currencies, interest rates and exit environment. Investors should focus on the most promising industries and geographies where they can add value.

Industry sector

Industry sectors differ in various aspects, such as their size and rate of growth, availability of targets and competitiveness. Specialist managers can build up proprietary insights about impending shifts in relative market share, emerging new opportunities and other industry-shaping trends, and turn these insights into themes underlying their investment strategy.

Also, spreading investments across different industry sectors protects against a sector temporarily going out of favour, like the Internet after 2000, or against cyclical industries. In case of intermediation through funds, investors have to rely on the fund managers' declared industry focus – which usually will be in accordance with definitions and categories set by industry data providers or used by industry associations like the EVCA. To some degree, relying on such standard industry codes could be seen as driving by looking in the rear-view mirror as they just reflect established industries and do not cater for the newly emerging sectors that, in fact, may offer the best opportunities. Consequently, investors are well advised to complement these standards with their own categorisations.

Geography

In the private equity industry, funds initially have been raised, investments have been made and exits have been achieved primarily domestically, but since the mid-1990s the private equity market has increasingly internationalised. This trend has been especially pronounced in the growth of cross-border capital commitments. However, geographical diversification principles tend to be based on rules of thumb rather than on systematic analysis.[4] In fact, interviewees in Heikkilä (2004) appeared to be more careful in diversifying their portfolios across investment stages – specifically venture capital versus buyouts – than across geographical areas. Some of the interviewees claimed that rather than spending too much time calculating potential benefits of geographical diversification, the more relevant issue is to consider the management teams of the funds, an assumption which – based on the discussion in the chapter on performance persistency – does not necessarily hold.

In terms of geography, investors can focus on one country, a few countries or a region. A distinction can also be made between investing in developed markets and those targeting emerging markets. Also related to geographies are access to credit, depending on interest rates, or the exit environment, via IPOs on local stock markets or through acquisitions by larger companies operating in the markets or a sale to other financial investors.

Vintage year

Market environments can change significantly over time. Therefore, private equity investments should be staggered over the full course of the economic cycle and should not be concentrated in any one year to reduce the risk of getting in or out at the wrong time. Practical experience has shown that vintage years diversification has the strongest impact.[5] If deals are done around the same time and with similar debt profiles, they would respond similarly to the development of the economy.[6] In standard private equity funds, the total capital available gets invested mostly during the investment period, i.e., the first three to five years of the fund's lifetime, but also afterwards, in a more targeted manner, to follow on the most successful investments. The distributions of capital to LPs are done as soon as investments get exited, mostly during the divestment period, i.e., the remaining fund's lifetime. One issue that investors can encounter in their effort to get an adequate vintage year diversification is when too many current GP relationships come back on to market in the same year. Obviously a trade-off between fund manager quality and vintage year diversification has then to be made.

Managing portfolio composition

In practice, classifications often go together: for buyouts opportunities tend to be of larger size, are predominantly in industries from the 'old economy' and with a more generalist nature, whereas venture capital typically comprises smaller and more technology-oriented investments that tend to be more concentrated in fewer industries.

Profiling investments

Profiling according to these classification dimensions leads to the main types of investment strategies used in private equity, such as buyouts and venture capital discussed already. Growth capital refers to the funding of more mature companies that are looking for capital to expand or restructure operations, enter new markets, or finance a major acquisition, most often as minority investment without a change in the control of the business. Growth capital can be in the form of debt, often additionally from traditional sources such as banks, or as equity and mezzanine with often a final 'kicker' payment or share in the company's equity. Distressed debt investing can be control-oriented in combination with restructurings or in a non-control and trading-type approach. Restructuring investments in financially distressed companies tend to provide equity in order to take control. Mezzanine, moreover, defies the traditional classifications of lenders and equity investors. Real estate private equity funds invest exclusively in properties, using debt and equity. Investments in public infrastructure (such as roads, bridges, airports and public transportation) are highly relevant for emerging markets where the demand for new infrastructure is growing rapidly. These three are relatively new forms of private equity that are also indicative of new areas and the shifting boundaries of this landscape.

Risk factors

Classifications tie into various risk factors (see **Figure 19.1**). A risk factor allocation seeks to exploit diversification gains from uncorrelated investment risks.[7] Here, different risk factors are explicitly taken into account as they are assumed to offer a particular reward for investors. The challenge is to structure the portfolio, so that the various risks are kept well in balance. For instance, a portfolio of ten

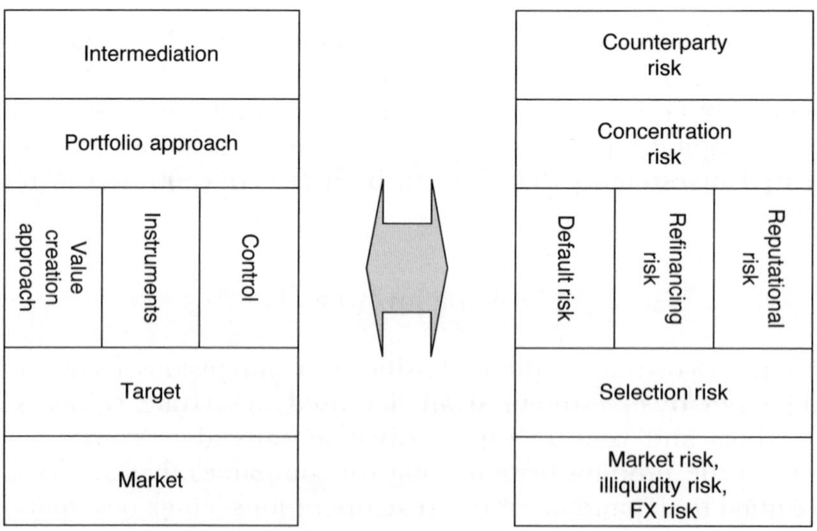

Figure 19.1 Classification and exposure to risk factors (simplified examples)

funds may look sufficiently diversified at first glance, but if they all belong to the same vintage year population, there is obviously too much concentration.

In fact, portfolios can be quite unbalanced when taking the time dimension into consideration, resembling the age pyramid of a human population: 50 per cent men and 50 per cent women may seem a good balance, but it is definitely a problem if the population only comprises women over the age of 90 and 'men' under the age of ten.

Achieving Portfolio Balance

One tool for managing a portfolio's balance is cluster analysis, a technique that is widely applied in a range of different research areas such as medicine, marketing and economics. It is used to classify similar objects into relatively homogenous groups and dissimilar objects into different groups. This technique cannot be applied wholesale to private equity, as the interpretation of the results is too subjective. Instead, in most cases it is sufficient to look at the degree at which a portfolio becomes 'clogged', i.e., tends to form clusters of sub-portfolios that cannot be seen as independent anymore. As an example consider two funds with three diversification dimensions: fund manager, vintage year and geography (see **Table 19.1**)

To analyse the tendency of a portfolio to clog, i.e., to form clusters, we look at different 'stress levels'. The stress level is the minimum distance two assets need to have in their classifications to be considered independent.[8] As in this case the classifications for 'fund manager' and 'vintage year' are different, the distance between these funds is two. One fund can be considered to be 'in reach' of another and be in the same cluster if the 'distance' is lower than the set stress level. Managing this properly allows investors to incur the same level of risk for lower diversification. Ideally a portfolio would

Table 19.1 Diversification dimensions

	Private equity fund 1	**Private equity fund 2**
Fund manager	ABC	UVW
Vintage year	2002	2006
Geography	Europe	Europe

be diversified over all risk dimensions and clog incrementally with increasing stress levels.

Such a classification is certainly to some degree judgmental and subjective. On the other hand, the classification process can be supported by a scoring process or by having several analysts assigning classifications to the same investments independently and reviewing their conclusions. This can mitigate the fear that classifications are manipulated to achieve a certain allocation target.

It is often said that fund managers should be monitored to assure that they stay within their competencies, which are typically specified in advance in the fund's limited partnership agreement. The classification of strategies may, at least in theory, establish a reference point for identifying style drifts. However, a classification by styles, while typical for managing assets with short-term investment horizons and where trading is possible, makes little sense for long-term oriented private equity with exposure to continuously changing economic conditions and where flexibility is required.

Speed Read

- Investors in search of diversification seek assets that behave differently to the rest of their portfolio.
- The label chosen for these assets is not relevant, and so a proper classification of private equity investments is an important tool for managing diversification.
- This can be achieved, albeit with a level of subjectivity. Ideally a portfolio would be diversified over all risk dimensions even under stress. This allows investors to incur the same risk for lower levels of costly diversification.

Chapter 20

Open-Ended Relationships

Nature's solution for bridging longer distances in the fitness landscape is – sex. Without stretching this analogy too far, engaging in a relationship between strong parents can increase the offspring's chances in the future significantly. During the lifetime of a fund, the interests of the GPs and the LPs are so closely aligned that the fund can be seen as an entity combining to some degree positive and negative characteristics, i.e., the 'genetic code', of fund managers and their investors. For the institutional investor, searching for suitable funds requires significant effort, and due diligence, structuring, and subsequent monitoring are quite expensive. The 'pairing' between LPs and GPs usually goes beyond the actual fund, with the 'genetic code' defining the relationship being passed on to follow-on funds.

Few, if any, private equity investment strategies recognise the presence of often simultaneously competing and collaborating LPs, but social relationships between market participants and their 'power' in the widest sense play an important role. LPs often also compete against each other; because of the funds' restricted scalability investing in this sector one LP's gain can be the other's loss. Conventional wisdom suggests that in the private equity market personal networks and alliances on the one hand, and personal rivalries, status or animosities on the other hand, play an important role and have an impact on the information flow and who gets access to funds.

Are LPs Just Passive Investors?

In efficient markets, managers can passively structure their portfolio to closely mimic the market. In inefficient alternative markets there are no 'safe' assets and managers continuously need to search for suitable opportunities. Particularly, private equity requires an active investment strategy by managers who typically try to be transformational and bring significant value-addition to the companies in which they invest. A passive index-tracking approach comparable to that of public market players is not feasible in private equity, as one LP's portfolio cannot be replicated by another LP.[1]

On the other hand, LP investing in private equity is viewed as passive, and because of the long lifetimes of funds, emphasis is put on extreme care and specialist skills when selecting GPs and not getting involved in the day-to-day management of the fund's portfolio.[2] This picture, however, is incomplete and there are various degrees of active involvement investors can take. For LPs there is wide spectrum between being passive and active.

One extreme are passive LPs that are not willing to back emerging managers and require a track record spanning several funds. They operate with standard terms and conditions and follow the recommendations of gatekeepers and consultants. Such LPs only commit to established 'institutional quality' GPs and 'brands', or follow the example of other LPs by coming in after a fund's first closing, essentially 'free riding' on other institutions' investment acumen. Proposals that do not fit into their standard due diligence will be rejected. Passive LPs take smaller stakes in funds, follow other LPs when fund-related issues need to be sorted out, do not step in for defaulting investors and do not make secondary transactions. In their monitoring, they rely on standard reporting and have little informal communication with the fund managers. They either do not co-invest at all or only evaluate opportunities that are offered to them by the GPs.

At the other end of the spectrum there are active LPs that aim to improve the payoff of their investments in funds, perhaps by negotiating more favourable terms and conditions. They explore the emerging spaces of the private equity market and cornerstone emerging teams. Such LPs research the market, conduct their own due diligence and take larger stakes in funds. Active LPs source co-investments instead of waiting for a GP's proposals, replace defaulting LPs and do secondary deals.[3]

The GP/LP Relationship

A number of studies discuss the relationship between managers of private equity funds and their investors in general.[4] GPs as well as their LPs have an interest in maintaining a relationship over the longer term. For a GP the certification effect brought by a reputable institution has a clear value, as it significantly eases the current and future fundraisings, and can give access to deep pockets in case something goes off course during the fund's lifetime. The costs of switching relationships are huge, as in such an opaque market also GPs that lose key investors can be perceived as 'lemons'. There is certainly a 'symbiotic' relationship between GPs and LPs.

Not surprisingly, 'marriage' and 'divorce' are often used in the context of relationships between fund managers and their investors.[5] It is an oversimplification to assume that investors only invest in top performers and that below-average funds are unable to continue. As in most relationships, there is a certain degree of tolerance for mistakes and failures, at least for some time.

GPs need to raise new funds as soon as the capital from the existing partnership is fully invested, that is, about once every three to five years. Relationships between LPs and GPs are forged over several rounds, resulting in a virtuous circuit of growing experience and fund size, and so on (see **Figure 20.1**).

The lifecycle of the GP/LP relationship matches the exploration, observation, amplification and exploitation cycle for searching and growing in the private equity landscape, as described before. For this discussion, we distinguish four phases in the lifecycle of the GP/LP relationship: entry, growth, maturity and 'death', i.e., decline (losing to competition, LPs do not commit further) or exit (GPs giving up or retiring).

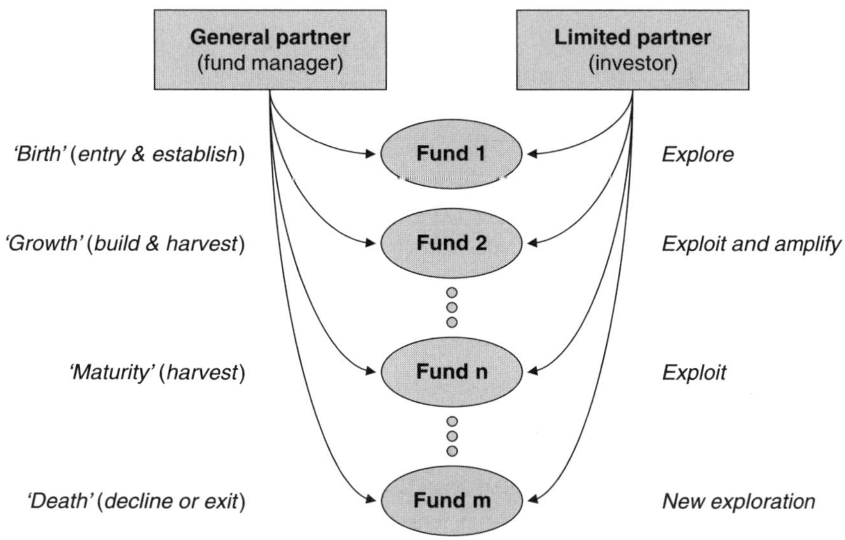

Figure 20.1 GP/LP relationship lifecycle model[6]

'Birth'

It is fair to interpret the occasionally difficult initial fundraising process as 'courtship'. Initially criteria are very stringent, and GPs usually cannot get rich through their first funds. Entry barriers exist for investors and for funds. It is clear that, lacking a verifiable track record, new teams find it difficult to raise their first fund. LPs that are pioneers are likely to be of more value to the GPs than followers. Their reputation is helpful for attracting other investors, they can bring investment opportunities to the funds, and they can provide additional funding in the form of co-investments.

New LPs, on the other hand, also face entry barriers. For example, they do not usually have access to the best funds, particularly where managers are oversubscribed and often need to use gatekeepers.

'Growth'

To minimise their expenses, fund managers, provided that their previous relationships were satisfactory, generally turn first to those who invested in their previous partnership. A favourable track record and experience is an asset in itself. It conveys information on ability and suggests that GPs take extra care to protect their reputations. Fundraising is less costly for more reputable funds.

During the growth phase the funds managed by the GP tend to be still relatively small and sometimes too small to allow larger commitments. GPs are said to search for 'deep pocket' LPs with a low probability of facing a liquidity shock that could lead to default or to withdrawing from the asset class, and who regardless of the financial markets' status are likely to quickly commit to the funds the GP raises in the future.[7] There is anecdotal evidence that investors that do not invest in one fund will be excluded from the best GPs' next fundraisings.[8]

For a GP switching to other LPs carries a high risk not just because of the delays associated with searching for new investors but also because of the strong dependence on loyal long-term relationships for future fundraisings. Moreover, GPs are looking for support in a wider sense, i.e., engagement with the firm over the long term. For example, endowments and foundations therefore belong to the most desired group of LPs. Being long-term oriented leads to a better understanding of market terms and conditions and allegedly to fairer negotiations between fund managers and investors, a stronger alignment of their interests, and efficient communication and constructive trouble-shooting throughout the relationship.[9] Foreign LPs also provide important international contacts for portfolio companies or exits.

'Maturity'

Mature GPs with a strong LP base face little difficulty raising follow-on funds. There are, however, limits to growth in terms of fund size and associated fees. As discussed in a previous chapter already, increasing fund sizes beyond a certain point are paralleled by a gradual decline in returns. Funds that are believed to be 'top-quartile' could try to charge higher fees. To some degree this does happen, as 'brand GPs' able to raise larger fund sizes tend not to reduce their relative fees as much as they theoretically could. However, raising fees above what is perceived to be market practice can be stopped by incumbent LPs. In case these LPs threaten not to re-invest, GPs tend to give in to avoid damaging their reputation.[10]

The chemistry between GP and LP is important, but on the other hand, inertia, i.e., the lack of being reactive to a changing environment, can become a problem and relationships need to be critically reviewed and, if necessary, reduced or even terminated. For instance, a GP creating too many funds in quick succession and increasing their sizes can be a signal to reduce or even exit the relationship.

'Death'

It is clear that there are limits to disappointing results but, all things being equal, investors would tend to go with fund managers they already know or who have been referred to them through their network, rather than with new teams. There is, of course, a downside, as many LPs will decide to invest in the follow-on, because they comfort themselves that it is 'too early to tell' and because they believe that maintaining the relationship is important. It may end, for instance, once the fund manager has 'made it' and is not interested in raising another fund. Few GPs manage to institutionalise and plan succession. Also, the LPs could eventually end the relationship if they lose confidence or trust in the team. It is probably rather a gradual decline. Some LPs do not invest in follow-on funds and need to be replaced with less than deep-pocket investors, or by secondary investors who see this rather as a 'one-off' financial play. In many ways the relationship might live on in its progeny, for instance, teams spun-out or approaches imitated by others. It is not just failures of GPs that make LPs end the relationship. It is also competition in the form of more promising spaces in the private equity market.

How much is a Relationship Worth?

Relationships are of different strength and quality and are indicative of the investor's 'game strength',[11] relating to his ability to successfully execute certain investment strategies.[12] Therefore relationships have a value which, however, is difficult to quantify. An important aspect is the targeted investment horizon, as a long-term relationship is of little relevance for a short-term oriented investor. There is clearly a link with the size of the investor's mandate and the resources the LP needs to put to work. For a mandate of small size, relationships with GPs raising small funds is valuable, whereas for investors with larger assets under management their impact on the portfolio may be too insignificant and the relationships becomes uneconomical. Also the ability to increase an LP's stake either in an existing fund or subsequent funds with growth in size, needs to be taken into consideration.

Other factors that may be taken into account are, for instance, how challenging it is to get access to the GP and how scarce, unknown or special it is. For the oversubscribed 'institutional quality' funds for many investors – in relative terms, as absolute amounts can be substantial – only small stakes are possible, and the high number of potential LPs allows the GPs to reject special deals. For niche players, that are often shunned by institutional investors because they are perceived to be of weaker quality, larger stakes are possible and allow the negotiation of more favourable terms and conditions.

Another aspect is the relative share an LP has in a fund. For example, a small stake in fund can result in a high ability to engage in secondary transactions with the other LPs, but it can also imply an ability to maintain the relationship with the firm in future funds. Likewise, a high stake in a fund can result in a high ability to maintain and influence the relationship, but would result in a low ability to execute secondary purchases, as additional stakes in the same fund would push the LP over its allocation threshold.

The costs associated with due diligence, management fees, monitoring, analysis and so on, tend to be larger for emerging GPs or for private equity firms that experience problems and are in decline. The ability to do co-investments along side the funds carries a significant value, perhaps in the form of a relative reduction in management fees or as a way to improve the LP's portfolio balance. For long-term oriented LPs the expected remaining lifetime of the relationship which depends on the GP's 'survival probability' is of additional relevance. LPs may also put a value on backing a potential 'spin-out' of a competent and experienced investment management team from a firm that otherwise is less attractive. The network, intelligence and inside information gained from the interaction with a firm's other LPs can also imply the 'right to play' in other areas of the private equity market.

Imitation and Independence

Being an investor dedicated to the private equity asset class, and being able to decide independently from one's peers or even being contrarian, is more likely to be the basis for generating superior performance.

The LP/LP relationship

Access may be a problem for a handful of buyout funds and some VC funds, typically 'Silicon Valley brands', but only a minority of institutional investors report that they ever had part of their money rejected and even where this was the case, the fraction of the rejected capital was said to be negligible.[13] Rather than access, lack of knowledge of the best opportunities and the fact that the best funds close too quickly for getting on the radar screen of most institutional investors pose an obstacle for LPs. In this respect, the network built with a GP's other LPs carries a significant value. LPs who are perceived as thought leaders, promote good corporate governance, and take a long view of what determines value, can open doors and provide market intelligence, and are imitated by less experienced LPs.

Like-minded LPs can form alliances for investing for specific objectives (such as ESG) and in specific market spaces. They can also create non-standard investment vehicles that take away the cyclicality of the typical fund life and make funding more permanent, decide the terms and conditions to reduce costs and even recruit a fund management team.

Follow the herd?

Obviously there is far less scope for differentiating oneself and for negotiating special terms and conditions when just following the example of the larger LPs and by investing in the mainstream of funds.

What is often termed as 'best practice' is often a lack of independent thinking: strategy is essentially replaced by following, often mindlessly, investors that are perceived as having high skills. To some degree, this imitation could be interpreted as a solution to a principle dilemma investment professionals as individuals face: how to invest in an alternative asset class where innovation is key while acting on behalf of risk-averse institutions that essentially shy away from any experimentation. 'Best practice' is one solution for avoiding being penalised for failures and bridging 'conservative attitude' with 'progressive investing'. Copying the behaviour and the decisions of respected peers that appear to have better insights helps to address environmental uncertainty as well as overcoming doubts within one's own organisation. On the other hand, simply imitating cannot result in above-average performance, unless there are cost advantages or the peers' mistakes can be avoided.

Being a follower has advantages as well, as it not only allows learning from and avoiding the mistakes made by the pioneers. A follower can also reduce uncertainty and base its decisions on identified opportunities and on current knowledge about a market's characteristics and players. Investors who copy the pioneers' practices can expect to incur lower costs and risks, but in the extreme this can result in herd behaviour where the majority are imitators and try to free-ride, assuming that their peers base their decisions on private information. 'Herding' can even be a sound strategy under uncertainty, but by running uncontroversial investment strategies run by many others in the industry, LPs end up with portfolios of funds that are exposed to the 'flavour of the day'.

Boldly go where no LP has gone before?

Being a pioneer essentially requires going alone which can be a problem for LPs who for a number of reasons cannot be the only investor in a fund and therefore rely on other LPs also wanting to enter an emerging market space. For entering such niches, private equity investors can partner with Development Financing Institutions (DFIs) that focus on emerging markets or venture capital in established economies. The role of DFIs in creating the landscape and to some degree enabling LPs to become a first mover is extremely important. For the DFIs attracting capital from highly regulated institutional investors and industrial countries also brings ESG-standards that avoid the extremes of conduct for which capitalism is often criticised in developing countries. The existence of large and cash-rich DFIs can support the emergence of a class of quality GPs and attract pools of capital from experienced and commercially oriented LPs.[14] Moreover, DFIs have a strong role as a 'credible threat' in case commercial investors are experiencing problems with the government officials, its bureaucracy or the legal system in a developing country.

Managing Portfolios of Relationships

Instead of looking at portfolios of funds, long-term oriented investors should rather look at managing portfolios of relationships. The idea of a relationship between LPs and GPs that can be managed but is also subject to a natural lifecycle may be difficult to accept and appear to be of little practical relevance to short-term oriented investors or LPs in the process of entering the private equity market. For many investors the long time period necessary to play on GP/LP relationship lifecycle goes far beyond their investment horizon and cannot be turned into an investment strategy beyond short-term oriented techniques, such as employing high leverage.

For example, private equity firms managing funds-of-funds provide a solution to this mismatch between relatively short-term investments in private equity funds and very long-term oriented GP/LP relationships. Players in the funds-of-funds industry could justifiably be called 'due diligence factories' and 'relationship warehouses' that package funds raised by GPs with whom they have built long-term relationships into commingled or tailor-made fund of funds vehicles.[15] The additional management fees charged for funds-of-funds implicitly compensate for the costs of exploration, i.e., the failed experiments. In this respect, investors in funds-of-funds get access to immediate exploitation of relationships with confirmed potential and can avoid the costly exploration stage.

Moreover, newcomers to private equity investing will find it difficult to judge whether a GP is beyond its 'sell by date' and in decline, a judgment that requires significant insight knowledge gained over long periods of monitoring.

Also, managing portfolios of relationships is about finding a trade-off between two types of modes – the 'exploitation mode' for existing relationships with consistently performing GPs and the 'exploration mode' to develop new relationships with emerging teams. Simplistically, and as explained before, relationships between institutional investors and private equity firms follow a lifecycle that is to some degree comparable to that described by the Boston Consulting Group's well known matrix, distinguishing four types of business units: 'question marks', 'stars', 'cash cows' and 'dogs' (see **Figure 20.2**). At the 'birth' of the relationship the 'question marks' are the funds raised by emerging GPs that are unproven but may develop into the future 'stars'. These 'question marks' require slack resources to absorb the losses of failed experiments.

Despite the higher perceived risks, an LP invests in a GP without a proven track record because being an investor in prior funds is the best – and in the case of some top GPs the only – way to gain

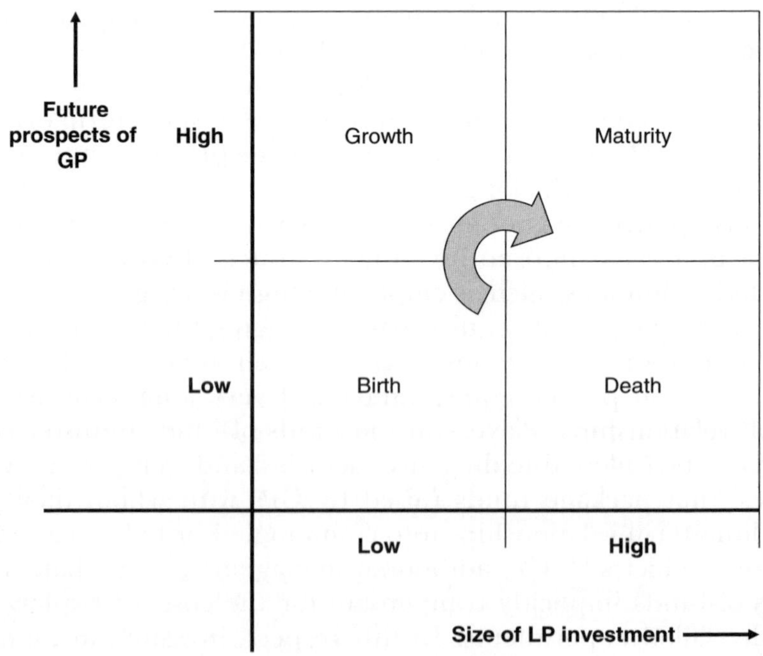

Figure 20.2 Managing portfolios of relationships

access to subsequent funds.[16] Being an investor in one of a GP's funds provides insights that make reinvestment decisions more reliable, so building access to emerging GPs is a critical part of the LP's approach to portfolio management.[17]

The 'stars' are going through their growth stage but funds raised by these GPs are not large enough to absorb larger commitments. Consequently, LPs need to consider techniques to amplify upside, for example by co-investments. In the 'star' category one could also put the oversubscribed 'golden circle' firms that have restricted the growth of assets under management to deliver consistent returns and typically do not accept investors outside their established group of LPs that often have been with them since the beginning. 'Stars' are arguably more a venture capital phenomenon, as buyout funds tend to be more scalable.

During maturity the relationships turn into 'cash cows', i.e., the institutional quality funds, mainly in the buyout sector that are relatively easy to access, but tend to raise funds above a size that is optimal for LPs and therefore deliver lower returns than 'stars' but also have a more substantial impact on the LPs' portfolio returns. 'Old dogs' are relationships at the end of their lifecycle, such as GPs facing succession crises, struggling with problematic portfolios or key persons leaving. Recognising these lifecycle characteristics allows LPs to build portfolios of relationships that find the right balance between exploration and exploitation.[18]

The LP/GP relationship can be thought of as a 'pairing' that supports a virtuous circle. Good historical performance results in higher trust in the fund managers' skills which leads LPs to give them more flexibility, which results in better returns. A stronger relationship allows a quicker reaction to newly emerging opportunities, as here GPs are able to access their LP basis and also other providers of capital and raise new funds more quickly than less trusted GPs. Similar reciprocal positive relationships between trust and success are reported to have a significant impact in other areas of the private equity market, such as the relationship between venture capitalists and the entrepreneurs they back.[19]

Speed Read

- The concept of the passive LP is an incomplete picture. In reality there is a spectrum, resulting in leaders and followers, and the former gaining a strong reputation among other GPs and other LPs.

- The GP/LP relationship is symbiotic and is often likened to a marriage where there can be a tolerance of faults for a certain period. The lifecycle of the GP/LP relationship encompasses four phases: entry; growth, maturity and decline or exit.
- Instead of looking at portfolios of funds, long-term oriented investors should rather manage portfolios of relationships. Investors where the long time period necessary to play on the GP/LP relationship lifecycle that goes beyond their investment horizon are restricted to relying on short-term oriented techniques, such as employing high leverage or going the fund-of-funds route.

Chapter 21

Hard and Soft Power

Management of uncertainty is central to strategy, with a struggle for freedom of action at its essence.[1] Success is inconceivable without the ability to tolerate uncertainty from the outset and during the implementation. It is a dictum not to invest in things one does not understand. On the other hand, no institution can bring all necessary expertise together to explore the private equity market and exploit identified opportunities. Instead, investment decisions need to be delegated to those best qualified to make them – an approach also embodied in the prudent investor rule.[2]

Centralised vs. Decentralised Decision-Making

The private equity industry is to a large degree organised around decentralised decision-making. Institutions tend to go through cycles in this regard, with the pendulum swinging in the direction of centralisation in recent years, as various prominent institutions have elected to invest directly. Of course centralised and decentralised decision-making are theoretical extremes and, for example, co-investments are a mixture of both.

The case for moving towards centralisation and investing directly is seductive. Not only is there a significant potential for cost savings, but investors have, at least in theory, far better control over portfolio composition. One major advantage of centralisation, and most probably one of the catalysts of this movement during and following the Great Recession, is that it offers senior management the opportunity to show strong leadership and tight control. It is also linked to the assumption that all information is available. In addition, the trend towards transparency invites micromanagement and can be seen as another catalyst.

However, bureaucracies of most large institutional investors will struggle to respond flexibly and with adequate speed – particularly as decisions are usually made in committees that strive for consensus. This of course brings different perspectives and insights to the discussion and in theory should lead to more robust decisions. On the other hand, it will take too much time to reach consensus and decisions are likely to end in the uncontroversial middle ground which is not conducive to experimentation and may prove ultimately more risky for alternative assets. Institutions who need to invest substantial amounts in private equity and therefore have to build up portfolios comprising many and geographically scattered, directly held companies, despite all progress in IT, will face an avalanche of information and requests for decisions, which could more than neutralise the theoretical advantages of centralisation.

Decentralisation, with GPs as intermediaries, allows quicker growth of portfolios and a wider geographical spread. Here decision-making is more diversified and thus enables more of the necessary experimentation. The downsides are significant inefficiencies, overlapping responsibilities between GPs and LPs, and it is far more difficult to ensure consistent practices and manage towards a targeted portfolio composition.

In the private equity market the 'pockets of profitability' and their opportunities are too small, too fleeting and too under-researched to allow central 'micromanagement' and interference in operations. To allow resilience, risk-taking, entrepreneurship and initiative, decentralisation based on accountability, trust and tolerance has been shown to be robust.[3] Funds could also be argued as a cultural transformation – from a bureaucratic institution where decision-making moves up and down a hierarchy and involves many parties, to an entrepreneurial-minded firm where decision-making is rapid and within a team of equals. Institutional investors are often criticised that their due diligence is excessive and their decision-making takes too much time. Fund managers as investment professionals are trained to understand where it becomes futile to look for more information and when they need to take a decision.

Adaptability and Flexibility

Growth and survival in an environment characterised by extreme uncertainty requires a high degree of adaptability and flexibility. For the purpose of this discussion, adaptation relates to changes in structure, whereas flexibility is adjusting to a new environment without changing the overall structure. Flexibility responds to short-term opportunities and threats in the private equity market landscape, whereas changes over the long term are addressed through adaptability. For example, adaptation happens when a new fund is raised with different investment strategy, focus, fund management team and LP basis. Flexibility and adaptation can take different forms, such as taking best practices from one market and applying them in a new environment or adjusting practices to cope with a changed environment.

The flipside of flexibility and adaptability are the so-called 'style drifts' and 'strategy drifts'. For hedge funds, style drift is one of the areas that causes concern for investors as it is seen as one of the major causes of investment failures.[4] A too close parallel to hedge funds, however, may be misguided as investors in private equity funds need to follow a different modus operandi. In the hedge fund world the concern regarding style drifts, where investors aim to control and regularly rebalance their portfolios of funds is justified, but in private equity a rebalancing of a portfolio of funds is clearly impractical. Because LPs cannot react to new information they should allow fund managers flexibility and allow them to adapt to changes in the market environment.[5]

Style drift

Style drift is a flexible response to changes in the market environment where fund managers identify areas outside their declared strategy that appear to offer better returns. In an environment of uncertainty, change and long investment horizons, the gap between the strategy originally declared and the one that is implemented will be wide. In the absence of a private equity index, identifying and measuring a style drift will be very judgmental and ultimately depends on trust and the intention on all sides to preserve the relationships.

A fund's investment strategy should be in line with the fund management team's abilities and past experiences. For this purpose, LPs may examine the existing portfolio to ensure that it is internally consistent and similarly matched with the previously described strategy. Nevertheless, any classification of industry sectors, geographies and so on, will be coarse and largely subjective. Style drifts may be picked up during the monitoring of a fund and actually pose the LPs a dilemma: should they allow the GP to deviate from what was agreed before but what may now be obsolete in a changed environment or is it better to let them take advantage of new and often unique investing opportunities?[6] Some LPs take the line that they would rather commit to other GPs with an appropriate focus in order to pursue such opportunities, but in practice this is not workable as it takes too much time to identify such GPs and do due diligence. As a new fund would start its investment with a significant time-lag the opportunities would be long gone, so giving the GP more flexibility in many cases will be the better solution.

Strategy drift

The strategy drift could be seen as adaptation, where GPs feel that their traditional focus looses attractiveness to LPs or holds less potential going forward and thus try to raise new funds based on strategies LPs appear to be looking for. Strategy drifts are more of a problem for the GP. The firm's track record is anchored in previous funds, therefore any change will be questioned by the existing LP base. Even where it becomes clear that a change in strategy is required, many LPs will not follow. This may not just be because they mistrust the GP's skills in executing a changed strategy but also because the new fund's focus may possibly not fit with the LP's targeted portfolio composition. GPs are caught in the dilemma between failing in the implementation of an unchanged strategy and failing with their next fundraising. They could opt for a very gradual adaptation where they do not stray away too much from their approaches but this may not be quick enough to keep abreast with changing markets. In this situation, style drift may actually provide a way out of a dilemma: while it may be initially resisted by the existing fund's LPs, it allows the GP to establish a track record with a new strategy based on which a future fund may be easier to raise.

Who needs to be flexible, who cannot be?

Opinions on style drifts vary. Even some GPs see it as critical not to let their style drift.[7] Others think that it can be advantageous to allow managers flexibility, provided that the investments meet a broad set of criteria that had been pre-agreed with the LPs.[8]

Is it better for an LP to commit to specialist funds in the case where the LP has a view on a geography, industry or stage focus, or should the selection be left to the GPs, by committing capital to generalist funds? According to Cornelius (2011), there are two competing hypotheses: specialist funds may possess informational advantages that make it more likely that they generate excess returns. Alternatively, such funds are more likely to underperform as they are less flexible to invest outside their special focus. If we accept the assumption that performance persistence is driven by markets, the flexibility given to a GP increases the real options they have, as they are able to move between industry sectors. There are various ways that LPs can provide flexibility to GPs, for instance, by pledging money for further investments and by allowing fund extensions. By definition, the room for manoeuvre is not necessarily used by the fund managers.

In illiquid markets, flexibility must be delegated to those who are best able to deal with uncertainty and change. LPs could be argued to be better positioned to manage the financial side of risk, for instance through diversification over fund types, geographies and currencies. Because of their limited size, most GPs will not be able to achieve such a level of diversification but are closer to their portfolio companies and thus better positioned to deal with compliance-related issues and operational risk. GPs actively reduce risk, whereas LPs are better placed to manage trade-offs and transfer risks. As LPs are unable to significantly change their portfolio composition over the short and medium term, they should give flexibility to the GPs in whose funds they have invested. A typical recommendation is that a GP should provide comfort to their LPs by being more transparent regarding their change in strategy and by giving information that verifies the market opportunity underlying the change.[9] Ultimately it comes down to the question of how much the LPs trust in the GP's skills going forward.

Mission Command

When thinking about private equity portfolios, the underlying principles are simplicity and modularisation. Speed is critical for value creation. It allows, for instance, to win a bid and keep the price within reasonable bounds.[10] In order to allow a quick reaction, a set a fundamentals that define the room for discretion in decision-making need to be agreed upfront. There is a trade-off between initiative and flexibility on one side and respect of guidelines and discipline on the other. These principles do not sit well together but need to be merged in the organisation, which requires an alignment of interest and approach that in military language is referred to as 'mission command'. It requires defining the 'mission' to be conducted and the freedom of action the agents are given.

'Mission command' is a concept that aims to foster cooperation in a flexible decentralised manner, based on a commonly understood overall concept, for instance the investment strategy agreed between the GP and his LPs, that allows considerable scope for individual initiative. This command style does not require acting according to rules or processes but instead, following principles.[11] Decisions should be made by the party that has the best information, is closest to the deal and whose judgment can be relied on most.

Like armies that are split up into coherent groups that comprise all operational functions, investors operating in the private equity market are building portfolios of funds that can act autonomously. Success depends on indirect coordination as direct guidance is not feasible. Rather than trying to assess a GP's track record, the important question from the LP perspective is to what degree they are able to adjust to changes in the environment. The broad range of fund managers' professional training and experience, often gained in different industries, allows flexibility in the approach, depending on the circumstances.

Flexibility is also a characteristic of the private equity firm. Often, particularly new GPs are quite entrepreneurial, less formal and quick with decision-making. As firms mature with a solid institutional LP basis they try to create structures that should outlast the founders, but such structures come with increased bureaucracy that stifles flexible reaction.

Commitment vs. Flexibility

It is the level of commitment that distinguishes strategy from tactics, as strategic decisions are difficult or costly to reverse once made.[12] This may also be a reason why investors shy away from strategy. Some institutional investors venture into private equity, particularly during boom periods, without the necessary team and infrastructure in place, almost inevitably resulting in an untimely jettison and huge losses. By definition, a position that does not require commitment is easy to give up. In fact, the short-termism of the financial industry in general is evidenced by a fascination with secondaries and liquidity solutions that are at odds with harvesting the illiquidity premium. While private equity as an asset class is not entirely illiquid, it is rather the lack of commitment to a long-term oriented strategy that could backfire and attract the wrong type of investors. To be able to cope with changes in the market, the organisation's will has to be invoked. Organisational commitment and an investment strategy helps to keep the objective in view, build up the necessary resources, methods and infrastructure, and not panic when things do not go well.

Commitment is crucial for success under uncertainty and to make proper use of flexibility. The often surprising resilience of private equity funds even during economic downturns may also come from the LPs forced to cling on to their investment and exercise pressure on the GPs to sort out problems. GPs are committed to their investee companies by virtue of being repeat players in the market and the need to preserve reputation and their lenders' and their own investors' trust.

The illiquidity and the long lifetime of funds set up as limited partnerships ensure the LP's commitment. 'Commitment' for private equity funds is well chosen as this term not only relates to the capital put forward by the LPs it also relates to their willingness to sign up for a relationship that, as Guy Fraser-Sampson observed, 'will last longer than the average marriage.'[13] In publicly listed companies the dispersion of ownership renders shareholders uninterested in monitoring and indifferent to risk.[14] It is also the short periods during which stock is held that diminishes the shareholders' involvement. Why spend time and effort in sorting out problems and then wait for two or three years for the payoff? Rather than addressing underperforming management and having all the other shareholders free ride on one's efforts, shareholders under such circumstances find it easier to just sell their positions.

More than most other structures tried in private equity, funds set up as limited partnerships represent what Colin Mayer in his book, *Firm Commitment*, referred to as a 'commitment device'.[15] Firms need to be able to determine the appropriate balance between commitment and control. Achieving this balance under these varied conditions does not require uniform or stifling regulation but enlightened forms of governance and government around the world – something LPs investing internationally will find important. In Mayer's view the potential of commitment has been inadequately appreciated and he proposes the protection of the long-term interests of stakeholders by creating overlapping generations of shareholders, where most control is in the hands of those with the longer horizon who are most likely to protect the interests of future generations of stakeholders. The private equity firm's modus operandi to raise overlapping series of funds does precisely this. Anecdotal evidence suggests 'elite' GPs occasionally do not allow secondary players buying fund positions from, for instance, defaulting LPs to participate in their follow-on fund. Effectively, by giving preference to short-term gains, secondary buyers signal that they are not reliable long-term partners for the GP.

Threats and Promises

In the relationship between GPs and LPs sometimes the distinctions between threats and promises are blurred. The LP's threat not to commit to the follow-on fund if the GP is not behaving as desired could also be seen as the implicit promise to invest in future funds as long as things move smoothly. Decisive for the GPs' as well as the LPs' influence is their reputation as repeat players in the market.

Limited legal enforcement

In private equity, very little can be legally enforced. In many countries, particularly emerging markets, the legal system is too slow and unreliable, not familiar with private equity, politically biased against these 'locusts', or simply corrupt. Taking matters to court carries high legal risk for an investor, as it is very difficult and lengthy to prove any wrong-doing. Under these circumstances, other ways of contract-enforcement that do not rely on the government have emerged. For instance, reputation plays a key role in addressing these problems because the market consists of few actors that repeatedly interact with each other. GPs that are removed for-cause may subsequently be unable to raise funds or participate in investment syndicates with other partnerships. In emerging countries co-investing with DFIs is perceived to provide some degree of protection as there is less scope for intimidating them and they are able to put indirect pressure on local governments. There is a parallel to the argument by Bruce Benson on merchants' courts, which traditionally had no legal authority and yet were able to enforce compliance with their judgment by the treatment of ostracism, the carrying out of which would put offending merchants out of business. Benson concludes that this pressure can be more effective than the pressure exercised by law.[16]

At least in its early phase, private equity was a small industry where GPs and LPs knew each other and reputation counted even more than today. Misbehaviour could be punished by ostracism. Essentially the industry was organised as a 'guild', avoiding legal courts and preferring amicable agreements. Affiliation also served as an endorsement, certifying a member's quality. However, the system is not scalable and there are, in fact, diseconomies of scale.

The massive inflow of capital during the industry's Golden Years changed this dynamic. Growing fund sizes led to a more fragmented LP base with less power and cohesion to influence a GP. This gave fund managers more flexibility but weakened the increasingly dispersed LPs' role as check and balance. The number of players in the industry has increased to such a degree that any sanctioning through exclusion from the industry has now simply become unworkable – a reason why there is more recourse to the legal system and why even regulation has been called for by various industry stakeholders.

Maintaining relationships with GPs and LPs

Occasionally LPs try to use the default option to exercise influence over fund managers and fail to answer capital calls. Litvak concludes that the threat of capital withdrawal is a useful contractual tool to reduce agency costs between investors and low-quality firms.[17] However, defaulting may harm other LPs in the fund by prompting underperformance and the default thus involves a 'reputational' penalty. In practice, the repercussions of being a defaulting investor go beyond the penalties described in the limited partnership agreement and may vary depending on the clientele of the fund[18]. Pension funds, university endowments and other repeat players care deeply about their reputations, while some individuals and corporate investors might be indifferent. The secondary market allows LPs to sell to another investor instead of defaulting.

While there is less of a stigma attached to secondary sales for GPs than in the past, some discretion may still be exercised to save relationships and face. When LPs need to reduce their allocation they may sell off only part of their fund stakes – interests of about 10 to 20 per cent, for instance – along with the commitments that stick with them, as opposed to their entire ownership in specific partnerships. This approach can mitigate the perception that the sell-off was driven by doubts in the fund manager. Likewise, LPs also often keep some stake in a fund to maintain the relationship and thus be able to commit to one of the funds raised by its GP in the future.[19]

A quite common way of dealing with this issue is by asking the GPs for help in order to transfer parts of its commitments to the fund's other LPs to avoid selling off stakes on the secondary market.[20]

Another option is 'structured secondaries', where the seller keeps the fund interests, at least in part, on its balance sheet. The buyer takes on the obligation to fund all the portfolio's future capital calls in exchange for a preferred return against its future distributions.[21] Here, at least in theory, the relationship between the selling LP and the GP of the sold fund remain unaffected.

Alignment of interests

The higher the deviation from the standard fund's risk profile, i.e., the higher the perceived 'riskiness', the stronger the alignment of interests in the form of the GP having 'skin in the game' that should be required by the LPs. LPs can tolerate deviations from the mainstream as long as the GP has put proportional 'hurt money' at risk.

Speed Read

- There is a trade-off between control and effectiveness, with the need to decentralise decision-making particularly poignant for uncertain and changeable alternative asset classes. This poses a dilemma for LPs – to what extent should you tolerate your GP's opportunistic approach?
- The answer partly lies in pragmatism – what are the opportunity costs – and partly in trust of the manager's skills. The key concept is 'mission command', defining the parameters of flexibility that can be exercised.
- Commitment – like trust – is a two-way street. LPs that demonstrate commitment and faith in GPs are seen as more desirable by other GPs. Reputation is a powerful check and balance, but its effectiveness weakens as the private equity industry grows and its investor base fragments.

Chapter 22
Real Options

In practice, investment decisions in private equity are irreversible in the sense that mistakes cannot be corrected through trading, at least not at an acceptable cost. Consequently, LPs need to be able to select or be in the position to alter their investments in funds post-commitment. Without the ability to respond in a meaningful way to a new development, the situation becomes a bet. This contrasts with 'real options' that can give investors the ability to respond to insights gained over time as a situation gradually becomes clearer. When primarily relying on selection skills, investors in funds are essentially taking a bet, hoping that calculated risks are taken and assuming the outcome is not dependent on pure chance.

Making irreversible 'all-or-nothing' decisions in the face of uncertainty is risky, but investors can at least prepare to manage the uncertain outcomes, once they happen. The 'real option' methodology recognises the value of deferring investment decisions and of learning over time. It is particularly useful when there is a high degree of uncertainty, some managerial flexibility, and not all the information is known ex ante. Foresight is essentially replaced by quick reaction to new information. Real options are an important but often overlooked tool for investors. They allow uncertainty to be managed and the impact of positive developments to be amplified.

The Value of Flexibility

Traditionally the time value of money of a long-term project is appraised by looking at its Net Present Value (NPV). As this, however, ignores flexibility, real options have increasingly become powerful tools for investment strategists. The classical real options presented in financial texts are:[1]

- The option to defer the start of a project or make staged investments, which reduces the uncertainty of an investment.

- The option to expand a project or to extend its life by which investors can benefit from an emerging upside.
- The option to contract or to abandon, which can serve to protect investors from the downside of an investment.

Generally, options to expand, extend or defer the start of a project can be classified as call options, whereas options to abandon, contract or switch between different modes of operation are seen as put options. Some real options, for example to abandon, are implicit and inherent in the investment decision, but others can be created in their own right. The value of a real option depends on several factors:

- Obviously, the so-called 'strike price', i.e., the price to exercise the option, decreases its value.
- On the other hand, the high volatility of the underlying asset makes the option more valuable – in other words, the option will have value only when there is uncertainty as to the possible outcomes of the initial investment.
- Moreover, the higher the uncertainty the higher its value. In practice, volatility is not a meaningful measure of risk in the case of an option, as low volatility would imply a low probability to profitably execute it.
- Also a prolongation of the time to an option's expiration is of additional value to an investor.

In the context of private equity, volatility is caused, for instance, by economic change that can be exploited by buyouts. Changes caused by technological innovation can benefit VC investments. The real world is too complicated a place to capture in a sophisticated financial model. Consequently, when using a real option framework, investors in private equity rely to a large extent on rough approximations and qualitative factors. Clearly for an LP real options would be the 'financially correct' answer to deal with a high uncertainty situation and would be, at least in theory, highly valuable. They allow the LP to observe a fund manager, monitor how the portfolio companies develop and manage towards growth as well as survival.

Rather than trying to predict the future, investors can guide their way into the future by building a portfolio of competing and independent real options that mirrors the evolution and competition going on in the markets.[2] Here real options form part of an evolutionary approach to strategy that emphasises the creation of choices, keeping options open, and making the 'tree' of possibilities as 'bushy' as possible at any point in time.[3] In situations of extreme uncertainty, one has to diversify in order to bet on many horses, a strategy that comes at a significant price, and/or one needs to be highly flexible. Comparable to mutations in biological evolution, real options are costly but also offer flexibility and thus have value in situations where changes are unpredictable.

Survival of the fattest

Having flexibility is a survival strategy and amounts to a collection of real options that allow investors to gain more on the upside than they would lose in the case of unfavourable outcomes. Structuring a portfolio as real options limits the consequences of failure. In this way, LPs can learn something from traditional venture capitalists. In this most uncertain of investment environments, structuring deals according to milestone achievements allows venture capitalists to gradually pick winners from within their own portfolios, over time. This gives flexibility, for example with a right to abandon, i.e., to write-off the investment, if certain milestones are not met.

To be able to benefit from a real option approach, investors need significant slack resources in the form of cash reserves, so they can wait for successful outcomes of their experiments and then amplify positive outcomes. Venture capitalists reserve capital for follow-on investments in their portfolio companies, often up to the size of their initial investments.[4] Likewise, the LP's dedicated resources serve as reserves for capital calls as well as for exploiting identified opportunities. Reserves are important in situations of extreme uncertainty where it is often the survival of the fattest rather than the fittest. For instance, portfolio strategies typically include a reserve of between 10 and 20 per cent to be allocated to co-investments.[5]

Implicit real options

Despite their relatively standardised structure private equity funds offer a range of real option-like features, for instance, allowing the GP to reinvest parts of the proceeds in follow-on investments, winding up the fund in a situation where a key person leaves, or extending the life of the partnership. In fact, incompleteness and ambiguities in the limited partnership agreement can be beneficial, as it gives rise to 'implicit' real options, although they often involve renegotiation with the rest of the parties, and in order to make changes, proposals must be accepted with either a simple or qualified majority.

For instance, co-investments can be decided by the LP, subject to approval by the GP. Others, like extension of the fund's lifetime, require the LP's majority vote. Whether consensus is reached depends on how the relationships are managed and ultimately on trust. Take the example where GPs ask LPs for more time to invest. In principle this would be interesting for LPs in situations where they have capital to deploy. LPs often see this to be a better alternative than forcing GPs to invest too quickly or to reduce the fund's commitment. The decision whether to go ahead or not will be on a case-by-case basis: 'For GPs with good track records, we actually encourage them to ask for an extension. For bad GPs, we'd want our money back.'[6] On the other hand, reducing a fund's commitments and asking the GP to return the capital, offers the option to allocate to funds that are better suited to a current environment, such as during market downturns to turnaround and special situation funds.

There are situations where LPs pay little or nothing for higher flexibility. For example, in exchange for a higher contribution, LPs that cornerstone emerging funds have more bargaining power, can enjoy more friendly contractual terms, and can influence the management of the fund. In such situations, LPs could make use of real option-like covenants in the limited partnership agreement ex-ante, as later on GPs are usually not willing to grant their investors this flexibility, particularly, as any contractual changes during a fund's lifetime inevitably bring in the other LPs as well – collective decision-making can be both costly and time consuming.

Limitations

The real option framework is a powerful technique for amplifying an emerging upside in order to support growth or to provide some degree of downside protection to help the investor in surviving market downturns or the failure of investments. The parallel with financial options, however, has limitations. A real option approach is difficult to apply in situations of decline as for private equity put options are not provided by the markets and a 'short selling' is therefore not possible.

Explicit Real Options

Co-investments, secondary transactions and side funds are explicit real options that are established parts of the private equity market. Interestingly, this is rarely how they are viewed. For instance, co-investments tend to primarily be seen as a way to cut costs. LPs often refuse to pay, and fund managers charge little or no fees for access to co-investment opportunities and claim no carried interest but just transaction fees without set-off.[7] However, the perception that all co-investment deals come without fees and carried interest is wrong. Indeed, some LPs find it wiser to keep the GP incentivised and pay 'promote', jargon that encompasses both carried interest and annual management fees on co-investments.

In addition, co-investments and secondary transactions are viewed to lead to a reduction of the J-curve effect and improve capital deployment and returns. Smoothing the liquidity J-curve, i.e., the concentrations in outflows due to capital calls during the early years of an investment program, may make sense, but will be difficult to achieve as secondary markets provide access to too little and to inconsistent quality deal flow to have a meaningful impact on sizeable portfolios. The same can be said about the objective of smoothing the accounting impact. Moreover, as previously mentioned, current accounting practices in many situations do not reflect the economic reality, so using co-investments and secondaries for this purpose would just be a 'balance sheet special effect'.

While portfolios of funds are effectively a diversification strategy, co-investments and secondaries allow concentrations of portfolios and allow LPs with a highly diversified primary fund programme to amplify exposure to industries they expect to have above-average upside potential, given the stage of the cycle.[8] The fact that fundraising cycles do not necessarily correspond to trends in industries can also be addressed by co-investments. Co-investments, secondary transactions and side funds appear to be comparatively short-term oriented real options in the sense that they are mainly of relevance for the existing portfolio of funds. However, they also need to be seen in the context of managing relationships between GPs, LPs and portfolio companies and in this respect are of a long-term nature, spanning beyond one fund.

Co-Investments

Co-investing is the syndication of a portfolio company's financing round between a private equity fund and one or more of its LPs.[9] Crucially, co-investments, unlike normal private equity investments via the limited partnership as 'blind pool', are not unknown quantities. The LP has an opportunity to assess the strength of the individual company and can target more mature companies with greater certainty, react faster to developments in the market, and thus amplify a well performing fund's overall returns. In this respect, co-investing conforms to the important characteristics of real options and can maximise the fund investment's upside by increasing the exposure to the best performing portfolio companies. Co-investing requires a different skill set to fund investing, as LPs need to have a much greater insight into individual deals. If they are unable to form a view on individual investments they can only save management fees and carried interest but will not be able to significantly improve the return profile of their portfolio of funds. In fact, LPs who strongly believe in their fund selection skills typically see no or little advantage and often even argue against co-investing.

For GPs, co-investments can be attractive when they lack sufficient funds for follow-on investment (particularly in a venture context) allowing smaller funds to boost their firepower on certain deals without resorting to collaboration with other GPs, which can potentially lead to conflicts and rivalry. However, if disputes on an investment arise, it can affect the relationship with the LP and negatively affect future fundraisings.

LP risks and rewards

If an LP follows the policy of co-investment only in portfolio companies that are profitable already or would reach profitability soon, this could, for example, mitigate the exposure to cash-burning start-ups. Also it may be difficult to find funds that specifically target, say, 'eco-innovation', but it is very likely that a number of funds have one or another company from this sector in their portfolio. Co-investing allows the LP to tilt the portfolio balance in a desired direction or fill specific target allocations in his portfolio. Because an LP builds up additional exposure to certain companies, industries or geographies, risks can increase very specifically with regard to individual portfolio companies. If too few co-investments are undertaken, there is also the danger of holding an overly concentrated portfolio of directly held investments. For investment decisions taken outside a formal partnership structure there is exposure to fiduciary risk. If things go wrong at the investment level, LPs may be exposed to legal and public relations liabilities.

In the context of an overcommitment strategy, it allows an LP not to execute the option if the liquidity is insufficient to honour the resulting increase in capital calls. Moreover, it could be used for managing foreign exchange risks as usual hedging products would be too uneconomical for private equity funds with their long lifetime and volatile cash flow.

For their risk and reward profile, co-investments are more risky than investing in a private equity partnership with a downside comparable to those of direct investments and require significant staff time and legal expenses. It is definitely not a panacea for higher returns in the asset class and, in fact, is often seen as quite difficult to execute. Therefore co-investing is clearly not for the risk-averse or inexperienced private equity investor.

Sourcing of co-investment opportunities

The main difference to direct investing is how it is sourced. Opportunities are generally deals a fund manager has pre-screened, structured, priced and is expected to invest in. Moreover, the fund generally organises the co-investment for the LP, who needs a significant number of primary fund commitments to generate a meaningful co-investment deal flow.

Co-investing is often pitched as a way to reduce costs where LPs are waiting for opportunities to be presented to them, thus creating concerns that those presented to them are 'lemons'. In fact, Fang et al. (2012) found evidence for underperformance of co-investments, which may be associated with the higher risk of such deals.[10] Importantly, the evidence found a sharp contrast between the performance of 'solo' deals where institutional investors source direct investments independently from GPs, and that of co-investment deals. They concluded there was an agency problem because GPs selectively offer deals to their LPs. Crucially, however, this conclusion describes an approach where LPs take no active role in sourcing opportunities.

On the other hand, LPs can express their interest in co-investments at the time of the fund commitment and reinforce this through regular follow-up calls and meetings: 'Just as equity sponsors call on intermediaries to generate deal flow, potential co-investors must be diligent in routinely conferring with their fund relationships regarding their ability to participate in potential co-investment opportunities.'[11] Efficient execution of the process, be it turning a deal down quickly or working in parallel and at the same pace as the GP, is critical to successful co-investing.

Secondary Transactions

At the first glance it may appear controversial to interpret secondary transactions as real options. Secondary transactions can be difficult to access, and only tend to be open to well-connected investors who are trusted to efficiently assess private equity assets, safeguard confidential information and execute with minimum fuss.[12]

In this context, LPs can negotiate pre-emption rights to buy shares before any third party, and so effectively exercise an option to increase its exposure. As a result, a portfolio of primary stakes in funds can develop into a powerful network with GPs as well as the other LPs represented in the funds. This network itself can be interpreted as a real option to access secondary deals.

Making secondary transactions into strong funds that have closed to new primary investment has similarities to co-investments. Both involve close contact and cooperation between GPs and LPs, as they rely on the GP's consent to get access to crucial proprietary portfolio company information. And in both cases the investment is not into a 'blind pool'. However, an important difference is that secondary fund investments are self-liquidating while co-investments are not necessarily so.

Side Funds

Side funds, depending on the situation also referred to as 'annex' or 'top-up' funds, are investment vehicles designed to increase the follow-on investment capabilities of an original fund with whom the side fund will invest in parallel. Generally side funds are launched some years after the creation of the original fund and are managed by the same fund manager but often under different terms and conditions. Investors joining a side fund are normally the original fund's LPs but can also be new ones. However, though the mechanism is apparently standard, there is no predefined structure and the motivation to establish a side fund can differ depending on the circumstances – usually related to problems such as higher than planned cash needs of the investee companies, a wrong assessment of the market conditions, a failed investment strategy or its flawed implementation. The only common characteristic is that the investee companies of side funds will always be a part of the portfolio of the original funds as it is described below.

Rather than cherry-picking companies – requiring that the LP has a direct investment capability – side funds could thus be interpreted as a further bet on a fund management team. Conceptually side funds sit between co-investments and secondary transactions, and indeed the lines are blurred. Theoretically any LP that has negotiated co-investment rights could create a 'virtual' side fund by simply exercising these rights and by proportionately topping up the fund's investments into portfolio companies, an approach that, in fact, is often followed as a way to offer some LPs effectively a lower fee level and create what is essentially price discrimination. In fact, there is a hierarchy of the LP's involvement:

- Investors who are purely passive LPs in funds;
- Investors who additionally use side funds;
- Investors who use side funds but selectively, opting out for specific investments;
- Investors who selectively co-invest alongside funds in individual portfolio companies;
- Investors who directly source, invest in and manage portfolio companies.

Variants of side funds are 'stapled' and 'top-up' secondary transactions.[13] In a stapled secondary transaction the new LP acquires not just a stake in an existing fund, but also the right to commit to the GP's next fund. In a top-up, a new LP invests fresh money and may also extend the life of a mature fund. GPs with a large portion of LPs unable to contribute further to a fund look for such top-ups. They are an option for existing LPs to limit their capital calls without becoming a defaulting investor and to block the fund from refinancing investments. The existing LPs have to give an approval as they need to pay for this option in the form of the preferential return required by the secondary investor.[14]

Relationship-Related Real Options

As discussed in **Chapter 9**, LP strategies are to a large degree driven by the relationship with fund managers that manifests itself in a series of commitments to funds raised by the same GP. Managing such relationships can be looked at from the real option perspective.

Staged investment

Committing to emerging GPs can be viewed as a staged investment containing a call option for the follow-on fund, which will be exercised only if the fund manager turns out to be skilled.[15] This offers an explanation for why some LPs invest in a first-time fund despite its disadvantages compared to funds raised by GPs with proven track records.[16] Searching for and committing to funds raised by new GPs without established track records can be a way to secure access to potentially high-performing funds raised in the future.[17] This strategy is nicely summarised by Sven Berthold's characterisation of WEGA's approach to emerging private equity managers in Asia:

> 'We think in the mid to long-term we need exposure in Asia. To date though we have only done one investment in the region. The team is very strong and well positioned so we took a small allocation to get our foot in the door. The fund we have chosen is highly sought after and should expectations hold up it might be difficult to get into the team's third fund if you have not been in the second one.'[18]

Taking into consideration that LPs tend to commit in a series of funds raised by the same GPs and that favourable terms and conditions can, at least to some degree, be transferred to future funds, there are considerable savings inherent in this approach.

Option to extend or abandon

When looking at the relationship as a series of funds, LPs have the option to continue or abandon this relationship. While the jury is out regarding the competence of fund managers, it is not necessarily an all or nothing decision. Instead of not committing to a next fund and thus essentially ending the relationship with the GP, LPs can also take a more nuanced approach and just commit a much reduced stake to this fund. This is certainly costly, but it limits the downside while still keeping the option to continue the relationship with larger investments in cases where the situation has improved.

LPs can collect a wide array of 'soft' information about the GP's skills, whereas outsiders, for example investors considering committing to the next fund and conducting a due diligence, can observe only 'hard' information such as realised returns. Investors in the previous fund are better positioned to assess fund managers and how they are developing. It is the access to the soft information that gives the investor an informational advantage when it comes to distinguishing between skill and luck.[19]

As incumbent LPs have an informational advantage when the GP raises his next fund, there may be a 'winner's curse' on outside investors.[20] LPs who were present in the previous fund and are convinced of the fund management team's skills tend to invest again and, as the GP will not want to jeopardise the fundraising, are essentially locking out outside LPs. This may be less a conscious strategy but more due to the fact that other market players will not hear about this opportunity or hear about it when it is too late. On the other hand, the incumbent LPs can hold up the GP's raising of the next fund if they do not agree with its timing or its terms and conditions. Previous LPs not backing the next fund is a powerful signal to potential investors who, in the absence of inside information, will become suspicious about the GP's skills.

Option to expand

When continuing a relationship, LPs can expand the relationship by committing higher amounts and by committing to other funds raised by the same GP in parallel. In the case where a private equity firm is experiencing problems or is approaching the end of its lifecycle, LPs can use their insights into a GP's team dynamics to encourage and sponsor a spin-out, resulting in an emerging fund manager with a high degree of motivation but without the typical uncertainty regarding skills and experience.

Implementation

The portfolio of options will only be of value if there is a high likelihood that they will be exercised and have a high impact once exercised. However, LPs often do not try or are unable to take advantage of their funds' emerging upside.[21] While theoretically the LP's case for a real option approach may be strong, in practice there are a number of significant problems that prevent its full scale application.

Tensions and disputes

Implicitly, a real option approach acknowledges that there are different classes of LPs, such as strong ones in good negotiation positions that come in at the first closing, and weaker or more passive LPs that come in later on. Different treatments may lead to tension and even dispute between the various LPs. Generally, it will become more difficult to align the interests between all parties – the GP, the LP and the other LPs. Finally, LPs still need to rely on the fund managers' expertise and exercise patience. Milestoned financing arrangements by LPs are likely to lead to interference, second guessing, and possibly 'creative' behaviour by the fund managers in return. Consequently, for any real option there is a range whereby the use of real options become detrimental to other critical success-factors. There is also the danger that selection standards slip when a 'strong' LP manages to get his 'uncertainty' taking compensated by concessions in the form of real options. This clearly carries the danger that necessarily strict selection standards slip.

To be able to exploit their real options portfolio, investors need to continuously monitor its development and be able to quickly execute in cases where the underlying investment develops positively. Some LPs generally ask for co-investments opportunities or even negotiate co-investment rights as a contractual feature of the limited partnership agreement, but co-investing is not an identical process to fund investing. To be able to do co-investments, LPs need to have skills that go beyond their core competence of fund manager selection. They need to be able to do – for them – non-standard due diligence within a short time and also need operational experience which is outside their traditional set of skills. Many LPs indicate interest in co-investments but few have the staffing and infrastructure to respond and commit to such opportunities in a timely manner.

Monitoring to evaluate real options

The main tool for an LP to gain intelligence on funds and emerging opportunities is through monitoring. While regular reporting from GPs provides data that becomes available to all the fund's, LPs informal and often personal contacts may provide background information and nuances that give important pointers, for instance, about LPs potentially defaulting and thus opportunities for secondary deals – something that in public markets would be insider trading. Other important information would be about co-investment opportunities coming up and whether an LP is interested in them or, alternatively, LPs explaining to the fund managers what type of portfolio companies they would be interested in.

Other intelligence gained through this monitoring relates to future funds to be raised, their anticipated focus, the targeted fund size and the intended timing of the fundraising. For direct and co-investments the ongoing monitoring role is seen as equally important as the initial structuring of the transaction.[22] Regardless how good the due diligence is before entering into the deal, the monitoring supports flexibility and proper reaction to adverse as well as positive developments.

The Prepared Mind

Uncertainty is the very source of investment opportunity for those willing to manage it. The fact that such management tools are more an art than a science deters many investors, who are trained to operate in fact-based, knowable environments. Indeed, organisational theorist, Russ Ackoff, observed that organisations fail more often because of what they have not done than because of what they have done. In the real option framework, knowledge, detailed management and the ability to forecast is replaced by monitoring, delegation, speed of reaction and adequate reserves. Optionality can substitute foresight, but favourable outcomes need to be recognised when they occur, and reacted upon quickly. For this purpose a process is required that tracks the market environment, enables the amplification of successful experiments and the quick elimination of unsuccessful ones.[23]

One explanation why the real option framework has so far been generally overlooked is that LPs are typically conservative in their approach to investing, and generally, in finance, the real option framework remains a comparatively new paradigm with a potential that is rarely fully realised. Real options in the context of private equity are of a more indirect nature and difficult to manage systematically. They are often not even recognised as such, are not covered in contracts and thus tend to remain underpriced. However, inaction carries opportunity costs. As the costs for the portfolio's explicit and implicit real options are often sunk, not exercising the option and wasting it carries a price, too. Seldom attempts are undertaken to systematically quantify their value and make this visible and therefore this value tends to be left on the table.

Speed Read

- Making irreversible 'all-or-nothing' decisions in the face of uncertainty is risky, but investors can at least prepare to manage the uncertain outcomes, once they happen. The 'real option' methodology recognises the value of deferring investment decisions and of learning over time.
- Real options are particularly useful when there is a high degree of uncertainty, some managerial flexibility, and not all the information is known ex ante. In private equity, for instance, co-investments or access to secondary opportunities are real options, but they are rarely viewed as such. Also, managing the LP/GP relationship can be looked at from the real option perspective.
- Investors in private equity tend to underestimate the relevance of real options for value creation. The real option framework remains a comparatively new paradigm with a potential that is rarely fully realised.

Chapter 23

No Plan Survives

Investment strategies are disclosed to prospective investors and in some circumstances also to regulators, who in all likelihood prefer a meticulous description of a series of connected and sequential steps to a general statement of principles. Conventional business strategies place emphasis upon planning and control. When considering a fund management team's track record, investors will look for discipline in implementation where a plan is only altered when necessary. For most managers it seems inconceivable that any other way of working could be acceptable.

But in the context of a private equity investment strategy, the idea of a 'master plan' that anticipates all contingencies is fundamentally flawed – like in war where Generalfeldmarschall Helmuth, Graf von Moltke famously observed that no 'operation plan extends with any certainty beyond the first encounter with the main body of the enemy.'[1] The fact that the future is unknowable and difficult to control means describing a reliable path towards an objective is unrealistic, aside from the fact that unalterable objectives are not in themselves realistic, as we have seen. Even if a plan was highly detailed, it would nevertheless be based on a simplified model of the private equity environment and thus likely to produce unintended outcomes. In previous chapters we have stressed the need to innovate by exploring under-researched spaces in the private equity market and to flexibly react to newly discovered opportunities.

Rather than relying on perfect foresight, emphasis should be put on efficient implementation, i.e., build a process that can cope with extreme uncertainty. There is no single performance driver such as selection skills that is deemed sufficient. To be successful, the entire private equity investment programme's components need to be managed well.

How Much Plan and How Much Flexibility?

In an uncertain and changing environment plans are an overly rigid response to achieve an objective. So should we drop the idea of a plan? Being able to quickly make investment decisions offers significant advantages, but this requires an intuitive understanding of a complex situation. Behaving opportunistically has the advantage of reacting flexibly but, on the other hand, in the extreme becomes chaotic and does not contribute to any objective. Often organisations try to cope with this dilemma by looking for unanimous decision-making within a team, by listening to their consultants or by imitating the behaviour of their respected peers, but this often leads to group think and uncontroversial but sub-optimal responses.[2]

Having planned and therefore evaluated various scenarios and discussed their implications helps making decisions and dealing with uncertainties as variations of these scenarios unfold. As Dwight D. Eisenhower remarked, '[p]lans are nothing, planning is everything.' Strategic planning thus becomes a tool to reduce a firm's reaction time. It should not be seen as an attempt to know what will happen, but as a learning exercise to prepare for an inherently unpredictable future.[3] When planning, situations and their consequences are thought through, whereas just reacting to unforeseen situations carries the danger that important factors are overlooked and not the right response to profit from a developing opportunity when it is found.

A decision-maker's most valuable resource is time and it is always in short supply.[4] As discussed before, real options have to be executed in order to have a value and procrastination and making no decision can often be worse than making a wrong decision. Time reserves for analysing and understanding consequences of decisions are important. If, for example, a company that fits a scenario comes up for sale, an investor can be far quicker with the offer and with fewer contingencies than his competitors, thus increasing the probability of success.[5]

Plans, investment guidelines and comparable rules are seen by some managers as unrealistically restrictive and as too constraining on their much-needed flexibility. Paradoxically, we argue that guidelines are necessary for providing flexibility as they help to focus the decision-makers' 'emotional resources' on the relevant and urgent matters at hand. Rather than constraining investment managers, guidelines can be efficient tools to accelerate their decision-making by providing focus on the essential questions to address. Making decisions for unforeseen situations is the business of private equity, and investment guidelines need to reflect this. Explaining, discussing and agreeing on the guidelines' underlying assumptions is an important first step and has to focus on difficult but routine questions that address 80 per cent of the situations.

Guidelines and plans can help to limit procrastination by defining upfront how much experimentation is necessary and how little information is deemed to be acceptable for allowing a decision. They establish a link between a firm's business model and its investment strategy. For a private equity firm, the right type of flexibility appears to be operating opportunistically within the framework set by its business model. Investment discipline is to operate within the constraints set by the value chain on one hand and continuously monitor and adapt the value chain to changes in the market place and the firm's business model when necessary.

Business Model

An investment strategy is only as good as its implementation: 'It remains a truism of investment that "people + process = performance"'.[6] A value chain model defines the process and the information flow required to produce and distribute the firm's products and service. The ultimate goal of this design tool is to maximise value creation within set cost constraints. A business model defines how a firm's products and services are positioned in the market place and what makes it valuable to its owners and investors. Both models interact and form the core of a strategy and its execution. The value chain's characteristics and strengths help to attract capital, but if the value chain is too 'sophisticated' and thus too costly, the business becomes less profitable. Consequently, there is a trade-off between a firm's value chain and its business model: the value chain needs to be strong enough to attract capital but costs need to be kept under control in order to generate a profit. As Kukla (2011) observed, there is no common understanding of the constituting components of a private equity firm's business model.

The components of the value chain are part of the resources necessary to implement an investment strategy and have to be made available when needed. Institutional investors creating a private equity investment programme are faced with a number of questions, such as how to scale up rapidly, whether to 'make or buy', go for a one-stop-shop solution or to look for several service providers. The assessment of internal capabilities and external parties is done against the background of the proposed private equity programme's value chain. At every step in the value chain a firm is faced with a 'make or buy' decision, to do a task in-house or to partially or entirely outsource it.

By way of illustration, we simplistically model the private equity programme's value chain as comprising six 'primary activities' (see **Figure 23.1**):

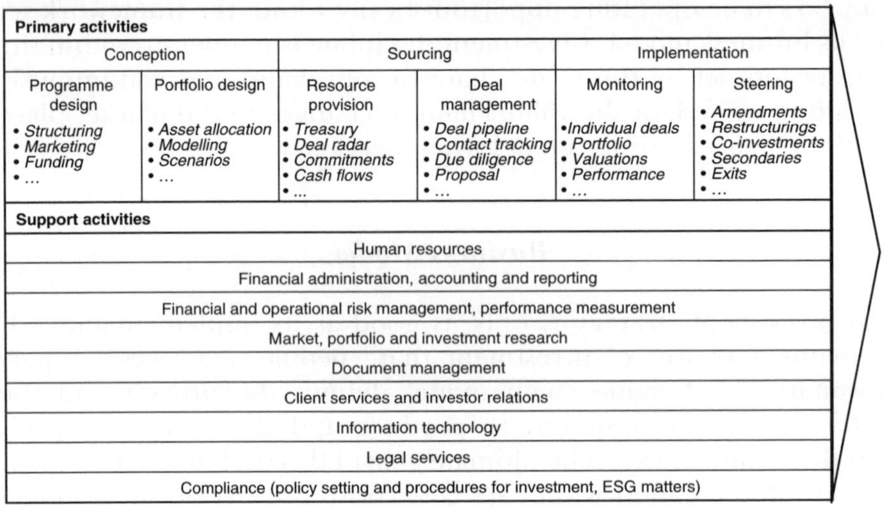

Figure 23.1 Private equity programme value chain

1. The design of the private equity programme (or the product, if conducted on behalf of external clients) is based on the objectives set by the sponsors. Depending on these objectives and the constraints, a wide array of different structures catering for various legal and tax environments is possible. In cases where the programme is targeting external clients the preparation of marketing material, road-shows, presentations, brochures or private placement memoranda requires significant effort and often cannot be achieved without involving placement agents. Investment objectives, constraints, and risk tolerance have to be formalised in investment guidelines as a reference point for managing the programme on a day-to-day basis.[7]
2. Portfolio design: the analysis of the market environment and the resulting return expectations is translated into a model of the programme for planning and controlling purposes.

3. Provision of resources: for instance, projecting cash flows for managing overcommitments can help to significantly improve the overall returns of a portfolio of private equity funds, while mistakes in this area can have a strong negative impact. Significant know-how is necessary to properly do this, creating competitive advantages for firms that are strong in this area.[8]
4. Deal making: this activity comprises a number of interrelated tasks. Deals are sourced in order to build a pipeline of interesting and accessible investment opportunities. This is a high barrier for newcomers in private equity. Evaluating the opportunity requires a structured approach, experience and judgment. Whether an investment proposal is selected, or which of several competing investment proposals is selected, depends on the fit with the chosen investment strategy and the pace of commitments.
5. Ongoing monitoring is the basic source of information regarding the progress of a private equity investment and necessary for valuation and portfolio analysis. However, financial reporting is just one aspect of monitoring, and proactive LPs maintain an ongoing dialogue with the funds in their portfolio, conducting regular visits and conference calls that also involve other LPs. This dialogue is particularly important for liquidity management, as short-time capital flows cannot be reliably modelled and in informal discussions fund managers often provide best-guess indications of future likely capital calls and draw-downs.
6. As LPs follow a buy-and-hold approach to investing, there is the impression that they are passive. However, there are a number of areas where LPs can steer their portfolio, either by stopping value destruction or even enhancing performance, for example through co-investing, or side funds or secondary transactions. In maturing programmes, LPs are increasingly faced with specific situations such as exit management for distributions-in-kind, workouts, or tail-ends.

A strictly regulated pension fund will internally operate differently than, say, a family office or an endowment and will thus put its emphasis on other activities and resources and consequently will build a different value chain. For example, a secondary specialist will need to develop distinctive capabilities and spend significant resources on developing the 'sourcing' activity in the value chain, particularly the deal pipeline. Other investors who do not see secondary transaction as their main activity will rather see this as a real option and thus work on the implementation activity, for instance the monitoring part where they try to identify such opportunities early. For these primary activities the value chain requires a number of 'support activities':

- Human resources, as having professionals with necessary skills and experience is a prerequisite for effective strategy implementation. There are a number of related issues, such as incentives and career development once an in-house team has acquired the necessary know-how and has gained more confidence.
- Client services and investor relations, as investing in private equity requires far more patience and tolerance for ups and downs than other asset classes. Communicating the progress – or the apparent lack of progress – to trustees, board members or managers from other parts of the investor's organisation who are familiar with private equity is a challenge.
- Financial administration, accounting and reporting, as gathering and tracking a huge amount of data is a major challenge. This can comprise hundreds and even thousands of portfolio companies, resulting in thousands of capital calls and distributions, as well as other administrative duties connecting the investors with the underlying partnerships, thus increasing the complexity of administration exponentially. This requires creating significant back-office infrastructure and personnel to support the rapid growth of administration tasks that comes with relatively few commitments to new funds.
- Market and portfolio strategy research, as a basis of a sound private equity investment strategy.
- Risk management and performance measurement, which can be markedly different compared to traditional asset classes.
- IT to support administration and portfolio modelling. Many private equity firms have invested heavily in administration and management information systems and in modelling for portfolio and risk management purposes or for sophisticated and tailored reporting. Likewise, there is anecdotal evidence that players with a powerful administration system infrastructure were able to attract mandates from institutions that were unable, or found it uneconomical, to build up capabilities in this function.
- Legal services get involved in negotiating terms and conditions of limited partnership agreements. One may have the impression

that legal services have little value to add to the private equity investment process. The reality is far from it. Over the years, terms and conditions for funds are continuously evolving, and it is difficult keeping abreast of the development, particularly if the investment programme has an international reach, and therefore the LP is faced with a multitude of different structures, tax regimes, co-investments, waivers in case of deviation from investment guidelines, renegotiation of management fees, tail-end situations and so on.
- Compliance to deal with regulation.[9] Also establishing appropriate procedures to address issues like insider trading when holding shares of listed companies after their IPOs usually fall to the responsibility of a compliance officer. In cases where an institutional investor manages third party assets and has to exercise fiduciary duties, resolving allocation conflicts may be overseen by a compliance function.

For most institutional investors hiring an extensive private equity investment and support staff with experience in all the relevant areas is not possible. The value chain's activities can either be operated insourced or outsourced to dedicated specialist firms. The question is rather, how to manage the allocation to these specialists.

Outsourcing for Flexibility

One aspect of outsourcing is as a temporary solution in situations where, for instance, internal staff are not fully recruited or not experienced enough yet, but where there is the intention to do everything in-house sooner or later. However, experienced investors may also find it preferable not to do everything in-house and outsource the activities that are either too expensive to replicate or are commoditised. We interpret outsourcing rather as a tool to create flexibility, based on a decision as to what are a firm's core competencies, what needs to be scaled rapidly to adapt to opportunities materialising and to bring in missing experience to address an unforeseen situation outside a firm's skills.

Given the increased investment obligations for fiduciaries, delegation has become an integral part of the investment process. As already touched upon in our brief history of private equity, the prudent man rule under the Employee Retirement Income Security Act (ERISA) could be seen as having paved the way to institutional investing into this asset class. Gradually, as explained in Cornelius et al. (2013), the prudent man rule has been replaced by what has been labelled the 'prudent investor rule' that includes the concepts of due diligence and, importantly, diversification, and as a legal doctrine focuses on the investment process, as opposed to labelling an investment or course of action as prudent or not. If the process followed was prudent, i.e., based on what was known and not known at the time of the decision, then the decisions that were made are prudent, regardless of subsequent results. The broader universe of possible investment options brings additional complexity and responsibilities that imply a different skill set compared with the traditional prudent man rule. Efficiency considerations force investors to delegate to qualified and supervised agents and it may now be deemed imprudent to fail to do so in some situations. However, trustees still must act in a prudent manner in selecting and supervising these agents.

Private equity service providers, such as consultants, administrators, analysts, accounting firms, legal firms and gatekeepers, are difficult to categorise, and it does not help that they offer comparable services with lines between them blurred: for instance, due diligence firms may overlap with executive recruiters, as due diligence firms also assess management ability to execute and thus do background checks and executive screening.

Fund administration is a daunting task and many investors outsource their middle and back offices. Specific service providers process capital calls and distributions, prepare and issue limited and general partner reporting, track distributions, proceeds and transfer of ownership interests, or prepare tax filings including annual returns, and also do investor allocations, including waterfall calculations. They track, monitor and report portfolio investments, prepare performance measurements, assure corporate regulatory compliance or prepare reclaims for tax exempt investors. Accounting and treasury services, global custody, foreign currency transactions with the associated multicurrency fund accounting, and off-shore cash administration are standard. Distribution managers focus on a specific area of fund administration, i.e., distributions in kind to assist clients with the orderly sale of securities distributed by private equity partnerships. All these tasks require strong system support. Software application providers and developers offer such services and help institutional investors to do project management, integrate administration applications with their back-office accounting system and databases with private equity market statistics or to develop specific applications such as cash flow forecasting models.

Such services are offered by various parties, but it is difficult to assess and to compare all of them, as literally no single provider operates like another. For some service providers, private equity is core business whereas for others, for example law firms, it is just part of a larger range of activities. Investors can use a gatekeeper who is able to provide all services as a 'one-stop shop'. Alternatively, they may consider combining various leading service providers in a 'best-of-breed' approach. Both approaches have pros and cons:

- A wholesale outsourcing to one party, for example a fund-of-funds, allows capital to be put to work in private equity quickly, particularly if a host of integrated services is offered as a 'one-stop shop'. There are disadvantages as well: it is unlikely that one gatekeeper can offer all the services in an equally strong fashion. In other words, a 'one-stop shop' tends to be a sub-optimal solution. Moreover, for institutional investors aiming to become autonomous in managing their programme, it is difficult to 'un-bundle' the services from one gatekeeper as they learn, because switching between services and providers is costly.
- Alternatively, investors can purchase private equity services from different providers in order to obtain the best service of its kind in each area. But such a 'best of breed' strategy is also problematic: trade-offs include the costs of defining, procuring and integrating several third parties and the need for managing and coordinating their contributions; they may well offset the benefits.

In reality neither a pure 'one-stop shop' nor a pure 'best-of-breed' approach is feasible. No player in private equity will be able to convincingly provide all relevant services. Likewise, it would be simply too difficult to search for and procure the best service for each relevant area.

What will be outsourced and what capabilities are to be built up internally over time will depend on the investor's long-term objectives and on the costs and value drivers for each activity in the chain. There is therefore no optimum solution, but it may be useful to reflect on whether tasks are 'core' or 'non-core' and whether they are 'routinely' or 'rarely' needed to achieve the set objectives. For illustration: in the case of core tasks that are required often, such as due diligence, investors should learn as much as possible from other market players while building up their own capabilities. This may temporarily require engaging various services providers to get access to the necessary know-how. Rarely executed but important tasks – specific legal services spring to mind – could require maintaining capabilities in-house, but scaling up with outside parties or asking for their specialist advice. For non-core activities that are needed regularly, such as accounting services, it makes sense to partner with some service providers over the longer term.

Speed Read

- Given private equity's uncertain operating environment, a master plan that seeks to cover all contingencies is impractical. Instead, planning should focus on building a process that can cope with extreme uncertainty.
- Plans and investment guidelines reduce a firm's reaction time, freeing up managers to focus on what matters and act opportunistically within the framework of their business model.
- Investment strategy is not just in 'what' but also 'how' a private equity firm invests. Its business model and value chain is at the core of what its investment strategy is. Designing a business model and the value chain establishes a link between long-term principles and inevitable short-term oriented evolutionary environment.

Chapter 24

The Heavy Hand of Regulation

Private equity is the most politicised of asset classes because it is an agent of change. It is the business end of the capitalist system's organisation of capital, resources and labour. Compared to, say, hedge funds, its actions and their effect on the socio-economy are very obvious and understandable to all. This brings into play ideological questions where positions, much less the answers, are not clear cut. Innovation is necessary for economic growth but is always accompanied by creative destruction. We all want to have the former but many resist change of the current system. Concerns such as market stability and systemic risk, which for most financial regulation are the big ones, are the easy bit in the case of private equity.

Regulation has been instrumental to the development and institutionalisation of the private equity asset class, but a number of regulatory initiatives are unfavourable to the industry, particularly those that inhibit exploration and innovation, create barriers to entry or lead to monopolies. Private equity as an industry is in an uncomfortable position: it is too small to attract sufficient attention for its technicalities and for meaningful support from the important stakeholders of the industry, the institutional investors. On the other hand it is too politicised to escape the regular populist backlashes against the financial industry in general. Consequently, there is always the threat that governments change laws and that such changes have a negative impact on investments or the industry as a whole.

How Regulation Has Shaped Private Equity

Regulation had – at least initially – a very positive influence on the asset class's development. As previously mentioned, the US Department of Labor's clarification of the 'prudent man rule' under ERISA allowed pension funds to invest in assets perceived to be risky and paved the way for the emergence of an institutionalised private equity industry. Unfortunately regulation has the potential to be detrimental as well. Limiting an investor's choice of strategies and instruments and restricting his flexibility can undermine financial performance and create new risks.

Since 2008, politicians have rejected the adoption of voluntary codes or self-regulation for private equity, feeling that their major concerns, notably 'non-transparency, asymmetric information, enormous growth in leverage, short-term financing, tax evasion, systemic risks on financial markets, and increasing vulnerability of public companies after the involvement of private equity funds',[1] are not properly addressed. However, for alternative assets trying to address every eventuality is not possible, at least not for acceptable costs. Regulation indirectly leads to a high degree of standardisation, an objective that is fundamentally at odds with an asset class that continuously has to adapt to an uncertain, changing environment.

Regulators define who is allowed to do what and what is permitted as behaviour and, in this way, determine an industry's structure. External asset managers falling under the Alternative Investment Fund Manager Directive (AIFMD), for instance, bear significant costs associated with regulatory compliance, whereas some institutional investors' in-house programmes are either exempted from regulation or are subject to a different type of regulation, such as Basel III or Solvency II, thus creating potential for regulatory arbitrage.

A Politicised Asset Class

Regulation is clearly associated with the promotion of moral conduct.[2] As mentioned already in our brief industry history, private equity, together with hedge funds, exemplifies in the eyes of many the unacceptable 'ugly face of free-market capitalism'[3] as firms 'chew up' good companies before 'spitting them out' again. The apparently adverse social impact of restructurings and rationalisations by outside investors – resulting in layoffs and increased unemployment, use of leverage leading to higher risk of bankruptcy and reductions of taxable earnings, for instance – mean many governments see private equity as undesirable.

The response throughout history to financial crises is to seek greater regulation[4] and Poul Nyrup Rasmussen, the then President of the Party of European Socialists and former Danish Prime

Minister position on this is just one of many examples. He based his call for tighter regulation of private equity funds on the perception that these were 'a menace to healthy companies, to workers' rights and to the European Union's Lisbon Agenda', thus subscribing to their – meanwhile classical – description as 'locusts' by Germany's former Vice-Chancellor Franz Müntefering.[5] In Rasmussen's view, LBOs follow a typical pattern where a 'once profitable and healthy company' is bought with borrowed money, then saddled with the debt and interest payments, workers are laid off and assets are sold. For him, the question is not about risk which could be dealt with by transparency and disclosure: 'They [i.e., LBOs] would still be objectionable.'

The private equity industry recognised early on that a negative public opinion can be detrimental for business and thus has been an apparently avid adopter of Environmental, Social & Governance (ESG) standards. Whether GPs are really convinced or whether they just pay lip service may be debatable. However, their LPs demand it and it is hoped that this will appease the public and politicians alike.

Another reaction to increasingly restrictive and cumbersome regulation is to avoid it altogether, for instance by venturing into emerging and less regulated markets. In fact, this question supports an entire industry for regulatory avoidance. Certain investors that do not have fiduciary duties – such as family offices, high net worth individuals, endowments – fall outside regulation. Single family offices are exempt from Dodd-Frank regulation in the US and the AIFMD in Europe, so it does not come as a surprise that some hedge funds were restructured as family offices to avoid unwelcome scrutiny and costs associated with compliance. Such moves could, however, contribute to increasing social divide, as the decision to become a family office is more common among hedge fund partners who have already made a lot of money and can thus afford to continue their operations without outside investors.[6] A possibly unintended consequence of such regulatory exemptions is that they support an unfair process where the rich pull up the ladder behind them, aggravating inequality as, for instance, pensioners pay a price for becoming essentially barred from the benefits of alternative asset investing.

Also Sovereign Wealth Funds (SWFs) – presenting the state – are exempted from regulation. SWFs have come up with a self-regulatory code, the International Forum of Sovereign Wealth Funds' (IFSWF) Santiago Principles. These Generally Accepted

Principles and Practices (GAPP) are subject to home country laws, regulations, requirements and obligations. As their adoption is on a voluntary basis, it is difficult to see how a SWF can be more transparent and have better corporate governance than the state it is serving. Arguably there are double standards: for instance, when calling for tighter regulation, former French president, Nicolas Sarkozy, described private equity firms as 'aggressive' gangs of 'speculators', 'bent on snapping up firms, sacking workers and creaming off profits'.[7] But a few years later, Mr. Sarkozy was reported to be 'wooed by sovereign wealth funds including Qatar's who are ready to back him to start a private equity fund' and apparently was not excluding this as an option for his further career.[8] The amounts invested by SWFs clearly move the market and set the behaviour. In sum, moralist criticisms on the one hand and lauded benefits of private equity on the other, are a never-ending debate across a wide political spectrum and conclusions are not easy to draw.

Current Regulation Does Not Help Investors in Private Equity

More intrusive regulation of markets is often justified because people are not fully rational and need to be protected from their own mistakes. Of course, financial regulation will invariably lag behind innovations in this industry, which is not surprising as it can only be drafted once a problem is more widely understood in order to enable regulators to effectively remove it. Consequently, with each financial crisis there is a rush to adopt frameworks that are not necessarily well drafted, particularly in the case of private equity as a niche activity, where politicians and bureaucrats tend to have little or no direct experience.

The case for regulating private equity

From a systemic risk perspective the case for regulating private equity is weak. Despite some noises to the contrary, private equity has neither caused nor contributed to a financial crisis and no such firm has required a bail out. The claim that buyouts are a threat to society is not supported by academic research and with the exception of the pay-to-play scandal,[9] and unlike in hedge funds (such as Madoff and the Galleon Group), there has not been a fraud or significant scandal in private equity, which – as we have seen – is to a large degree thanks to the limited partnership structure, which precludes Ponzi schemes. Clearly some funds have used too much leverage and contributed to the demise of acquired companies, but the majority of private equity managers have acted rationally and in numerous cases turned around investee companies that otherwise would have failed.

On the other hand, hedge funds played a crucial role in generating the crisis and it was necessary to bring them under the umbrella of international financial regulation. As there is obviously a potential for regulatory arbitrage, such as hedge funds re-labelling themselves as private equity groups in the area of distressed debt, for instance, it is probably the simpler and more 'water-tight' solution to regulate all alternative investment vehicles, regardless of whether they are private equity or hedge funds.

Illiquid assets and the liquidity bias

As Modern Portfolio Theory (MPT) shows that diversification may reduce risk at a given level of returns (and vice versa), newer financial regulation emphasises investment risk at the portfolio level rather than at the level of single assets.[10] While in theory this should result in a larger share of capital being allocated to alternative asset classes, MPT is anchored in the Efficient Market Hypothesis, and thus accounting standards require marking assets to market prices and regulatory regimes emphasise the liquidity associated with active markets.

We do not challenge the need for regulating private equity. The point is rather that some initiatives could result in regulatory failure, e.g., not addressing the true financial risks such as not meeting pensioners' liabilities because of underperformance. Regulation forces institutional investors such as banks, insurers and pension funds to hold increased amounts of liquid, high-quality assets that can be readily sold or used as collateral in private markets, even when those markets are under stress. New rules are designed to ensure these institutions are in a strong position to weather any future financial crisis. They are not necessarily driven by the objective of discouraging investments in alternative assets, rather to tilt allocations towards such supposedly liquid and 'safe' government debt. For private equity, however, there is no active market where assets can be turned into liquidity, at least not on short notice and when needed to cover liquidity shortfalls, and consequently regulation implicitly discourages institutional investors from material allocations to this asset class.

Creating Jurassic Park

For the private equity industry there are costs associated with regulatory compliance which are not matched or not believed to be compensated by additional gains. Regulatory overheads are the same independent of assets under management. This does not really affect established players with less need for flexibility and therefore also provides incentives to get bigger.[11] The smaller and mid-sized GPs that tend to operate more in the entrepreneurial system are thus disadvantaged. In this way, ironically regulation favours those large players that have the most controversial impact and may approach a size where they could be seen as 'systemic'.

Regulators are faced with a trade-off between two complex approaches that are subject to manipulation and simple standards that remove scope for flexibility. Regulation erects barriers for 'GP entrepreneurs' trying to enter the private equity industry with innovative approaches, who are unable to establish themselves anymore in an environment dominated by the industry's 'dinosaurs'. It may thus contribute to 'evolutionary stasis' in this area of the financial markets and therefore is likely to carry huge indirect costs for society. Reducing the investor's flexibility and adaptability can only result in lower financial returns on average. The danger of such a development is that regulation becomes too restrictive and discourages or even eliminates variety and experimentation, which is the raison d'être of the private equity industry and probably one of its most important societal benefits.

Transparency

Disclosure is generally seen as a sounder safeguard than prescriptive regulation. While the industry is 'private' and legitimately exploits opportunities associated with opacity, would an increased transparency and disclosure – as stipulated by politicians and many investors as well – be the solution?

A crisis of trust

We could interpret the recent regulatory initiatives as the result of a crisis of trust where suspicion about financial actors has become routine. However, private equity is operating in environments where information is difficult to get, non-standardised, difficult to understand and where its interpretation requires professional judgment and experience. Any disclosure is likely to trigger a cycle of follow-on questions. As philosopher Onora O'Neill stated in the 2002 BBC Reith Lectures: 'Transparency and openness may not be the unconditional goods that they are fashionably supposed to be.' Public distrust grew in the very years in which transparency and accountability have been so avidly pursued. 'By the same token, secrecy and lack of transparency may not be the enemies of trust.'[12]

The crisis of trust also extends to those who are supposed to make use of the increased transparency. For instance, it is argued that 'allegedly sophisticated middlemen' are incapable of monitoring, pointing to cases like Madoff, and as a consequence regulatory reporting requirements have risen. Such transparency leads to an implicit setting of rules for how to manage investments instead of regulating for the outcomes and leaving it to the (mistrusted) financial market to find ways of achieving them.

Regulate the car or the driver?

One of this book's core theses is that the limited partnership structure is the 'natural' solution to address uncertainty and while we can 'see' a fund's individual components, they are, in fact, inseparable. For instance the 'look-through' requirement to risk-weight the underlying exposures of a fund as if the exposures were directly held leads to a distorted picture of the limited partnership's risk. Additionally, this perspective, plus a 'close to public market' transparency invites micromanagement and second guessing of GPs by LPs or, even worse, may lead to a situation where regulators start to interfere in how to invest in private equity.

The question is, whom do we trust to look through the veil of opacity and make the judgment on risks and opportunities? The thrust of regulators to cater for the needs of all types of investors, including retail customers, in the same way and make alternative assets 'safe' is almost comparable to the attempt to increase safety standards in Formula One by requiring a first aid kit and a spare tyre onboard every racing car. This attempt to regulate risk out of alternatives is obviously absurd. Instead the right approach would rather be to make sure that investors in this asset class have the right skills, profile, processes, systems and resources – to stay with the analogy, are qualified Formula One drivers instead of somebody with average driving skills.

Interestingly, regulatory arbitrage appears to increasingly cut out the experienced middlemen. As the GP's costs to assure regulatory compliance make investing through funds as intermediaries too expensive, many institutional investors, instead of acting as LPs, try to invest in companies directly. However, they are rarely prepared to do this and are more likely to fail, which cannot be the regulator's intention. Maybe doubts regarding the institutional investors' sophistication are justified, but this is the problem that needs to be addressed: regulate the driver and do not try to build a 'zero accident' Formula One racing car.

In extremis, GPs may unwittingly be regulated out of the private equity market, which actually would prove harmful to society. As mentioned already in **Chapter 7**, Acemoglu and Robinson (2012) credit what they term 'inclusive institutions' for Venice's riches in medieval times and explain the republic's end of prosperity with its switch towards more extractive economic institutions, eventually also outlawing the commenda. Private equity is a fundamentally anti-establishment force – at least anti-inefficient establishment. As the establishment pushes back and protects itself, so everyone will lose. The debate on the social benefits and the damage caused by private equity will continue and – as ideologies and interests of the various parties involved are often diametrically opposed – are unlikely to ever be settled.

Speed Read

- Regulation has been helpful to private equity, and hostile. Hostile regulation tends to lead to regulatory arbitrage or avoidance, followed by countermoves, such as closing loopholes.
- In fact, the limited partnership structure has protected private equity from wrong-doing, since it is not conducive to Ponzi schemes and fraudulent activity.
- Private equity is an inherently politicised asset class that will always attract polarised views. Rather than protect investors, existing regulation tends to protect the largest players, creating a Jurassic Park of private equity.
- Regulatory approaches that seek to make alternative asset classes safe will be counterproductive. Regulate the driver, not the vehicle.

Chapter 25

Private Equity Unchained

Private equity has come this far without much said on the subject of strategy, so why start now? Newcomers may find it surprising that until fairly recently strategy did not even play a significant role in the management of illiquid investments at all, and what many investors call 'strategy' has been more akin to 'tactics' or 'learned reflexes'. Even large institutions still appear to manage private equity on such a case-by-case basis. But the environment has changed, the industry has matured, more players seek to deploy ever larger amounts in a market where opportunities necessarily become difficult to identify and access. The few principles that institutional investors have relied on up till now have been anchored in a less competitive past. Nick Cavalla from Cambridge's endowment is not alone in his assessment: 'But we think, structurally, private equity [...] is a much, much harder business than it was 2002 to 2007.'[1]

The limitations of a framework such as Modern Portfolio Theory (MPT) have been well rehearsed. It is not that MPT is necessarily flawed, it is just that most of its fundamental assumptions are not met for private equity. Investors have tried to work around this complication in two ways. One avenue is trying to replace the limited partnership structure used for funds with something closer to traditional asset classes – for example, publicly quoted private equity or securitisations – in order to make the asset class more liquid and easier to price. This, however, is counterproductive, bringing in through the backdoor precisely the problems the limited partnership structure has successfully overcome: the inability to put a price on extreme uncertainty and the lack of investor's commitment over the long horizons necessary for success.

Other practitioners have accepted private equity's strengths (or probably resigned themselves to its weaknesses) and work with them, in many ways along the lines of what is described in this book as an interpretation of the Adaptive Market Hypothesis. Successful investors in private equity appear to share certain characteristics: they manage assets of a size within a certain band, they are very long-term oriented, i.e., aiming to create and preserve wealth over several generations, have the right decision-making processes and are not impeded by a regulatory framework that is anchored in the MPT and therefore puts a premium on instant liquidity. The longer the time horizon, the more valuable optionality investors find in their private equity portfolios.

There Are No 'Brilliant' Investment Strategies

Strategy is about shaping the future as we wish it to be, but regarding the degree investors are able to manage towards desired outcomes one can only come to a quite sobering assessment. As there are various objectives with changing priorities depending on changes in the environment, no rigid plan can be successful. The lack of vision, muddled leadership, and inept execution are, in the words of Duncan Watts, 'not the stuff of success for sure, but more likely to lead to persistent mediocrity than colossal failure'.[2] This contrasts with 'brilliant' strategy that is typically referred to as being 'marked by clarity of vision', 'decisiveness' and 'bold' execution. Being applied in the right context it can lead to 'smashing' success. If it fails, however, 'great' strategy paradoxically is more likely to lead to a complete disaster. Whether it fails or not, depends entirely on whether the initial vision happens to be right or not.[3] We are back to the question of forecasting, which we cannot do over the long time frames necessary for investment success in private equity.

While one often reads about 'brilliantly' executed strategies in war, business, sports or games that have (allegedly) yielded fantastic results, these assessments usually relate to the results realised but not to the original intentions. In fact, it is unlikely that strategies ever realise exactly as aimed for and the question whether one intended strategy is better than the other is probably meaningless. We have to conclude that an environment characterised by extreme uncertainty and subject to unpredictable developments over long time horizons like private equity cannot be the domain of a 'brilliant' strategy.

This book began with the caveat that a play-by-play account of private equity investment strategy for institutional investors is not feasible in such a fascinatingly complex and changeable industry. Now we find that not only is there no 'right strategy' but also no brilliant ones. What can be said definitively on the subject, if anything? Perhaps anti-climactically, there are some simple rules that seem to hold across most private equity investment situations.

The Six Principles of Private Equity Investment Strategy

A good strategy must reflect a purpose, in the sense of projecting far into the future, anticipating several rounds of competitive moves, responses and countermoves.[4] Lawrence Freedman in his book on strategy develops the idea of strategic scripts as a way of thinking about strategy as a story told in the future tense.[5] This approach resonates with Kees van der Heijden's thinking, who saw a scenario as a story, a narrative that links historical and present events with hypothetical events taking place in the future.[6] Scenarios aim to make sense of future events in the same way as historical accounts make sense of the past. Strategies try to pave a path into this future, based on decisions that are more robust under a variety of alternative futures. Strategy must promote effectiveness, efficiency and honesty in the assessment of the situation, the market environment and one's capabilities. Strategy should establish a system of rules and behaviours that does not rely on talent and certainly not on genius.

Common pitfalls

There are common pitfalls of failing to have a strategy or failing to follow it. Avoiding experimentation and merely following the herd; a lack of creativity, looking backward, leaving strategy to outsiders, such as consultants; choosing uncontroversial and uniform approaches rather than being original, based on one's own insights and assessments. It can also lead to over-confidence in one's selection skills. Organisational theorist, Henry Mintzberg, pointed out that strategy is consistency in behaviour, whether or not intended.

There is a difference between failures from not having a strategy and strategic mistakes, such as a wrong analysis of a situation, which is not necessarily caused by incompetence but simply a fact of life under uncertainty. However, the failure to adapt and to continue relying on the past, the failure to correct mistakes or to put perverse incentives in place are clearly faults in management.

Our analysis does not challenge or seek to amend the structure of the private equity industry, which is in fact an effective response to the extreme uncertainty that it poses investors. Rather, we propose a narrative that aims to make more sense of this structure and offers a more effective framework for navigating it. So without further ado, here are the six principles investors in private equity should follow:

1. Instead of looking at investments in funds in isolation, investors should manage a portfolio of long-term relationships with GPs in whom they trust and whom they do not micromanage.
2. Good due diligence is a necessary but insufficient ingredient for investment success and investors should accept its limits.
3. Denial about uncertainty leads to real options being ignored. In order to be able to exercise real options, the capability and infrastructure, e.g., in the form of a value chain, needs to be put in place.
4. Instead of trying to eliminate all uncertainty and falling victim to 'paralysis by analysis', investors should not just rely on data but seek the 'blue ocean' of opportunities ignored by their peers. Military strategists stress the importance of flexibility to negotiate such uncertain terrain.
5. Processes, procedures and guidelines appear to be constraining, but they speed up decisions, focus decision-makers on the essentials and thus enable flexibility.
6. Most of all, investors should avoid the temptation of trying to time the market or to frequently alter their approaches, and instead invest steadily with a long-term horizon.

In spite of all uncertainty, one can do more than be swept along by events. Investing in private equity needs to be understood as the management of long-term relationships that allow collaboration. Consequently, concepts such as reputation and trust are important and lessons from diplomacy can be applied as well.

And soft factors matter too

As in warfare, morale is an important factor. Although most investors intellectually understand that private equity is a long-term oriented asset class, temporary market downturns – even with completely immaterial impact on the portfolio's final return – leave them regularly dispirited and trigger a change of heart and a shutdown of their activities in this area. Strategy means perseverance, stamina, not giving up. Lasting success is not achieved overnight and is a result of visions and activities that span decades.[7] In private equity, due diligence makes sure that only the skilful and committed fund managers participate. Typical incentive structures are based on the fund managers putting their reputation at stake, their investment of own personal wealth in the fund, and the chance to participate in substantial carried interest. This plays a strong role in keeping individuals focused on the fund over the long term.

Unchaining Investors

An investment strategy is a way of providing clearer guidance and a more reliable map. Data and intelligence are inevitably unreliable, tend to take a pessimistic bias and are often contradictory. Without a framework of how the industry operates and how to apply judgment, recent data is prone to misinterpretations and leads to overreactions. Risk would not be called 'risk' if everything worked out in a predictable way. Instead of trying to make investments in private equity a 'sure thing' they should be viewed as probability distributions, where it is possible to engineer a targeted portfolio with a desired risk–return profile.

Despite reservations about plans, strategic planning is necessary to think through all contingencies in advance and to make fewer tactical execution errors. The plan clarifies where to search, where and when to concentrate, which trade-offs are acceptable, what is performance and how it is incentivised. It also answers what capabilities and capacities the organisation has to build up and what resources are needed. Investment guidelines should be put in place in order to accelerate decision-making.

We have seen how the traditional ways of viewing private equity through the prism of models suitable for efficient financial markets have 'chained' investors to a way of thinking that is detrimental to success; and we have attempted to sketch alternative ways of modelling private equity that appear more conducive to critically thinking about investing.

In a market that owes so much to pioneering spirit and individual skill, the concept of any sort of pre-planning can be viewed dimly. But we have seen that a sound strategy is one that liberates investors, by providing a clear and flexible framework for investment partners to operate under in the face of uncertainty, while explicitly acknowledging the real options that are available to fund investors. Private equity fund commitments are commonly characterised as passive, illiquid and blind. Investors that can see beyond that by building and implementing a strategy for dealing with uncertainty, one that is unchained from inapplicable financial theories and the comfort of facts will have deserved success.

Notes

1 Introduction

1. See Bance (2004).
2. See also Janeway (2012) who saw for the modern venture capitalist the arbitrage typically to be between a technical innovation and the commercial product or service that can be derived from it.
3. In his 1921 work, *Risk, Uncertainty, and Profit*, the University of Chicago economist, Frank Knight, established a distinction between 'risk' and 'uncertainty'. While in the case of risk, probabilities can be assigned to outcomes, such quantification is not possible in the case of uncertainty. For an in-depth discussion of the distinction between 'risk' and 'uncertainty' in the context of private equity, please refer to Cornelius et al. (2013) and Mathonet and Meyer (2007).
4. See Lhabitant (2004).
5. Quoted from Söderblom (2011).
6. See Heuser (2002).
7. See Fraser-Sampson (2013).
8. See Johnson (2012).
9. The expression 'deserve' is another reference to Winston Churchill, who once said (in effect) that one can never be sure of success, one can only deserve it. See Vasconcellos e Sá (2005).

2 A Neo-Classical Asset Class

1. See Rubenstein (2008), quoted in Cornelius (2011).
2. See Phalippou (2011).
3. See Wright and Robbie (1996).
4. See *The Economist* (2004).
5. See interview in Finkel and Greising (2010).
6. See Baker and Smith (1998) and Kosman (2010).
7. See Cornelius et al. (2013).
8. See Baker and Smith (1998).
9. See Kosman (2010).
10. See Firstbrook (2007).
11. See interview with Steve Kaplan in Finkel and Greising (2010).
12. Franz Müntefering, the then head of the SPD, the leading party in Germany's governing coalition at the time. See *The Economist* (2005).
13. See Baker and Smith (1998).
14. See Phalippou (2011).
15. See Baker and Smith (1998).
16. See Private Equity News (2013).
17. See Schultes (2012).

3 *The 'Repair Shop of Capitalism'*

1. See Cornelius et al. (2013).
2. See interview with Steve Kaplan in Finkel and Greising (2010).
3. See Cornelius et al. (2013).
4. See interview with Ajit Nedungadi in Bishop (2012).
5. See interview with Steve Kaplan in Finkel and Greising (2010).
6. See interview with Mark Goldsmith from Actis in Bishop (2012).
7. Venture capital could be described as one extreme where a portfolio company would not be able to operate before further injections of working capital and a significant build-up of products and services, organisation and client base. At the other end of the spectrum there would be 'asset strippers' that only need to spin off what shareholders perceive as 'dead weight' in an otherwise undervalued company. In reality, private equity investors employ all of these techniques together. It is obvious that adding something to a portfolio company will usually take longer than subtracting unnecessary assets from it.
8. See Gadiesh and MacArthur (2008).
9. Quoted in Baker and Smith (1998).
10. See Barber and Goold (2007).
11. See Cornelius et al. (2013).

4 *Strategy Challenges*

1. See Fraser-Sampson (2006).
2. Quoted from Simpson (2013).
3. See Porter (1980).
4. See De Vany (2004).
5. See Mei and Moses (2002).
6. See Campbell (2008).
7. See Kim and Mauborgne (2005).
8. See Desportes (2007).
9. See Watts (2011) and *The Economist* (2012).
10. Quoted from Manchester and Reid (2012), p. 706.
11. See Vasconcellos e Sá (2005).
12. See Huffman (2001) or Fraser-Sampson (2006).

5 *Strategic Asset Allocation*

1. See Fraser-Sampson (2006).
2. See Cornelius (2011).
3. MPT assumes normally distributed returns, but empirical evidence shows that the distribution of private equity returns is highly non-normal – many small losses but few extraordinary 'home runs'. In contrast to public markets, private equity valuations are infrequent and more likely to be estimates than actual transactions that establish a fair market price. Therefore it is not possible to measure risk as the volatility of a time series and the subsequent interpretation of correlation as a measure of dependence usually is misleading.

4. Phalippou (2011) argues that institutional investors do not stay out of private equity because they could not cope with its illiquidity and thus questions whether there really is a premium paid for those that have long horizons.
5. Quoted from Söderblom (2011).
6. See Lerner et al. (2005) and Hobohm (2008)
7. See Hobohm (2010).
8. See Söderblom (2011).
9. See Settboun (2005) and Dimmock (2008).
10. See interview with John Hess, Altius Associates Ltd in Bishop (2012).
11. See Copeland (2008).
12. See Vardi (2009a).
13. See Webber (2008).
14. See Vardi (2009a).
15. A collection of disjointed subsets of a given set where the union of the subsets must equal the entire original set.
16. See Vardi (2009b). As Harvard follows David Swensen's endowment model with more than one-third allocated to alternative assets, this implies an overcommitment ratio of over 115 per cent, which would be consistent with usual overcommitment ratios reported in the fund-of-funds industry.
17. Dimmock (2008) found no evidence that university endowments take the correlation between their non-financial income and asset returns into account when investing. Endowments apparently are not optimising their portfolios with respect to all forms of institutional risk.
18. See Miller and Fabrikant (2008).
19. See Swensen (2000).
20. See Phalippou (2011).

6 *The Sky is Not the Limit*

1. See Mayer (2013).
2. See Demaira (2010), based on studies by McKinsey and Watson Wyatt.
3. See Phalippou (2011).
4. David Swensen from the Yale Investment Office did not see an allocation to venture capital as meaningful for his $18 billion portfolio. See Cornelius (2011).
5. See interview with John Hess, Altius Associates Ltd in Bishop (2012).
6. Based on Cornelius et al. (2013).
7. See Mathonet and Meyer (2007).
8. See Söderblom (2011).
9. See Lopez-de-Silanes et al. (2010).
10. See Chung (2010) and Metrick and Yasuda (2010).
11. See Chung (2010).
12. See *The Economist* (2013).
13. See Manninena et al. (2010).

7 *The Limited Partnership as Part of Humanity's DNA*

1. Also tax and regulatory requirements drive the structuring of these investment vehicles with the additional objectives of tax transparency, i.e. investors are treated as investing directly in the underlying portfolio companies.

2. Also in the earlier Edo period (between 1603 and 1867) in Japan, a trade financing method called 'nagekane' was used, apparently being introduced by the Portuguese, based on their experience with the commenda. Wealthy merchants from Nagasaki, Hakata and Sakai provided funding to Portuguese, Chinese and Japanese ships in 'shuinsen' trade voyages. To the lenders these high interest rates compensated for the huge risks involved in distant journeys on the high seas. If the ship got lost on a journey, however, the loss was shouldered by the lenders and the debtors were not obliged to return the funding.
3. See Borden (2009).
4. In a societas maris, the travelling tractator took the capital of the investors into his service. If the ship sank, the investment was lost. Such partnerships were compliant with the canonist law against usury: according to Swabey (2008), Pope Innocent III advised the Archbishop of Genoa in 1206 that: 'In some cases a dowry should be committed to some merchant, that an income might be derived by honest gain.'
5. Also see Garis (2007) discussion of market risk management based on the Holy Qur'an's explicit and implicit teachings.
6. See Gilson (2003).
7. See Evans (2006).
8. There are a number of variations, driven mainly by level, basis, hurdle, and timing of the carried interest. The carry basis refers to how profits are measured, e.g., the profit and loss for the fund can either be aggregated (European Waterfall) or the general partner can be allowed to take a share of the profit on each individual investment (US Waterfall). For the timing of carried interest distributions, various approaches are possible, e.g. the 'fund-as-a-whole' where no distributions are made to the general partner until the limited partners have received distributions equal to the amount of their capital contributions. A detailed discussion of the carried interest and other waterfall concepts, such as claw-backs and catch-ups, goes beyond the scope of this book. For more technical explanations, please refer to, for instance, Mathonet and Meyer (2007), Metrick and Yasuda (2010) and Cornelius et al. (2013). In the US, historically, recipients of a carried interest have been taxed as though they were investors who had supplied 20 per cent of the fund's capital instead of at the individual income tax rate that would otherwise apply. Tax treatment in general is likely to change and be less favourable in the future.
9. Metrick and Yasuda (2010) and Phalippou (2009) find that non-performance related management fees account for around two-thirds of the total compensation of fund managers. According to Sørensen et al. (2013), of the LP's total cost of the investment in funds, approximately 50 per cent are due to illiquidity, 25 per cent are due to management fees, and the remaining 25 per cent are due to carried interest.
10. See McCahery and Vermeulen (2013) for an overview over recent changes in industry practices. One exception is the comment made by Nick Ferguson from SVG Capital in Bishop (2012): 'I'm always amazed that, given all this difficulty of raising funds, you never hear anybody suggesting that they sell on a 15 per cent carry instead of 20. It's unbelievably rigid.' It is not surprising that the comment comes from an LP. It may not just be the question of fairness that stops GPs from proposing this. They may fear that by proposing this below standard term they signal their inferiority, taking into account that a

small number of mainly US private equity firms marketed themselves as 'elite' requiring a 'premium carry' of 25 per cent or 30 per cent, based on the justification that they consistently outperform the typical fund. In the same way, LPs may reject this suspecting adverse selection.

11. Schelling himself gave the following example for a focal point: assume that tomorrow you have to meet a stranger in New York. Unfortunately you have no further piece of information and there was no coordination between the two of you when or where to meet. So what would you do? You go to the place you expect the unknown person is likely to choose: when Schelling asked his students this question the most common answer was to be at 'noon at the Grand Central Station's information booth'.
12. 'Then Joseph said to the people, Behold, I have bought you this day and your land for Pharaoh: Io, here is seed for you, and ye shall sow the land. And it shall come to pass in the increase, that ye shall give the fifth part to Pharaoh, and four parts shall be your own, for seed of the field, and for your food, and for them of your households, and for food for your little ones.' Genesis, Chapter 47; as pointed out by Metrick (2006) and Metrick and Yasuda (2010).
13. See Fernández-Armesto (2007).
14. The game is played only once and anonymously, so that reciprocation is not an issue. This stylised negotiation was first studied by experimental economists Güth et al. (1982).
15. See Jensen et al. (2007).
16. A sense of fairness may be less exclusive to humans than these results suggest. In 2003 the primatologists Frans de Waal and Sarah Brosnan from the Emory University in Atlanta conducted a study with capuchin monkeys and chimpanzees. Their results suggest that all primates evolved a sense of justice, in the sense of a moral emotion that signals whether an exchange was perceived to be fair or unfair.
17. An alternative (and slightly depressing) theory is that humans are simply good at sizing each other up. Being able to infer how another person will react to being short-changed in combination with knowledge about the concept of fairness would to some degree also explain the results found in studies of the ultimatum game. One could also argue that the limited partner more often than not has the upper hand. Here in the extreme the set-up would degenerate into the so-called 'dictator game', where the proposer determines the allocation and the responder simply receives what the proposer has not allocated to himself. As the responder's role is entirely passive, the dictator game is not formally a game at all. Economically rational 'dictators' would give nothing to the responder, but experimental results have indicated that even then proposers do not maximise their own expected utility. Nevertheless, the ultimatum game seems to be a better model for the LP/GP relationship.
18. See Mathonet and Meyer (2007).
19. See Bernstein (2008).
20. See Dobbs (2013).
21. Communication between Hans Lovrek and author, 22 Oct 2012. See also Lovrek (2012).
22. See Mayer (2013).
23. See Snow (2006).
24. See, for example, Scott (2012).
25. See Lerner and Schoar (2002).

26. Also the so-called 'endowment effect', which is also known as the 'divestiture aversion effect' or 'status quo bias', may also contribute to the illiquidity of funds. A classic example of the endowment effect is a family's reluctance to sell an old painting, which has been in their possession for a considerable amount of time, (more or less) regardless of the price that is being offered. In private equity it is important to take into account that interactions between LPs in a fund and the fund manager are particularly close, which distinguishes these asset classes from publicly traded assets. With access to funds sometimes being restricted and mutual trust being built up over several years, investors in a fund may be reluctant to terminate a relationship. See Cornelius et al. (2013).
27. See Fraser-Sampson (2007).
28. In fact, little or no dividend payout is more favourable for investors, as taxation on a dividend is higher than on a capital gain.
29. See Mayer (2013).
30. For the purpose of this discussion we focus on institutional financing and ignore the continuous innovation and experimentation with vehicles such as business angel networks, pledge funds, crowd funding etc. that are mainly found at the boundary between formal and informal capital markets in early stage entrepreneurial investing.
31. See interview with Jon Moulton in Bishop (2012).
32. See Mayer (2013).

8 *Do-It-Yourself?*

1. See Fang et al. (2012).
2. See Fang et al. (2012).
3. See Witkowsky (2012).
4. See Chassany (2013).
5. See Hutton (2007) and Kapoor (unknown).
6. See interview with John Hess from Altius Associates in Bishop (2012).
7. See Cornelius et al. (2013).
8. See for example Fann and Bernhardt (2013).
9. For their study, Fang et al. (2012) compiled a proprietary dataset of direct investments – comprising solo investment and co-investments – from seven large institutional investors.
10. See for instance Gallagher (2011).
11. Quoted from Chassany (2013).
12. We thank John Renkema from APG for this clarification.
13. See Hochberg et al. (2013).
14. See Cornelius et al. (2013).
15. See also Lerner et al. (2011).
16. In Meyer and Mathonet (2005).
17. Also called reward-to-variability ratio.
18. For a more in-depth discussion of funds-of-funds see also the chapter 'Gatekeepers' by T. Meyer in Talmor and Vasvari (2011).
19. They nevertheless could be a meaningful way of entering the asset class as they increase flexibility in tactical asset allocations and allow fast exposure to private equity fund investments, while maintaining some degree of liquidity.
20. See Lai (2006).

21. Jo (2002) analysed 48 US-based funds-of-funds (13 asset managers, 15 banks and 20 independent funds).
22. See for example Pease (2000), Otterlei and Barrington (2003), Sormani (2005) or Mathonet and Meyer (2007). Smith (2000) argues that expenses for in-house teams and management fees charged by funds-of-funds are comparable.

9 *Economics of Private Equity Firms*

1. For further details on the private equity fund's economics we recommend the seminal article on this subject by Metrick and Yasuda (2010).
2. Usually a percentage of the net asset value of investments which the fund holds.
3. See Metrick and Yasuda (2010).
4. See Primack (2010).
5. See interview in Bishop (2012).
6. See Hochberg et al. (2013).
7. See Mathonet and Meyer (2007).
8. See Kosman (2010).
9. See Metrick and Yasuda (2010).
10. See Chung et al. (2010).
11. See Fraser-Sampson (2013).
12. See Emshwiller and Corkery (2010).
13. See for example interview with Richard Kramlich in Finkel and Greising (2010).
14. See interview with Jon Moulton in Bishop (2012).

10 *Objectives*

1. See Fraser-Sampson (2013).
2. Clausewitz's letter to Friedrich Karl Ferdinand Freiherr von Müffling (1775–1851), quoted in Heuser (2002).
3. See Aragon (2008) and Knepley and Bailey (2009).
4. See Harris (2009).
5. See Simpson (2013).

11 *Performance Persistence*

1. See also, for instance, von Braun (2000), Tierney and Folkerts-Landau (2001), Scardino (2004), Kaplan and Schoar (2005), Rouvinez (2006), Hendershott (2007), Sørensen (2007) and Phalippou and Gottschalg (2009).
2. As data providers such as Thomson Venture Economics, Preqin or Cambridge Associates do not cover all funds in their databases, there is also a sample selection bias – in theory, funds that do not report performance may exhibit stronger performance persistence.
3. Assuming that private equity holds a higher risk than public equity, an assumption we need to qualify later on when discussing the risk topic in more detail.
4. According to Phalippou (2011) no less than 77 per cent of fund managers claim to be in the top quartile.

5. See Rouvinez (2006).
6. Some LPs try to do the analysis on the underlying portfolio company data, where the statistical significance will be reached quicker. This may give information on many aspects of the GP's investment approach but not on its portfolio management.
7. See for instance Chung (2010).
8. See also Phalippou (2011).
9. See Burgel (2000) or Conner (2005).
10. See Mathonet and Meyer (2007).
11. See for instance Fraser-Sampson (2007).
12. 'Relationships' should be looked at critically and not from the perspective of human interaction: to quote Sood (2003), '[if] you believe that you have a relationship with your fund managers you are going to be less inclined to pass on future investments [...] It's the re-ups that have really hurt investors'.
13. See Beinhocker (2006), Rosenzweig (2007) and Raynor et al. (2009).

12 Nobody Knows Anything

1. See for example Söderblom (2011) and Cornelius et al. (2013).
2. See Meyer and Mathonet (2005) and Mathonet and Meyer (2007).
3. See Taleb (2012).
4. According to Manninena et al. (2010), previous academic studies have favoured the selection skill explanation. An exception is Mulcahy et al. (2012), taking the practitioner's perspective.
5. See Mills (2005).
6. See Nelson (2003).
7. Source: http://www.investorwords.com/1596/due_diligence.html, [accessed 13 May 2008].
8. See Camp (2002).
9. See Meyer and Mathonet (2005).
10. See, for example, Camp (2002) in the context of due diligence: 'But, there is no way venture capitalists can ever say, with absolute certainty, that a particular deal will make a great investment or will turn out to be a dog.'
11. Quoted from Date (2013). This is a phenomenon common to alternative assets in general. See for example Kelleher (2013): 'It suggested that institutional investors are ratcheting up their due-diligence requirements, partly because they are dissatisfied by the high fees and weak returns their investments carry. They require more reporting and documentation, greater detail on valuation and operational dealings, and more guidance from consultants on their investments.'
12. See Fraser-Sampson (2007). According to Camp (2002), it 'is important to note, however, that venture capital due diligence is, by its nature, an imperfect process because it has no clear end. Certainty is unattainable. It is easy, therefore, for some venture capitalists to drag the process out, grasping and hoping for something certain. Precious time and effort is often wasted performing due diligence on irrelevancies'. This quote relates to direct investments, but the same can be said for the evaluation of private equity funds.

13. In B.F. Skinner's experiments, pigeons associated the delivery of food with the chance actions they had been performing just before. By repeating these actions the pigeons expected to be rewarded by food again, over time enacting entire 'rain dances'. Skinner concluded that the formation of superstition lies in establishing a connection between rituals and favourable but unrelated outcomes.
14. See Kahneman (2011).
15. Estimates based on returns for US buyout funds between 1995 and 2005. The author thanks John Renkema from APG Asset Management for this analysis.
16. Keynes: 'Worldly wisdom teaches that is better for the reputation to fail conventionally than to succeed unconventionally.'
17. See Kosman (2010), Manninena et al. (2010), Fraser-Sampson (2013) and Kelleher (2013).
18. See Kelleher (2013).
19. Swensen (2000) argues that investors should consider alternatives outside the mainstream such as managers without the requisite institutional characteristics.

13 Spreading Risks – Thinly and Thickly

1. See Taleb (2012).
2. Moreover, for investors being worried about reputational damage it does not make sense to diversify, as it just increases this exposure associated with ESG-related failures.
3. See Davies (2008).
4. In principle there are three types of secondary transaction. One situation is an LP acquiring a stake in an active fund from another GP. The same happens on the GP level, where one fund is acquiring a portfolio company from a fund managed by another GP. More challenging from an LP's perspective are 'direct secondaries', where an LP acquires a GP-like interest in one or more portfolio companies.
5. See Cornelius (2011).
6. Securitisation is the mechanism by which financial assets (such as loans, bonds, credit cards receivables, derivatives, investments in hedge funds or private equity funds) are packaged together in a pool which is sold to a special purpose vehicle (SPV). The SPV refinances itself by issuing debt instruments, i.e. the ABS, with various risk profiles, sold to investors with different appetites for risk. Securitisation of private equity investments are classified as collateralised debt obligations (CDO), or more specifically as private equity collateralised fund obligations (CFO). Therefore, private equity CFOs simply represent an application and an adaptation of traditional technologies of securitisation to portfolios of private equity investments.
7. In the case of buyout funds, performance apparently is less driven by market-timing. See Schmidt et al. (2004).
8. See Cornelius (2011).
9. See Kaplan and Stromberg (2009), Kaplan and Lerner (2010) and Cornelius (2011).
10. See Swensen (2000).

11. See Meyer and Mathonet (2005), Cornelius (2011), Phalippou (2011).
12. See Meyer and Mathonet (2005).
13. This method can also deal with the 'next fund risk': here the same amount is committed across fund managers and the funds they raise subsequently, thus mitigating the effect of GPs increasing the size of their funds.
14. See Cornelius (2011).
15. See Meyer and Mathonet (2005).
16. See Cornelius (2011).

14 Private Equity Risk

1. See Knight (1921).
2. See Cornelius et al. (2013).
3. See EVCA (2013) and Cornelius et al. (2013).
4. See EVCA (2005).
5. See Phalippou (2011): 'Recently, there have been some attempts to standardise these valuations and bring them closer to market values (FAS 157 rule).'
6. See Cumming et al. (2013).
7. See, for example, Meyer and Mathonet (2005), Fraser-Sampson (2007), Demaira (2010) or Phalippou (2011).
8. Unfortunately, as Demaira (2010) goes on in his criticism, the fund-of-funds managers as the perceived thought-leaders in the industry have been 'deafeningly silent in the debate'.
9. To some degree, the real option framework also gives insights into the question of valuation for private equity funds: under the fair value framework all assets are assumed to be sellable, but this option has a price. When allocating to illiquid assets, LPs gave up a number of options, notably those to sell-off or abandon the investment, and consequently the changing valuation of these options should not affect the valuation of the fund.
10. Regarding the concept of modelling a fair transaction please refer to EVCA (2013) or, for a more technical discussion, to Cornelius et al. (2013).
11. See EVCA (2013).
12. See BCBS (2013). This Consultative Document, however, did not differentiate between fund types, such as open-ended mutual funds and closed-ended limited partnership funds.
13. Fraser-Sampson (2013) points out that these are 'cash-flow type assets' and 'while finance theory is happy to apply a different approach to the ones they like (bonds, that are measured using compound returns) they illogically deny it to the others, which include private equity, infrastructure and real estate as well as various energy type assets such as oil and gas royalties.'
14. Cornelius et al. (2013) mention a number of examples such as Harvard Management Corporation (HMC), which manages the endowment of Harvard University, and CalPERS, the largest US pension fund.
15. From the LP's perspective the stake in the fund cannot be broken up into individual portfolio companies as long as they are in the intervention phase.
16. See Cornelius et al. (2013).
17. See Janeway (2012).
18. See Fraser-Sampson (2006).

19. Let us assume an LP that committed to a fund with an estimated remaining lifetime of several years and the value of an asset held by this fund has increased. However, from the LP's perspective no profit should be attributed until the outcome can be determined with reasonable certainty, e.g., in the case of funds when the amount is eventually paid to the LPs. It could be paid out to the LPs tomorrow but it may also be at the end of the fund's lifetime, so the LPs would expect a lower time value for the gain. The same holds for losses and consequently changes of the NAV are 'dampened' in line with the fund's remaining lifetime.
20. See Baker and Smith (1998): 'Again, those expectations were locked into the financial structure, in the form of payment schedules and debt covenants, encapsulating a virtuous circle of debt discipline, equity ownership, and high standards for performance.'
21. The gap to bridge is too high. Even for industry standard funds Weidig and Mathonet (2004) estimated a loss of 30 per cent, given any capital loss (seeing this as a default).
22. See Mathonet and Meyer (2007).
23. See Cornelius et al. (2013).
24. Dinneen (2004) gave a number of criteria that can form the basis for a categorisation. See also Mathonet and Meyer (2007).
25. See Kahneman (2011) and Taleb (2012).

15 Performance Measurement

1. To calculate the MIRR a fund's start and end date need to be known. Usually, the start date is the time of fund inception and the end date its contractual termination date.
2. See Fraser-Sampson (2006): 'I know one pension fund that committed all its allocation on the first year (a terrible practice) and was complaining three years later that they were only about 10% invested.'
3. See Meyer and Mathonet (2005) and Fraser-Sampson (2007).
4. See Fraser-Sampson (2007).
5. See Fraser-Sampson (2007) and Mulcahy et al. (2012).
6. In case there are additional resources dedicated to the programme, or resources are withdrawn from the programme, one would need to determine the ratios for the various time periods.
7. To recall, the IRR is the discount rate which makes the Net Present Value (NPV) of a series of cash flows equal to zero. Hence, a positive NPV implies an expected return higher than the cost of capital. The present value of EVAs from a given investment can be shown as mathematically equivalent to the NPV of the investment. See Desai and Ferri (2006).
8. See Desai and Ferri (2006).
9. The amount of money on a fictitious account at liquidation, divided by the amount of capital committed to the power of one over the fund duration.
10. This perspective actually resonates with our argument put forward in the previous chapter that the undrawn capital forms part of a fund's exposure.
11. See Mathonet and Meyer (2007).
12. See Mathonet and Meyer (2007).
13. See Harris et al. (2012).

14. There are divergent views on whether overcommitments generally constitute leverage. For an in-depth discussion we refer to Cornelius et al. (2013).
15. A reason why EVCA's Risk Measurement Guidelines foresee a so-called 'funding test' whether the LP is able to honour all capital calls and thus does not need to value the portfolio under what is essentially a 'fire sale' assumption. See EVCA (2013).
16. See Desai and Ferri (2006).

16 The Galapagos Islands of Finance

1. See Mathonet and Meyer (2007) and OECD (2007).
2. See Lo (2005).
3. See Wile (2012). Another challenger to the EMH is behavioural finance. Behavioural models use social, cognitive and emotional factors in understanding investment decisions and are primarily concerned with the bounds of rationality (selfishness, self-control) of market participants. A central feature of behavioural portfolio theory is the observation that investors view their portfolios not as a whole, as prescribed by MPT, but as distinct layers in a hierarchy of assets, where layers are associated with particular goals and where attitudes towards risk vary across layers. One layer might be a 'downside protection layer' to protect investors from suffering losses whereas an 'upside potential layer' aims to give investors a chance at being rich. Investors are assumed to be risk averse in the downside protection layer whereas they are risk-seeking in the upside potential layer. The typical core-satellite portfolios built by private equity investors would be consistent with behavioural portfolio theory. However, behavioural finance models are not offering a satisfying explanation: why should investors protect their downside within an allocation to private equity, if the same effect can be achieved much cheaper with conventional assets? The core-satellite is also called a 'core and explore' approach (see Pietranico and Riepe, 2002) and therefore, as we discuss later in this chapter, appears to be closer to AMH than to behavioural finance.
4. An analogy also used by Niall Ferguson: 'In evolutionary terms, the financial services sector appears to have passed through a twenty-year Cambrian explosion, with existing species flourishing and new species increasing in number [...] funds are the Galapagos Islands of finance [...] the rate of innovation, evolution, competition, adaptation, births and deaths, the whole range of evolutionary phenomena, occurs at an extraordinarily rapid clip.' See Ferguson (2008).
5. See Dawkins (2000).
6. See Stacey (1996).
7. See the discussion around war as a non-linear phenomenon and Clausewitz's work in Beyerchen (1992).
8. See interview with Steve Kaplan in Finkel and Greising (2010).
9. See interview with Jon Moulton in Bishop (2012).
10. See Lo (2005).
11. See Tett (2010) and Authers (2014).
12. See also Beinhocker (2006), who argued that change in the economy is driven more by the entry and exit of firms than by the adaptation of individual companies.

13. DNA (deoxyribonucleic acid) contains the genetic instructions for the biological development of a cellular form of life or a virus.
14. The idea was first introduced in 1932 by Sewall Wright, an American geneticist known for his influential work on evolutionary theory.
15. See Baker and Smith (1998).
16. See interview with Garry Wilson, Endless LLP in Bishop (2012).
17. See interview with Ajit Nedungadi, TA Associates L.P. in Bishop (2012).
18. See Cornelius (2011) and Fraser-Sampson (2013).
19. See interview with Jon Moulton in Bishop (2012).
20. As reported by Reuters in 'Private equity poised for push into Africa', 14 November 2012.
21. According to Nobel laureate Kenneth Arrow, the impossibility theorem states that no voting system based on the ranking of candidates can be converted into a community-wide ranking while also satisfying a particular set of four criteria – unrestricted domain, non-dictatorship, Pareto efficiency, and independence of irrelevant alternatives.
22. To underline the argument: Baker and Smith (1998) describe the LBO as a 'classic entrepreneurial coup'. Like other important innovations in economic life, its invention is obscure and outside the economic mainstream, in this case on the peripheries of the established financial industry. LBOs 'spurred a dual revolution in the American economy – one in corporate finance, another in corporate governance – that profoundly altered patterns of managerial power and behavior'.
23. See EMPEA (2005).
24. See Kukla (2011).

17 The Locust and the Deep Blue Sea

1. See Kim and Mauborgne (2005).
2. See Söderblom (2011).
3. See Lerner et al. (2005) and Manninena et al. (2010).
4. See Janeway (2012).
5. See Lo (2008).
6. See Mathonet and Meyer (2007).
7. See March (1991).
8. See Beinhocker (2006).

18 Don't Confuse Transparency with Intelligence

1. See Desportes (2007).
2. See Phalippou (2011).
3. Phalippou (2011) found that for emerging market spaces, the number of funds is so small that this benchmark is even less reliable than those for the 'mature segment'.
4. For example, Lo and Mueller (2010) proposed a finer taxonomy and suggested a differentiation between fully reducible, partially reducible, and irreducible uncertainty for the various components of a quantitative investment strategy, thus underscoring the fact that there is a continuum of randomness between risk and uncertainty.
5. Quoted from Karmin (2009).

6. See Manchester (1996).
7. See *The Economist* (2009).

19 *Spreading Risks – Part II*

1. See UBS (2010).
2. See Cornelius et al. (2013).
3. See Mathonet and Meyer (2007).
4. See Mathonet and Meyer (2007).
5. See Cornelius et al. (2013).
6. See interview with John Canning in Finkel and Greising (2010).
7. See Cornelius et al. (2013).
8. See Lhabitant (2004) for typical metrics like the Manhattan distance, the Euclidean distance or the Minkowski distance.

20 *Open-Ended Relationships*

1. To some degree funds-of-funds could be considered to be an index, albeit with many limitations. Also, close correspondence to standard market practices, such as the ILPA Principles, could be seen as tracking 'private equity index'. Funds outside this mainstream may offer better value but require more LP skills.
2. See Fraser-Sampson (2007).
3. Comparable to the concept of 'active share' used in studies on mutual funds, institutional investors in private equity can evaluate how active they are compared to their peers, for instance by looking at the number of first-time funds, co-investments and secondary deals compared to 'brands' or funds of generation three and higher. A mutual fund's active share is calculated by taking the sum of the absolute value of the differences of the weight of each position in the portfolio compared to the weight of each position in a given index and dividing this figure by two.
4. See Byworth (2005), Fruchbom (2005), Gompers and Lerner (2001) and Lerner and Schoar (2002).
5. See Hellman and Katz (2002) and Fraser-Sampson (2006).
6. Based on Meyer and Mathonet (2005).
7. See Lerner and Schoar (2002).
8. Phalippou (2011) found no empirical evidence on this point.
9. See Fruchbom (2005) and Lerner et al. (2005).
10. See Phalippou (2011).
11. One way to measure the strength of the relationship between a GP and a given LP is by counting the number of similar funds this GP had raised in previous years and in which the LP had invested as well (see Manninena et al., 2010). The stronger this relationship, the less work LPs expect to have to spend on due diligence. Consequently, this could be seen as a measure of inertia as familiarity with a GP will make reinvesting in its new funds easier for an LP. In the same way, an LP's relevant experience can be measured by counting the number of the same type of funds this LP had invested in previously. This figure is actually also argued to be a good measure of the LP's access to investment opportunities, as GPs raise new funds at fairly regular intervals. Finally, the number of funds of the same type managed previously could be a reasonable

proxy for a GP's experience. Also a high share in a fund, whether the LP has a board seat, co-investment rights or side letters can be indicative of the relationship's strength.

12. Examples for LPs with a typically high 'game strength' are fund-of-funds players. A high 'game strength' can imply low returns on an overall portfolio level, as it is associated with many relationships that can come at a significant price.
13. See Phalippou (2011), quoting an investor survey compiled by Da Rin and Phalippou.
14. See interview with Martin Escobari from Advent International, in Bishop (2012).
15. For instance, Adam Street Partners created their first fund-of-funds in the late 1970s. See http://www.adamstreetpartners.com/about-us/history.html, [accessed 23 January 2014]. HarbourVest Partners has been investing in partnerships since 1978. See http://www.harbourvest.com/about, [accessed 23 January 2014]. Pantheon Ventures was founded in 1982. See http://www.pantheonventures.com/about, [accessed 23 January 2014].
16. See Manninena et al. (2010).
17. More reliable assessments would in theory imply larger commitments in subsequent funds. However, some LPs are less certain about this – they consider the 'next fund risk' and therefore commit always the same amount across fund managers, funds and time.
18. For instance, New York Life Capital Partners follow a so-called 'core partner strategy' that involves a comprehensive review of a wide spectrum of GPs and has led to early identification of many leading private equity firms. See http://www.nylim.com/nylim/0,2058,12_1002870,00.html, [accessed 12 September 2012].
19. See Duffner et al. (2009).

21 Hard and Soft Power

1. See Desportes (2007), referring to General André Beauffre in Beauffre (1998).
2. See Fraser-Sampson (2013) and Cornelius et al. (2013).
3. See Desportes (2007).
4. See Knepley and Bailey (2009).
5. Schwienbacher et al. (2005) even found some evidence of a positive relation between style drifting and investment performance. They hypothesised that due to the potential reputation costs of deviation, style drifts are more common in cases where investments are expected to yield favourable realisations.
6. Phalippou (2011) suggests that funds engaging in secondary buyout transactions, investing in public equity or taking over publicly listed companies may have an insufficient deal flow.
7. See interview with Ajit Nedungadi, TA Associates L.P., in Bishop (2012).
8. See interview with Garry Wilson, Endless LLP, in Bishop (2012).
9. See Knepley and Bailey (2009).
10. See Baker and Smith (1998).
11. Based on the German Military's 'Auftragstaktik'.
12. See Beinhocker (2006).
13. See Fraser-Sampson (2007).

14. See Mayer (2013).
15. See Mayer (2013).
16. See Benson (1990).
17. See Litvak (2004).
18. See Fleischer (2004).
19. See Vardi (2009a).
20. See Aragon (2008).
21. See Talmor and Vasvari (2011).

22 Real Options

1. A detailed explanation of the theory goes beyond the scope of this book. For a practitioner's guide to real options we refer to Copeland and Antikarov (2003).
2. See Beinhocker (2006).
3. See Beinhocker (2006).
4. See Ibrahim (2010).
5. For funds-of-funds, co-investing is becoming much more mainstream and important and can comprise 25 per cent and more of their overall exposure.
6. Anonymous LP quoted by Schwimmer (2010).
7. Also often funds-of-funds do not charge carried interest or a special fee for co-investments, although there are exceptions.
8. See Cornelius (2011).
9. Date (2013) refers to a Preqin study from April 2012 that found that 43 per cent of LPs were seeking co-investment rights when committing to funds, and that a further 11 per cent were considering this.
10. One explanation put forward for this result is that it reflects the fact that the sample consists of large and sophisticated investors. Small investors replicating a direct investment strategy may have different experiences.
11. Quoted from Gallagher (2011).
12. Phalippou (2011).
13. See Harris (2009).
14. For example, up until 1.5x its money, and pari passu afterwards. See Harris (2009).
15. See Meyer and Mathonet (2005), Hochberg et al. (2013) and Manninena et al. (2010). Some academic studies, such as Lerner et al. (2005), also put forward the argument that emerging GPs generate significantly higher performance than their established peer group. Nevertheless, it is difficult to generalise such findings. In any case, funds raised by emerging GPs tend to be comparatively small and thus typically have an immaterial impact on an institutional investor's overall portfolio.
16. See Manninena et al. (2010).
17. See Manninena et al. (2010).
18. Quoted from an interview with Sven Berthold from WEGA support GmbH in AltAssets (2005).
19. See Hochberg et al. (2013).
20. See Hochberg et al. (2013).
21. See Paulina Junni in Mathonet and Meyer (2007).
22. See Baker and Smith (1998).
23. See Beinhocker (2006).

23 *No Plan Survives*

1. The saying that 'no plan survives contact with the enemy' has variously been attributed to Napoleon, George Patton or Dwight D. Eisenhower, but it originated with Moltke 'the Elder'.
2. See Morel (2012).
3. See Beinhocker (2006).
4. See Fraser-Sampson (2013).
5. See Beinhocker (2006).
6. Quoted from Fraser-Sampson (2013).
7. The main question that needs to be considered is whether the programme is really so important, unique and strategic for an institutional investor that internal resources are to be spent to put team, infrastructure and processes in place, or whether it is a more opportunistic and temporary initiative that is better outsourced partially or in full to external service providers.
8. Grundt (2003) was referring to one fund of funds with more than one-third of staff involved in forecasting cash flows.
9. See Mears (2004).

24 *The Heavy Hand of Regulation*

1. Quoted from van den Burg and Rasmussen (2008).
2. See Mayer (2013).
3. See *The Economist* (2010).
4. See Mayer (2013).
5. See Rasmussen (2008).
6. See Marriage (2013).
7. See Charlemagne (2009).
8. See Chassany and Barber (2013).
9. In the US some pension fund employees and intermediaries were paid by private equity funds in order to invest in the said fund. See Phalippou (2011).
10. See Cornelius et al. (2013).
11. See Mallaby (2011).
12. Quoted from Thornhill (2013).

25 *Private Equity Unchained*

1. See Authers (2014).
2. See Watts (2011).
3. See Watts (2011).
4. See Huffman (2001).
5. See Freedman (2013).
6. See van der Heijden (1996).
7. See Simon (2001).
8. See Huffman (2001).
9. See Huffman (2001), Manarin (2007) or Jargon Darbar (2008).
10. See Huffman (2001).

Bibliography

Acemoglu, D. and J. A. Robinson (2012) *Why Nations Fail – The Origins of Power, Prosperity and Poverty* (London: Profile Books).

Acharaya, S. and E. Dimson (2007) *Endowment Asset Management – Investment Strategies in Oxford and Cambridge* (Oxford University Press).

Achleitner, P. and S. Albrecht (2011) 'Private equity in an insurance company's strategic asset allocation', in *Inside the Limited Partner – A compendium of investor attitudes to private equity* (PEI Media).

AltAssets (2005) *Institutional Investor Profiles*, Various Interviews, AltAssets. Available at http://www.altassets.com, [accessed 16 September 2006].

Aragon, L. J. (2008) 'LPs Are on the Ropes', peHUB, 7 July. Available at http://www.pehub.com/2008/11/07/lps-are-on-the-ropes, [accessed 5 September 2013].

Authers, J. (2014) 'Cambridge honours the Yale model by not following it', *Financial Times*, 27 January.

Baker, G. P. and G. D. Smith (1998) *The New Financial Capitalists – Kohlberg Kravis Roberts and the Creation of Corporate Value* (New York: Cambridge University Press).

Bance, A. (2004) *Why and How to Invest in Private Equity?*, 2nd edn, Zaventem, EVCA Investor Relations Committee Paper, European Venture Capital and Private Equity Association.

Barber, F. and M. Goold (2007) 'The strategic secret of private equity', *Harvard Business Review*, September.

BCBS (2013) *Capital Requirements for Banks' Equity Investments in Funds – Consultative Document – Issued for comment by 4 October 2013*. Basel Committee on Banking Supervision. July 2013.

Beauffre, A. (1998) *Introduction à la stratégie* (Hachette).

Beinhocker, E. D. (2006) *The Origins of Wealth* (London: Random House).

Benson, B. (1990) *The Enterprise of Law: Justice without a State* (San Francisco: Pacific Research Institute for Public Policy).

Bernstein, W. J. (2008) *A Splendid Exchange* (New York: Grove Press).

Beyerchen, A. (1992) 'Clausewitz, Nonlinearity and the Unpredictability of War', *International Security*, Vol. 17(3), Winter.

Bishop, M. (2012) *The Future of Private Equity – Beyond the Mega Buyout* (London: Palgrave MacMillan).

Bongaerts, D. and E. Charlier (2006) 'Risk Management for LBOs in Buy-and-hold Portfolios', 27 August. Available at http://www.greta.it/credit/credit2006/poster/2_Bongaersts_Charlier.pdf, [accessed 30 June 2008].

Borden, B. T. (2009) 'The Aggregate-Plus Theory of Partnership Taxation', *Georgia Law Review*, Vol. 43. Available at http://ssrn.com/abstract=1121351, [accessed 18 July 2008].

von Braun, E. (2000) *Selektion und Strukturierung von Private Equity Fonds-Portfolios* (Munich: IIR Private Equity & Venture Capital Konferenz).

Browne, K. R. (2006) 'Appropriateness and Feasibility of Targeted Diversification in a Private Equity Portfolio', MBA Thesis, Massachusetts Institute of Technology.

Buchanan, J., D. H. Chai and S. Deakin (2012) *Hedge Fund Activism in Japan – The Limits of Shareholder Primacy* (Cambridge University Press).

van den Burg, I. and P. N. Rasmussen (2008) *Hedge Funds and Private Equity – A Critical Analysis*, Report PES-Group in the European Parliament, 5 September. Available at http://www.pes.org/downloads/Hedge_Funds.pdf, [accessed 12 May 2012].

Burgel, O. (2000) *UK Venture Capital and Venture Capital as an Asset Class for Institutional Investors* (London: BVCA).

Byworth, A. M. (2005) 'Qualities of a Good Limited Partner', CDC Presentation, 7 February. Available at http://www.altassets.com/features/arc/2005/nz6292.php [accessed 9 February 2005].

Camerer, C. and R. Thaler (1995) 'Anomalies: More Ultimatum and Dictator Games', *Journal of Economic Perspectives*, No. 9, February.

Camp, J. J. (2002) *Venture Capital Due Diligence* (New York: John Wiley & Sons).

Campbell, R. A. J. (2008) 'Art as a Financial Investment', *The Journal of Alternative Investments*, Spring.

Charlemagne (2009) 'Battle of the big beasts', *The Economist*, 23 July.

Chassany, A.-S. (2013) 'Flying solo', *Financial Times*, 10 September.

Chassany, A.-S. and L. Barber (2013) 'Sovereign Wealth Suitors Woo Sarkozy', *Financial Times*, 10 March.

Chung, J.-W. (2010) *Performance Persistence in Private Equity Funds* (The Chinese University of Hong Kong) 24 November.

Chung, J.-W., B. A. Sensoy, L. H. Stern and M. S. Weisbach (2010) 'Pay for Performance from Future Fund Flows: The Case of Private Equity', November. Available at http://www.ssrn.com/abstract=1554626, [accessed 12 July 2013].

Conner, A. (2005) 'Persistence in Venture Capital Returns', *Private Equity International*, March.

Copeland, M. V. (2008). 'Private equity's basic math problem', *Fortune Magazine*, 17 November. Available at http://money.cnn.com/2008/11/14/news/companies/privatemoney_copeland.fortune/index.htm, [accessed 1 August 2011].

Copeland, T. and V. Antikarov (2003) *Real Options – A Practitioner's Guide* (New York: Thomson-TEXERE).

Cornelius, P. (2011) *International Investments in Private Equity* (Burlington, MA: Academic Press).

Cornelius, P., K. Juttmann and R. de Veer (2009) 'Industry cycles and the performance of buyouts funds', *Journal of Private Equity*, No. 12.

Cornelius, P., C. Diller, D. Guennoc and T. Meyer (2013) *Mastering Illiquidity – Risk Management for Portfolios of Limited Partnership Funds* (Chichester: John Wiley & Sons).

Cumming, D., L. H. Haß and D. Schweizer (2013) 'Private Equity Benchmarks and Portfolio Optimization', *Journal of Banking and Finance*, Draft, 9 March.

Date, S. (2013) 'Positive partners', *Capital Insights*, Issue 7, 3rd quarter.

Davies, M. (2008) 'CalPERs [sic] private equity stakes under microscope', Reuters, 20 November.

Dawkins, R. (2000) *The Blind Watchmaker* (London: Penguin Books).

Demaira, C. (2010) *Introduction to Private Equity* (Chichester: John Wiley & Sons).

Desai, M. A. and F. Ferri (2006) 'Understanding Economic Value Added', Harvard Business School Note 9-206-016, 11 July.

Desportes, V. (2007) *Décider dans l'incertitude* (Paris: Economica).

De Vany, A. (2004) *Hollywood Economics – How Extreme Uncertainty Shapes the Film Industry* (Milton Park: Routledge).

Dimmock, S. G. (2008) 'Portfolio Choice, Background Risk, and University Endowment Funds', Working paper, Michigan State University.

Dinneen, P. (2004) 'Emerging Markets Private Equity: Performance Update', IFC Conference, 6 May. Available at http://www.ifc.org/ifcext/cfn.nst/AttachmentsByTitle/Patricia+Dinneen/$FILE/Panel4-PatriciaDinneed.pdf [Accessed 1 February 2006].

Dobbs, D. (2013) 'Restless Genes', *National Geographic*, January.

Duffner, S., M. M. Schmid and H. Zimmermann (2009) 'Trust and Success in Venture Capital Financing – An Empirical Analysis with German Survey Data', *Kyklos*, Vol. 62, No. 1, February.

Economist, The (2004) 'The New Kings of Capitalism', 25 November.

Economist, The (2005) 'Locust, Pocus', 7 May.

Economist, The (2009) 'Full Disclosure – The case for transparency in financial markets is not clear cut', 19 February.

Economist, The (2010) 'The Wrong Targets', 20 May.

Economist, The (2012) 'Fashion Forward – Zara, Spain's most successful brand, is trying to go global', 24 March.

Economist, The (2013) 'Clayton, Dubilier & Rice – Engineers of a different kind', 22 June.

EMPEA (2005) 'New Funds of Funds Increase Options for Emerging Markets Private Equity Investors', Emerging Markets Private Equity Association, 20 March. Available at http://www.empea.net/docs/Emerging_Markets_Private_Equity_Issue_1.pdf, [accessed 31 October 2005].

Emshwiller, J. R. and M. Corkery (2010) 'Calpers Review Recommends Fee Changes', *Wall Street Journal*, 14 December. Available at http://online.wsj.com/article/SB10001424052748703727804576017970639353898.html, [accessed 15 December 2010].

Evans, P. (2006) 'An Alternative to Usury?', May. Available at http://www.moneyabuse.org/pdf/An%20Alternative%20To%20Usury%20(CCR%20article,%20May%202005).pdf, [accessed 6 August 2008].

EVCA (2005) *International Private Equity and Venture Capital Valuation Guidelines*.

EVCA (2013) *Risk Measurement Guidelines 2013*, European Private Equity and Venture Capital Association, January. Available at http://www.evca.eu/uploadedfiles/EVCA_Risk_Measurement_Guidelines_January_2013.pdf, [accessed 11 October 2013].

Fang, L., V. Ivashina and J. Lerner (2012) 'The Disintermediation of financial Markets: Direct Investing in Private Equity'. Available at http://www.stern.nyu.edu/cons/groups/content/documents/webasset/con_037960.pdf, [accessed 17 October 2012].

Fann, D. and T. Bernhardt (2013) 'Working with investment advisors and consultants', *Private Equity International*, 12 August.

Ferguson, N. (2008) *The Ascent of Money: A Financial History of the World* (New York: Penguin Press).

Fernández-Armesto, F. (2007) *Pathfinders – A Global History of Exploration* (Oxford University Press).

Finkel, R. A. and D. Greising (2010) *The Masters of Private Equity and Venture Capital* (McGraw-Hill).

Firstbrook, C. (2007) 'Private Equity: High Quality Due Diligence', Accenture Blogs, 27 March. Available at http://www.accenture.com/Global/Accenture_Blogs/Accenture_High_Performance_Business_Blog/March_2007/Private+Equity+High+Quality+Due+Diligence.htm, [accessed 23 July 2008].

Fleischer, V. (2004) 'Fickle Investors, Reputation, and the Clientele Effect in Venture Capital Funds', UCLA School of Law, Law-Econ Research Paper No. 04–14, 2 October. Available at SSRN: http://ssrn.com/abstract=600044 [accessed 5 May 2006].

Fraser-Sampson, G. (2006) *Multi Asset Class Investment Strategy* (Chichester: John Wiley & Sons).

Fraser-Sampson, G. (2007) *Private Equity as an Asset Class* (Chichester: John Wiley & Sons).

Fraser-Sampson, G. (2013) *Intelligent Investing – A Guide to the Practical and Behavioural Aspects of Investment Strategy* (Hampshire: Palgrave MacMillan).

Freedman, L. (2013) *Strategy – A History* (New York: Oxford University Press).

Fruchbom, P. (2005) 'GPs on LPs', *Private Equity International*, June.

Gadiesh, O. and H. MacArthur (2008) *Lessons from Private Equity Any Company Can Use (Memo to the CEO)* (Harvard Business Review Press).

Gallagher, B. (2011) *Co-investments in funds of funds and separate accounts*. Available at http://www.twinbridgecapital.com/pdf/m_Co-Investment.pdf, [accessed 10 September 2013].

Garis, D. (2007) *Manna from Heaven* (George Ronald Publications).

Gilson, R. J. (2003) 'Engineering a Venture Capital Market: Lessons from the American Experience', *Stanford Law Review*, Vol. 55, April. Available at http://ssrn.com/abstract=353380, [accessed 2 February 2006].

Gompers, P. A. and J. Lerner (2001) *The Money of Invention – How Venture Capital Creates New Wealth* (Boston Massachusetts: Harvard Business School Press).

Grundt, M. (2003) *Private Equity als Anlagekategorie einer Versicherung* (Diplomarbeit, Fachbereich Wirtschaft, Hochschule Wismar, April).

Güth, W., R. Schmittberger and B. Schwarze (1982) 'An Experimental Analysis of Ultimatum Bargaining', *Journal of Economic Behavior and Organization*, December.

Haight, G. T., S. O. Morrell and G. E. Ross (2007) *How to Select Investment Managers & Evaluate Performance* (Hoboken, New Jersey: John Wiley & Sons).

Harris, J. (2009) 'Default debacle', *PEI Manager*, June.

Harris, R., T. Jenkinson and S. N. Kaplan (2012) 'Private Equity Performance: What Do We Know?', NBER Working Paper 17874.

van der Heijden, K. (1996) *Scenarios – The Art of Strategic Conversation* (Chichester: John Wiley & Sons).

Heikkilä, T. (2004) 'European Single Market and the Globalisation of Private Equity Fundraising: Barriers and Determinants of Foreign Commitments in Private Equity Funds', Master of Science in Engineering Thesis, Helsinki University of Technology.

Hellman, R. B. and E. Katz (2002) *The Evolution of Partnership Terms – Aligning GP and LP Interests* (Sacramento, CA: Institute of Fiduciary Education).

Hendershott, R. (2007) 'Using Past Performance to Infer Investment Manager Ability', Preliminary paper, November. Available at http://www.scu.edu/business/mindwork/ winter08/upload/hendershott-past_performance_nov07.pdf, [accessed 12 May 2008].

Heuser, B. (2002) *Reading Clausewitz* (London: Pimlico).

Hobohm, D. (2008) 'Investors in Private Equity Funds: Large-Scale Performance Analysis and the Question if Location Matters', 22 October. Available at http://ssrn.com/abstract=1286139, [accessed 7 July 2009].

Hobohm, D. (2010) *Investors in Private Equity Funds: Theory, Preferences and Performances* (Gabler).

Hochberg, Y. V., A. Ljungqvist and A. Vissing-Jørgensen (2013) 'Informational Hold-up and Performance Persistence in Venture Capital', *The Review of Financial Studies*, 17 December.

Huffman, B. (2001) 'What Makes a Strategy Brilliant?', *Business Horizons*, Vol. 44, No. 4, July.

Hutton, W. (2007) 'Private equity is casting a plutocratic shadow over British business', *The Guardian*, 23 February.

Ibrahim, D. M. (2010) 'Debt as Venture Capital', *University of Illinois Law Review*, Vol. 2010. Available at http://illinoislawreview.org/wp-content/ilr-content/articles/2010/4/Ibrahim.pdf, [accessed 22 July 2013].

Idzorek, T. (2007) 'Private Equity and Strategic Asset Allocation', Report Ibbotson Associates. 31 October. Available at http://corporate.morningstar.com/ib/documents/methodologydocuments/ibbassociates/ibbotsonprivateequity.pdf, [accessed 16 August 2011].

Inderst, R. and F. Muennich (2003). *The Benefits of Shallow Pockets* (London School of Economics).

Janeway, W. H. (2012) *Doing Capitalism in the Innovation Economy* (Cambridge University Press).

Jargon Darbar (2008) 'How to Evaluate a Strategy?', 26 January. Available at http://jargondarbar.blogspot.com/2008/01/how-to-evaluate-strategy.html; [accessed 6 February 2008].

Jensen, K., J. Call and M. Tomasello (2007) 'Chimpanzees are Rational Maximizers in an Ultimatum Game', *Science*, 5 October.

Jo, H. (2002) *Perspectives and Problems of Private Equity Funds-of-Funds* (Leavey School of Business & Administration).

Johnson, L. (2012) 'Muddling through is a strategy that works', *Financial Times*, 9 May.

Kahneman, D. (2011) *Thinking Fast and Slow* (London: Allen Lane).

Kaplan, S. N. and A. Schoar (2005) 'Private equity performance: returns, persistence, and capital flows', *Journal of Finance*, No. 60.

Kaplan, S. N. and J. Lerner (2010) 'It ain't broke: The past, present, and future of venture capital', *Journal of Applied Corporate Finance*, No. 22.

Kaplan, S. N. and P. Stromberg (2009) 'Leveraged buyouts and private equity', *Journal of Economic Perspectives*, No. 23.

Kapoor, S. (unknown) 'A few random thoughts on hedge funds, private equity, the financial system, tax justice & capital flight', Presentation. Available at www.tni.org/archives///crimes-docs/kapoor.ppt, [accessed 17 February 2014].

Karmin, C. (2009) 'Yale's Investor Keeps Playbook', *Wall Street Journal*, 13 January.

Kelleher, E. (2013) 'Unfair Darwinian churn drowns small hedge funds', *Financial Times*, 16 September.

Kim, W. C. and R. Mauborgne (2005) *Blue Ocean Strategy – How to Create Uncontested Market Space and Make the Competition Irrelevant* (Boston, MA: Harvard Business School Publishing Corporation).

Knepley, K. and B. D. Bailey (2009) 'Peeling Back the Onion: LPs Get Tougher on Due Diligence', SVB Capital Venture Capital Update, May.

Knight, F. H. (1921). *Risk, Uncertainty, and Profit* (Boston, MA Hart: Schaffner and Marx. Houghton Mifflin Company).
Kosman, J. (2010) *The Buyout of America – How Private Equity Is Destroying Jobs and Killing the American Economy* (New York, NY: Portfolio/Penguin).
Kukla, D. (2011) 'Competitive Strategy of Private Equity: Boundary of the Investment Firm', Doctoral Thesis, Technische Universität Berlin.
Lai, R. K. (2006) 'Why Funds of Funds?', 15 January. Available at http://ssrn.com/abstract=676999, [accessed 6 January 2010].
Lerner, J. (2009) 'Private Equity and Venture Capital in the Wake of the Crisis', Presentation at Super Investor Conference, Paris, November.
Lerner, J., F. Hardymon and A. Leamon (2011) *Venture Capital and Private Equity: A Casebook* (Hoboken, New Jersey: John Wiley & Sons).
Lerner, J. and A. Schoar (2002) 'The Illiquidity Puzzle: Theory and Evidence from Private Equity', *Journal of Financial Economics*, Vol. 72, No. 1.
Lerner, J., A. Schoar and J. Wang (2007) 'Secrets of the Academy: The Drivers of University Endowment Success'. Available at http://www.barwon.net.au/pdfs/Secrets-Academy-Drivers-Uni.pdf, [accessed 6 July 2009].
Lerner, J., A. Schoar and W. Wong (2005) 'Smart Institutions, Foolish Choices? The Limited Partner Performance Puzzle'. Available at http://www.law.harvard.edu/programs/olin_center/corporate_governance/papers/SmartInstitutionsFoolishChoices_041011.pdf, [accessed 6 July 2009].
Lhabitant, F.-S. (2004) *Hedge Funds – Quantitative Insights* (Chichester: John Wiley & Sons).
Litvak, K. (2004) 'Governance through Exit: Default Penalties and Walkaway Options in Venture Capital Partnership Agreements', University of Texas, Law and Economics Research Paper No. 34, October. Available at http://ssrn.com/abstract=613142, [accessed 5 May 2006].
Lo, A. W. (2005) 'The Adaptive Market Hypothesis', *The Journal of Investment Consulting*, Vol. 7, No. 2.
Lo, A. W. (2008) *Hedge Funds – An Analytical Perspective* (Princeton and Oxford: Princeton University Press).
Lo, A. W. and M. T. Mueller (2010) 'WARNING: Physics Envy May be Hazardous to Your Wealth'. Available at http://papers.ssrn.com/sol3/papers.cfm?abstract_id=1563882, [accessed 21 June 2010].
Lopez-de-Silanes, F., L. Phalippou and O. Gottschalg (2010) 'Giants at the gate: On the cross-section of private equity returns', Working paper, quoted in Phalippou (2011).
Love, G. (2009). 'Praise for Evergreen Funds', *Venture Capital Journal*, 1 December.
Lovrek, H. (2012) 'Die mittelalterliche Commenda und die moderne Private Equity Industrie. Lösungen eines Prinzipal-Agent Problems, Diplomarbeit', A312. Universität Wien.
Luttwak, E. N. (1976) *The Grand Strategy of the Roman Empire* (Baltimore, Maryland: The Johns Hopkins University Press).
Mallaby, S. (2011) *More Money than God: Hedge Funds and the Making of a New Elite* (UK: Bloomsbury Publishing).
Manarin, R. (2007) *Wealth Building Report*, Issue 13, 16 October. Available at http://www.manarin.com/wfdata/frame717-1080/File15.pdf; [accessed 3 January 2008].
Manchester, W. (1996) *A World lit only by Fire – The Medieval Mind & the Renaissance* (London: Papermac).

Manchester, W. and P. Reid (2012) *The Last Lion: Winston Spencer Churchill. Defender of the Realm, 1940–1965* (New York: Little, Brown and Company).

Manninena, O., M. Jääskeläinena and M. Maula (2010) 'Access versus Selection: What Drives Limited Partners' Private Equity Returns?', 1 November. Available at http://efmaefm.org/0EFMSYMPOSIUM/Toronto-2011/papers/Manninen.pdf, [accessed 10 April 2014].

March, J. G. (1991) 'Exploration and Exploitation in Organizational Learning', *Organizational Science*, Vol. 2, No. 1.

Marriage, M. (2013) 'Hedge funds copy Soros's regulatory sidestep', *Financial Times*, 5 August.

Mathonet, P.-Y. and T. Meyer (2007) *J Curve Exposure – Managing a Portfolio of Venture Capital and Private Equity Funds* (Chichester: John Wiley and Sons).

Maula, M. and G. Murray (2003) *Finnish Industry Investment Ltd: An International Evaluation*, Ministry of Trade and Industry publication 1/2003, Industries Department.

Mayer, C. (2013) *Firm Commitment – Why the corporation is failing us and how to restore trust in it* (Oxford University Press).

McCahery, J. A. and E. P. M. Vermeulen (2013) 'Recasting Private Equity Funds After the Financial Crisis – The End of 'Two and Twenty' and the Emergence of Co-Investments and Separate Account Arrangements', Topics in Corporate Law & Economics 2013-2.

Mears, S. (2004) 'Taking Stock of Stock Distributions', Testa, Hurwitz and Thibeault, 21 July. Available at http://www.altassets.com/knowledgebank/learningcurve/2004/ nz5222.php. [accessed 13 May 2008].

Mei, J. and M. Moses (2002) 'Art as an Investment and the Underperformance of Masterpieces'. Available at http://people.stern.nyu.edu/jmei/artgood.pdf, [accessed 22 July 2013].

Metrick, A. (2006) *Venture Capital and the Finance of Innovation* (New York: John Wiley & Sons).

Metrick, A. and A. Yasuda (2010) 'The Economics of Private Equity Funds', *The Review of Financial Studies*, Vol. 23, No. 6.

Meyer, T. and P.-Y Mathonet (2005) *Beyond the J-Curve* (Chichester: John Wiley & Sons).

Miller, C. C. and G. Fabrikant (2008) 'Beyond the Ivied Halls, Endowments Suffer', *The New York Times*, 26 November. Available at http://www.nytimes.com/2008/11/26/business/26endowment.html, [accessed 16 April 2009].

Mills, L. (2005) 'The New Road', *Real Deals*, 27 January.

Morel, C. (2012) *Les Décisions Absurdes II* (Paris: Gallimard).

Mulcahy, D., B. Weeks and H. S. Bradley (2012) 'We Have Met the Enemy... and He Is Us – Lessons from Twenty Years of the Kauffman Foundation's Investments in Venture Capital Funds and the Triumph of Hope over Experience', Kauffman Foundation, May.

Murphy, D. (2007) 'A Practical Guide to Managing Private Equity Commitments', Goldman Sachs Asset Management, Strategic Research, June.

Nelson, H. (2003) 'Note on Due Diligence in Venture Capital', Tuck School of Business at Dartmouth, Center for Private Equity Research and Entrepreneurship.

Noonan, J. T. (1957) *The Scholastic Analysis of Usury* (Cambridge, MA: Harvard University Press).

OECD (2007) 'The Implications of Alternative Investment Vehicles for Corporate Governance: A Synthesis of Research about Private Equity Firms and "Activist Hedge Funds"'. Issued by the OECD Steering Group on Corporate Governance, July.

Oosterbeek, H., R. Sloof and G. Van De Kuilen (2001) 'Cultural Differences in Ultimatum Game Experiments: Evidence from a Meta-Analysis', October. Available at http://ssrn.com/abstract=286428, [accessed 24 July 2008].

Otterlei, J. and S. Barrington (2003) 'Alternative Assets – Private Equity Fund of Funds', Special report, Piper Jaffray Private Capital.

Phalippou, L. (2009) 'The Hazards of Using IRR to Measure Performance: The Case of Private Equity'. Available at http://ssrn.com/abstract=1111796, [accessed 22 April 2013].

Phalippou, L. (2011) 'An evaluation of the potential for GPFG to achieve above average returns from investments in private equity and recommendations regarding benchmarking'. Report for the Ministry of Finance and the Norwegian Parliament, February.

Phalippou, L. and O. Gottschalg (2009) 'The performance of private equity funds', *Review of Financial Studies*, No. 22.

Pease, R. (2000) 'Private Equity Funds-of-Funds – State of the Market', Research Report, Asset Alternatives Inc.

Pietranico, P. and M. Riepe (2002) 'Core & Explore – Details', Charles Schwab and Company, http://www.schwab.com.

Porter, M. (1980) *Competitive Strategy – Techniques for Analyzing Industries and Competitors* (New York, NY: The Free Press).

Primack, D. (2010) 'Random Ramblings', *peHUB Wire*, 22 June.

Private Equity News (2013) 'Institutionalisation and the dilution of private equity', 29 May.

Rasmussen, P. N. (2008) 'Taming the private equity fund "locusts"', *Europe's World*, Spring.

Raynor, M. E., M. Ahmed and A. D. Henderson (2009) 'A Random Search for Excellence – Why "great company" research delivers fables and not facts', Report, Deloitte Development.

Rosenzweig, P. (2007) *The Halo Effect and the Eight other Delusions that Deceive Managers* (New York: Free Press).

Rouvinez, C. (2006) 'Top Quartile Persistence in Private Equity', *Private Equity International*, June.

Rubenstein, D. (2008) 'The Post-Banana World of Private Equity', presentation given at the conference of the National Bureau of Economic Research, 5 April (quoted in Cornelius, 2011).

Scardino, J. (2004) 'Past Performance – a Guide to Likely Future Performance in Private Equity', *Private Equity Monitor*, Redhill, UK, Initiative Europe Ltd.

Schmidt, D., E. Nowak and A. Knigge (2004) 'On the Performance of Private Equity Investments: Does Market Timing Matter?', CEPRES, March.

Schultes, R. (2012) 'Private Equity's Darwinian Moment', *The Wall Street Journal Europe*, 21 December.

Schwienbacher, A., G. A. Fleming and D. J Cumming (2005) 'Style Drift in Private Equity', 25 April. Available at http://ssrn.com/abstract=729684, [accessed 18 July 2008].

Schwimmer, R. (2010) 'The Future of Private Equity', Churchill Financial Special Report, Churchill Financial LLC, July.

Scott, B. (2012) 'LP model in the dock', *Real Deals*, 8 March.

Settboun, H. M. (2005) 'The Investors' Composition in Private Equity Funds'. Available at http://pluto.huji.ac.il/~chanamuriel/5all-improved-mickel%20edition.pdf, [accessed 7 July 2009].

Simon, H. (2001) 'What is Strategy?', Strategy International – Series 1, *Frankfurter Allgemeine Zeitung*. Available at http://www.simon-kucher.com/Internetdatabase/publication.nsf/72bedc9299946461c12568ac002b4c9e/eabf6666b3fa249ac1256a4d0029f6a3?OpenDocument; [accessed 5 February 2008].

Simpson, E. (2013) *War from the Ground up* (London: Hurst & Company).

Small, P. (2003) 'A biological way to think about information, systems, people and collaboration'. Available at http://www.stigmergicsystems.com/simpleexplain/biopaper1.html, [accessed 9 October 2012].

Smith, M. D. (2000) 'Private Equity Funds-of-Funds: Getting What You Pay For', Presentation at Asset Alternatives' Fund-of-Funds Summit 2000.

Snow, D. (2006) 'An Asymmetric Success Story', *The Private Equity Fundraising Compendium*, November.

Söderblom, A. (2011) 'Private Equity Fund Investing – Investment Strategies, Entry Order and Performance'. Dissertation for the Degree of Doctor of Philosophy, Stockholm School of Economics.

Sood, V. (2003) 'Investment Strategies in Private Equity', *The Journal of Private Equity*, Summer.

Sørensen, J. (2006) *Acting under uncertainty: Ritual actions and predictions of success in pragmatic endeavors.* Institute of Philosophy, Education and the Study of Religions, University of Southern Denmark.

Sørensen, M. (2007) 'How smart is smart money? A two-sided matching model of venture capital', *Journal of Finance*, No. 62.

Sørensen, M., N. Wang and J. Yang (2013) 'Valuing Private Equity', Network for Studies on Pension, Aging and Retirement, Discussion Paper 04/2012-041, 13 June.

Sormani A. (2005) 'Fund-of-Funds: Working to Stand', *European Venture Capital Journal*, August.

Stacey, R. (1996) *Complexity and Creativity in Organizations* (San Francisco: Berrett-Koehler).

Stern, C. W. and M. S. Deimler (2006) *The Boston Consulting Group on Strategy: Classic Concepts and New Perspectives* (New York: John Wiley & Sons).

Swabey, H. (2008) 'Usury and the Church of England', CESC Publication, May. Available at http://www.cesc.net/adobeweb/scholars/swabey/swabey.pdf, [accessed 29 August 2008].

Swensen, D. F. (2000) *Pioneering Portfolio Management – An Unconventional Approach to Institutional Investment* (New York: Simon & Schuster).

Taleb, N. N. (2012) *Antifragile – How to Live in a World We Don't Understand* (London: Penguin Books).

Talmor, E. and F. Vasvari (2011). *International Private Equity* (Chichester: John Wiley & Sons).

Tett, G. (2010) 'Singapore Looks to Move Away From Harvard Model', *Financial Times*, 9 April.

Thornhill, J. (2013) 'How can we defeat terrorism if all the trust has gone?', *Financial Times*, 24/25 August.

Tierney, J. F. and D. Folkerts-Landau (2001) *Structured Private Equity – An Old Market Becomes an Emerging Asset Class* (Frankfurt: Deutsche Bank Global Markets Research).

Toll, D. (2001) 'Private Equity Partnership Terms and Conditions', Research Report, Asset Alternatives.

UBS (2010) 'Private Equity Education Series, Part 3: Private Equity Strategies', UBS Alternative Investments Report. Available at http://ssrn.com/abstract=1776471, [accessed 13 December 2012].

Vardi, N. (2009a) 'The Reason Stanford is Selling Private Equity', Forbes.com, 6 October.

Vardi, N. (2009b) 'Did Harvard Sell At the Bottom?', Forbes.com, 24 October.

Vasconcellos e Sá, J. A. (2005) *Strategy Moves* (Prentice Hall).

Watts, D. J. (2011) *Everything is Obvious – How Common Sense Fails* (London: Atlantic Books).

Webber, S. (2008) 'Harvard, Other Big Endowments Selling Private Equity Stakes at Big Losses', 1 December. Available at http://www.nakedcapitalism.com/2008/12/harvard-yale-other-big-endowments.html, [accessed 16 August 2011].

Weidig, T. and P.-Y. Mathonet (2004) 'The Risk Profile of Private Equity', January. Available at http://ssrn.com/abstract=495482, [accessed 16 June 2008].

Wile, R. (2012) 'Adaptive Market Hypothesis: Andrew Lo's Groundbreaking Work Combining Rational and Behavioral Market Theory', 6 May. http://www.businessinsider.com/andrew-lo-adaptive-market-hypothesis-2012-5?op=1

Witkowsky, C. (2012) 'OMERS PE loses fund investments expert', 12 March. Available at http://www.privateequityinternational.com/article.aspx?article=66254, [accessed 25 May 2012].

Wright, M. and K. Robbie (1996) 'The investor-led buy-out: A new strategic option', *Long Range Planning*, Vol. 29, Issue 5, October.

Index

References to notes consist of the page number with, in brackets, the chapter number followed by the letter 'n' followed by the number of the note, e.g. 281(12n4) refers to note no. 4 under chapter 12 on page 281. References to figures are shown in *italics*. References to tables are shown in **bold**.

Printed and bound by CPI Group (UK) Ltd, Croydon, CR0 4YY